Democracy and the Limits of Self-Government

The political institutions under which we live today evolved from a revolutionary idea that shook the world in the second part of the eighteenth
century: that a people should govern itself. Nevertheless, if we judge
contemporary democracies by the ideals of self-government, equality,
and liberty, we find that democracy is not what it was dreamt to be.
This book addresses central issues in democratic theory by analyzing the sources of widespread dissatisfaction with democracies around
the world. With attention throughout to historical and cross-national
variations, the focus is on the generic limits of democracy in promoting equality, effective participation, control of governments by citizens,
and liberty. The conclusion is that, although some of this dissatisfaction
occurs for good reason, some is based on an erroneous understanding
of how democracy functions. Hence, although the analysis identifies
the limits of democracy, it also points to directions for feasible reforms.

Adam Przeworski is the Carroll and Milton Petrie Professor of Politics
at New York University. Previously, he was the Martin A. Ryerson
Distinguished Service Professor at the University of Chicago. He is the
author of thirteen books and numerous articles. His recent publica-
tions include *Democracy and Development*, co-authored with Michael
R. Alvarez, José Antonio Cheibub, and Fernando Limongi (2000);
Democracy and the Rule of Law, co-edited with José María Maravall
(2003); and *States and Markets* (2003). He is the recipient of the 2001
Woodrow Wilson Prize and the 2010 Johan Skytte Prize.

Cambridge Studies in the Theory of Democracy

General Editor

Adam Przeworski *New York University*

Other Books in the Series

Robert Barros, *Constitutionalism and Dictatorship: Pinochet, the Junta, and the 1980 Constitution*

Jon Elster, ed., *Deliberative Democracy*

José María Maravall and Adam Przeworski, eds., *Democracy and the Rule of Law*

José María Maravall and Ignacio Sánchez-Cuenca, *Controlling Governments: Voters, Institutions, and Accountability*

Adam Przeworski, Susan Stokes, and Bernard Manin, eds., *Democracy, Accountability, and Representation*

Adam Przeworski et al., *Democracy and Development: Political Institutions and Well-Being in the World, 1950–1990*

Melissa Schwartzberg, *Democracy and Legal Change*

Roberto Gargarella, *Constitutionalism in the Americas, 1776–1860*

To Joanne,
long overdue.

Democracy and the Limits of Self-Government

ADAM PRZEWORSKI

New York University

CAMBRIDGE
UNIVERSITY PRESS

CAMBRIDGE UNIVERSITY PRESS
Cambridge, New York, Melbourne, Madrid, Cape Town, Singapore,
São Paulo, Delhi, Dubai, Tokyo, Mexico City

Cambridge University Press
32 Avenue of the Americas, New York, NY 10013-2473, USA

www.cambridge.org
Information on this title: www.cambridge.org/9780521140119

First published 2010

Printed in the United States of America

A catalog record for this publication is available from the British Library.

Library of Congress Cataloging in Publication data

Przeworski, Adam.
Democracy and the limits of self-government / Adam Przeworski.
    p.   cm. – (Cambridge studies in the theory of democracy ; 9)
Includes bibliographical references and index.
ISBN 978-0-521-76103-1 – ISBN 978-0-521-14011-9 (pbk.)
1. Democracy – History.   2. Democracy – Philosophy.   3.
Representative government and representation.   I. Title. II. Series.
JC421.P795   2010
321.8–dc22   2010000028

ISBN 978-0-521-76103-1 Hardback
ISBN 978-0-521-14011-9 Paperback

Contents

Preface

This book has autobiographical roots and they may help explain its motivation and its goals.

Growing up in communist Poland, I imagined democracy only dimly across a curtain, attracted mostly by the thrill of elections: parties compete, someone wins, someone loses, and even if their chances are unequal, no one knows how the game will end. It was like football, and I was passionate about football. So I read results of elections in foreign countries the same way I read scores of foreign soccer games. And, to increase the emotional stakes, I had my favorites in both: Swedish Social Democrats and Arsenal.

I was first exposed to democracy during the two years I spent in the United States between 1961 and 1963. Although the first textbook I was forced to read as a graduate student opened with the sentence "The United States has the best system of government in the world," the experience was not inspiring. Still recovering from McCarthyism, the country was not the bastion of freedom it portrayed itself to be. I even had a personal adventure: A group of graduate students planned to picket a movie theater that would not show a sexually explicit foreign film. To organize the picket, we formed a political group, Student Association for Liberal Action. Then the leader of the group received a call from the local police chief, who met him at midnight in an underground garage and pointed out that our leader had several unpaid parking tickets, thus being liable to arrest. That was the end of liberal action. Even more than this Polish-style police repression, what I found dismaying was that both censorship and repression enjoyed the support of a majority of citizens of American democracy. Neither would have been true in Poland: Although communist leaders tended to be prudes, they just stuck age limits on movies and let it go at that. And even though police were omnipresent, I knew no one in Poland who thought that they were anything but a bunch of thugs. So instead of dutifully following the graduate program, I spent my time avidly swallowing Tocqueville's warnings about the tyranny of the majority and the reactions of German refugees from fascism to what they saw as "totalitarian democracy." I almost flunked out of the program, because some of my teachers thought that my readings were not "political science." Some of them defended me, so I made it through, and I returned to Poland with this image of democracy.

The experience, however, was not completely dissuasive, for I still thought that selecting rulers through elections was a good idea and, indeed, that it would make things better in my native country. There must have been someone within the communist leadership who thought the same, because in 1965 the Party suddenly decided to grant the people some voice in elections at the village level. Because communists were maniacs about keeping records, detailed results of these elections became available, and together with a colleague I analyzed them. We found that the people who were newly elected did not differ by any observable characteristics, party membership included, from those who were eliminated. Hence, we said, "Look, people were allowed to choose representatives they liked and to send away unpopular ones, and nothing else followed, nothing that could be seen as hurting communism or the Party." The article was published in the theoretical organ of the Polish United Workers (Communist) Party, *Nowe Drogi*. Two weeks later we were called in, together with our boss at the Polish Academy of Sciences, by the Party tsar in charge of ideology to his headquarters, a building that now houses the stock exchange. He must have seen through our intentions, for in his rage he called us "reformists, revisionists, Luxemburgists," and I do not remember what else. He also said "You will see," which was not a forecast about our eyesight. In the end, the sanction was that I could not travel abroad, but the Polish repressive system was not very efficient – nothing was – so that if you knew somebody who knew somebody, you could get around most political sanctions. The ban lasted about a year.[1]

---

[1] In retrospect, I wonder why the comrade in question allowed the publication to begin with – ex officio he was the editor of the journal – and why my travel ban was relatively easily lifted. It may have been a setup; perhaps he wanted the message to become public but did not want to be associated with it, so he made a show of condemnation.

When I returned to the United States in 1967, it was a different country. A suggestion to picket a movie theater would have been shouted down as "reformist." The country emanated the fervor of a revolution: cultural and personal, not just political. It was one of those rare historical moments in which one felt free, perhaps because, as one of le Carré's characters observes (in *Small Town in Germany*), "Freedom's only real when you're fighting for it." One of the slogans directed against "the system" was "Power to the people," which I found curious because I had been taught that power of the people *was* the system: This is what "democracy" means. Obviously, electoral power was not the power claimed by this slogan. Elections were about nothing: Democrats, Republicans, what's the difference? The freedom to control one's own life is not the kind of power that results from elections. I intensely shared this quest for freedom. I was also sympathetic to the claim that elections do not offer real choices, that as Bobbio (1989: 157) would later advise, "to pass a judgement today on the development of democracy in a given country the question must be asked, not 'Who votes?' but 'On what issues can one vote?'" I did see the difference between systems in which, again in Bobbio's language, "elites *propose* themselves and elites *impose* themselves." But people have no power in a system ruled by elites: This is what we thought.

Power did fall into the hands of the people in a country where I arrived in 1970 – Chile. The people chanted euphorically that "*El pueblo unido jamás será vencido*," the people united will never be defeated. However, either this inductive generalization is false or the people were far from united. President Allende was elected by a tiny plurality as the candidate of a coalition of divergent and quarrelsome forces. Stabbed in the back by a party that portrayed itself as centrist, Christian Democrats, Allende soon lost control over his own coalition, parts of which hallucinated about socialist revolution. Henry Kissinger proclaimed that Allende was elected "due to the irresponsibility of the Chilean people" – such was his understanding of democracy – and the U.S. government decided to restore responsibility by force. When the force was unleashed, on a September 11 (1973), it was ferocious.

The Chilean debacle transformed the Left. Until 1973 many people on the Left were ambivalent between the quest for their normative goals and their respect for democracy. I believe, by the way, that Allende himself was a committed democrat, whose vision of "the road to socialism" was one of gradual steps, only as large as would be supported by the popular will expressed at the polls. He was prepared to see socialist reforms defeated in elections and he never entertained the possibility of holding power against their result. In any case, the Chilean tragedy forced a choice, reminiscent of that faced by Social Democrats in the interwar period: Socialism or democracy first? The clearest response emerged from the debates within the Italian Communist Party and it was resolutely in favor of democracy. This response may have been originally motivated by strategic lessons from the Chilean experience; pushing the socialist program too vigorously, without sufficient popular support, would lead to tragedies. But soon the unconditional embrace of democracy found philosophical, normative, roots: With all its deficiencies, democracy is the only mechanism by which the people can implement their power and the only form of political freedom feasible in our world.

These reflections were taking place in a world in which barbarism was widespread. Brutal military governments ruled Argentina, Brazil, Chile, Greece, and Uruguay; authoritarian regimes were still killing people in Portugal and Spain; communists did the killing earlier so that intimidation was sufficient to maintain their oppressive rule. This was not the time to engage in critical reflections about democracy: Democracy was what was missing, an absence. So when a group of scholars, many of them pro-democracy activists in their countries, gathered at the Wilson Center in Washington in 1979 to analyze and strategize how this barbarism could be stopped, we thought in terms of "transition from," from authoritarianism – that is, not "to" anything. Democracy was just what we did not like about authoritarianism. Hence, we studied transitions *to* democracy without asking questions about democracy. And we were not the first to do so: Shapiro (1999: 2) comments that "John Dewey's comment on older democratic revolutions rings equally true of our own: They aimed less to implement an abstract democratic ideal than 'to remedy evils experienced in consequence of prior political institutions'."

The advent of democracy repeatedly, and inevitably, generated disenchantment. Indeed, O'Donnell (1993) colored the democratic grass from green all the way to brown: Democracy is compatible with inequality, irrationality, injustice, particularistic enforcement of laws, lies and obfuscation, a technocratic policy style, and even with a fair dose of arbitrary violence. Everyday life of democratic politics is not a spectacle that inspires awe: an endless squabble among petty ambitions, rhetoric designed to hide and mislead, shady connections between power and money, laws that make no pretense of justice, policies that reinforce privilege. No wonder, then, that having followed liberalization, transition, and consolidation, we have discovered that there is something still to improve: democracy.

The new catch phrase became "quality of democracy." And it should be. As I look back, I cannot help but think that the world has become much better if this is what we worry about. Only now can people around the world engage in the luxury of taking a critical look at democracy. And they are taking that look. Moreover, as democracies emerged under exotic conditions, the complacency about institutional blueprints was shaken. Even the most parochial area students of them all – Americanists – ventured into a world outside the U.S. Congress, only to discover what a unique institution it is. Although the very first attempts to look beyond were terribly naive, some in fact just mindlessly arrogant – "imitate the U.S. institutions" – it quickly became apparent that democracy can come in all forms of variations and gradations. If we are to understand democracy, we have to be able to think of Chile, Poland, and the United States at the same time.

What I fear is that the disenchantment is as naive as was the hope. I am not afraid that a critical look would make democracy more brittle: I am convinced that in almost all countries that today enjoy democracy, it is there to stay. Nevertheless, unreasonable expectations about democracy feed populist appeals (see O'Donnell's 1985 brilliant analysis of Argentina) while blinding us to feasible reforms.

There are different ways to think about the quality of democracy. Certainly, it cannot mean resemblance to the United States, "the best system of government in the world," as all kinds of rating agencies would have it. According to the Freedom House, for example, citizens of the United States are free. They are free to vote, free to express their views in public, to form associations and political parties – except that almost one-half do not vote even in presidential elections, public speech is not free but sponsored by private interests, and no parties are ever formed. Are they free? To paraphrase Rosa Luxemburg, *is* one free or can one only *act* freely? Developing this theme would take us too far away from the topic of these ruminations, but there is one point I want to emphasize. Democracy is a system of positive rights but it does not automatically generate the conditions necessary for exercising these rights (Holmes and Sunstein 1999). As J. S. Mill observed, "without decent wages and universal reading, no government of public opinion is possible." Nevertheless, there is nothing about democracy per se that guarantees that wages would be decent and reading universal. The nineteenth-century solution to this problem was to restrict citizenship to those who were in condition to use it. Today citizenship is nominally universal, but many people do not enjoy the conditions necessary to exercise it. Hence, we may be seeing a new monster: democracy without effective citizenship.

The approach in this book combines two perspectives. I found it enlightening to think about the historical evolution of representative institutions into what today we call democracy. My impression is that we still tend to evaluate contemporary democracies in terms of the ideals of the founders. Because some of these ideals were incoherent or unfeasible, we find democracies in which we live lacking. I believe that we need to free ourselves of these shackles. I am not claiming that this is a pioneering undertaking: I cite herein many authors whose traces I follow. Robert Dahl, for one, spent most of his life ruminating about the same issues. Along with Dahl, Hans Kelsen, Joseph Schumpeter, Anthony Downs, and Norberto Bobbio are among my intellectual guides. If I write this book, it is not because I find their answers faulty but because I find that many questions remain open.

As a history, my account is at times deliberately anachronistic. Taught by subsequent experience, we today can make distinctions our historical protagonists could not. Such distinctions vocalize their silences, illuminate their hidden assumptions, delineate their conceptual horizons. Hence, although the voices heard below are theirs, the analytical apparatus is ours.

History illuminates variations and gradations but cannot speak to limits and possibilities. To determine what democracy can and cannot achieve, we need analytical models. Hence, I am following different footsteps by relying on social choice theory. The four axioms introduced in the short mathematical note by May (1952) are normatively attractive and analytically useful for identifying limits of democracy and directions of feasible improvements. However, social choice theory goes only part way in elucidating some important aspects of democracy: equality in the economic realm, effectiveness of political participation, control of governments by citizens, and the scope of issues that should be subject to collective decisions. Hence, I also rely on other models.

Although the material of this book is historical and comparative, the motivation is normative. When I was in graduate school – some time ago – every political science department offered a course in Comparative Government and one in Political Philosophy, popularly dubbed "From Plato to NATO," often taught by the same person. Comparative politics was the material with which to think about the great issues posed by venerated thinkers of the past. Yet over the past four decades these subjects became separated; indeed, history of political thought pretty much vanished from the curricula. But the history of thought is a history of issues about which we, in the end, care. I find it thrilling to ask what we have learned about these issues from our empirical knowledge of political institutions and events. I think we did learn, we are wiser, and we often see things more clearly than our intellectual forefathers. Unless, however, we bring our knowledge to bear on the big issues, it will remain sterile.

Throughout the book, I accompany textual analyses and historical narratives with analytical models and at times with statistical analyses. Like all authors, though, I want the book to be read. Hence, I hide technical material as much as possible. The inevitable cost is that some assertions may seem to be glib, but their origins should be transparent to a technical reader. Some issues, notably those concerning causality, are truly technical. I do not believe that history is driven by any "primary causes" or "ultimate instances," whether ideas, forces of production, or institutions – but that means that everything is endogenous. If it is, then identifying causes is hard, if not impossible. Hence, often I can say only that some aspects of ideational, economic, and political life evolved together, without even trying to detect which were the causes and which the effects.

Because this is an autobiographical preface, it is also a place to acknowledge intellectual debts due to personal interactions, not just reading. I have been privileged by the willingness of several friends to teach me what I do not know and to warn me that I am wrong. Although I studied philosophy as an undergraduate, my learning of history of thought has been guided by Bernard Manin and Pasquale Pasquino, whose erudition has no limits. Jon Elster, John Ferejohn, Russell Hardin, Stephen Holmes, José María Maravall, John Roemer, and Pacho Sànchez-Cuenca repeatedly opened my eyes to issues I did not see and often made me change views. I learned from conversations with Luiz Carlos Bresser Pereira, Fernando Cortés, John Dunn, James Fearon, Krzysztof Ostrowski, Ian Shapiro, and Jerzy J. Wiatr. Finally, I am deeply grateful to Neal Beck for instructing me in statistics and to Jess Benhabib for private lessons in economics.

I have also been lucky to be able to learn from many of my former students. Quite a few thoughts that enter these pages are a result of collaborations with Mike Alvarez, Zé Cheibub, Carolina Curvale, Jen Gandhi, Fernando Limongi, Covadonga Meseguer, Sebastian Saiegh, James Vreeland, and the late Michael Wallerstein. Much of what I know and think about legislatures is due to Argelina Figueiredo, Fernando

Limongi, and Sebastian Saiegh. Much of what I know about Latin American constitutionalism comes from José Antonio Aguilar, Robert Barros, and Roberto Gargarella. I learned about Argentine politics from Carlos Acuña and Julio Saguir, about Korea from Hyug-Baeg Im and Jeong-Hwa Lee, about China from Zhiyuan Cui and Gaochao He, about Chile from Patricio Navia, about Mexico from Jorge Buendia, about Brazil from Fernando Limongi. Tamar Asadurian, Anjali Bohlken Thomas, Carolina Curvale, and Sunny Kuniyathu participated in collecting the historical data used in this volume.

These personal debts find reflection in the pages that follow. I also have institutional debts: to the National Science Foundation for financing the project of which this book is a product and to New York University for awarding me ample opportunity to research and write.

As I repeat, I have been lucky. But my greatest luck has been to have spent most of my life – all the way through Poland, Chile, France, and the United States – with Her to whom this book is dedicated.

I

Introduction

The representative institutions under which we live today evolved from a revolutionary idea that shook the world in the second part of the eighteenth century, namely, that a people should govern itself. Only when equal citizens determine the laws under which they live are they free. Furthermore, liberty was the ultimate political value, "everything," as many said. Yet if we judge contemporary democracies by the ideals of self-government, equality, and liberty, we find that democracy is not what it was dreamt to be. Could it have been? If it could have been, can we better implement these ideals today? These are the questions that motivate and structure what follows.

We tend to confuse the ideals of founders for a description of really existing institutions. This ideological veil deforms our understanding and our evaluations. It is politically pernicious because it simultaneously feeds unreasonable hopes, including quite a few hallucinatory projects, and blinds us to feasible reforms. Hence, my intent is to demystify, to free our understanding of real democracies from the perspective of their origins.

"Democracy," with all its changing meanings, has recurrently confronted four challenges that continue to feed widespread and intense dissatisfaction today. These are (1) the incapacity to generate equality in the socioeconomic realm, (2) the incapacity to make people feel that their political participation is effective, (3) the incapacity to ensure that governments do what they are supposed to do and not do what they are not mandated to do, and (4) the incapacity to balance order and noninterference. At the same time democracy incessantly rekindles our hopes. We are perennially eager to be lured by promises, to put our stakes on electoral bets. A spectator sport of mediocre quality is still thrilling and engaging. More, it is cherished, defended, celebrated. True, those who are more dissatisfied with the functioning of democracy are less likely to see it as the best system under all circumstances. Nevertheless, even more hope that democratic institutions can be improved, that all which is valuable in democracy can be maintained while the malfunctions can be eliminated. Whether this is a reasonable hope is to be investigated.

Thus, the big question is which of these "incapacities" are contingent – specific to particular conditions and institutional arrangements, and thus remediable – and which are structural, inherent in any system of representative government. My ultimate concern is with the limits: How much economic and social equality can democracy generate? How effective can it make participation of various kinds? How effectively can it equip governments to act in the best interest of citizens and citizens to control governments? How well can it protect everyone simultaneously from each other and from the government? What should we expect of democracy? Which dreams are realistic and which futile?

Obviously, democracies appear in variations and their incapacities come in gradations. To assess the range of variation, I pay attention to all democracies that have existed around the world in the modern era. Reading histories of democracy, one quickly discovers that they focus predominantly on the experience of a handful of countries: Ancient Greece, England, the United States, and France. Indeed, one American reading of this history draws a lineage that extends from Greece, passes via England, and finds its culmination in the United States, the "New Athens." This lineage is not only ethnocentric; it is simply inaccurate. Europeans, in turn, see the two divergent experiences that dominated their history – constitutional monarchy as it evolved in England and republicanism ushered in by the French Revolution – as the first paths to democracy, ignoring the awkward fact that experiments with representative institutions in Latin America preceded those in most European countries. Hence, if we are to understand what democracy is, how it works, and what it does, we need to take a broader look. As Markoff (1999: 661) observed, "Not everything happened first in a great power."

I find little merit, however, in the exercise of looking for "democratic traditions" around the world (Sen 2003). It is easy to find elements of democracy in ancient India,[1] medieval Iceland, or precolonial Africa, but the implication that modern politics in these places owes something to their own political traditions is at best farfetched. Indeed, modern Greek democracy has no roots in the democracy of Ancient Greece. English constitutional monarchy had more impact on modern Greek political history than Athens did. I understand the political intention behind the project to find native roots of democracy, to make it appear less of a Western creation. Particularly now that the very word "democracy" has been sullied by its instrumental use in American imperialist excursions, native authenticity can be a source of vitality. Nevertheless, in most countries that became independent at various periods during the twentieth century, representative institutions were an export or at best an import: Even in those places where political institutions emerged without foreign domination, they were designed in the world as it was at the moment. The repertoire of institutional choices is a world heritage, not a native tradition. Although innovations did occur, the choices available to any country are to a large extent confined to those that are around. While some people advocated basing the 1950 Constitution of India on the tradition of the panchayat raj system, in the end the constitution "was to look toward Euro-American rather than Indian precedents" (Guha 2007: 119). Still, the experience of latecomers is not any less a part of democratic experience and, as such, a source of rich information. Indeed, my second goal is to free the study of democratic history from its ethnocentric bias by extending the scope of vision to the entire world.

Yet limits cannot be derived inductively from observing even all the historical variations. Even the best democracies we observe may be far from all that is possible. To identify limits, we need analytical models.

1.2 DEMOCRACY AND "DEMOCRACY"

When representative institutions were first established, they were not democracy as we see it today, nor were they seen as such by their founders (Dunn 2005; Hansen 2005; Manin 1997; Rosanvallon 1995). As Dunn observed, this fact raises two questions that must be treated as distinct: (1) How did it happen that political institutions evolved into arrangements under which political parties compete in periodic elections and assume

---

[1] During the Indian constitutional convention of 1946–9, someone invoked a 1,000-year-old inscription "that mentioned an election held with leaves as ballot papers and pots as ballot boxes" (Guha 2008: 121).

office as a function of their result? (2) How did it happen that we came to call such arrangements "democracy"? Moreover, there is no reason to suppose the actual institutions and our labels for them evolved together: Words and realities have their own histories.

Consider the second question first, because it is easier to answer and ultimately less consequential. The story is bewildering. The word "democracy" appeared during the fifth century BC in a small municipality in Southeastern Europe, acquired a bad reputation, and vanished from usage already in Rome. According to the *Oxford English Dictionary*, its first appearance in English was in 1531. The 1641 constitution of Rhode Island was the first to refer to a "Democratical or Popular Government." In Europe the term entered public discourse only in the 1780s, significantly at the same time as the word "aristocracy" came into common usage as its antonym (Hanson 1989: 72; Palmer 1959: 15; Rosanvallon 1995: 144); "democrats" were those who wanted everyone to enjoy the same rights as aristocrats. "Democracy" as a system of government was still employed almost exclusively with reference to its ancient meaning: The first edition of the *Encyclopedia Britannica* referred in 1771 to "Democracy, the same with a popular government, wherein the supreme power is lodged in the hands of the people; *such were Rome and Athens of old* . . . " (quoted after Hansen 2005: 31; italics added). The word continued to carry a negative connotation, so that both in the United States and in France, the newly established system was distinguished as "representative government" or "republic."[2] "Under the confusion of names, it has been an easy task to transfer to a republic, observations applicable to democracy only," complained Madison in *Federalist #14*. A positive view of Ancient Greece as a democracy emerged in the first half of the nineteenth century (Hansen 2005). Still, identifying good governments as democracies became the norm only after World War I, when, at the instigation of Woodrow Wilson, "Democracy became a word of common usage in a way that it had never been previously. An examination of the press, not only in the United States but in other Allied states as well, shows a tendency to use the word democracy in ways that Wilson made respectable and possible" (Graubard 2003: 665). According to Manela (2007: 39 ff.), Wilson accepted Lenin's language of "self-determination," but to counter its political impact he combined it with the "consent of

---

[2] The first thinker to use the term "representative democracy" in place of "republic" in Latin America may have been the Peruvian constitutionalist Manuel Lorenzo de Vidaurre, in 1827 (See Auguilar 2009).

the governed." As a result, he used this term "in a more general, vaguer sense and usually equated this term with popular sovereignty, conjuring an international order based on democratic forms of government." And "democracy" ended up to be the label all governments would claim. Even the "Democratic and Popular Republic of North Korea" mimics the self-reference of Rhode Island. I can only echo the astonishment of Dunn (2003: 5): "But what I want to emphasize is not just the implausibility of the idea of a single global criterion for legitimacy; it is the strangeness of the criterion we have chosen: the sheer weirdness... of picking on democracy as our name for how politics should be conducted everywhere and under all but the very worst of circumstances."

When one speaks about words, one must ask whose. Who were "democrats"? Was Madison a democrat? Were Robespierre, Bolívar? In itself, this question is not interesting, for any answer immediately becomes ensnared in definitions. If Dahl (2002) considers Madison to have been more of a democrat at the age of 80 than at 36, it is because he, Dahl, has a particular conception of democracy. Someone else may argue – Wills (1981) does – that Madison was as much of a democrat in Philadelphia as in his old age. Gargarella (2005) thinks that he was not one at any time during his life. But this is not a discussion about Madison, but about definition of a "democrat."

The 1955 (fifteenth) edition of the *Encyclopedia Britannica* defined "democracy" as "a form of government based upon self-rule of the people and in modern times upon freely elected representative institutions and an executive responsible to the people, and a way of life based upon the fundamental assumption of the equality of all individuals and of their equal right of life, liberty (including liberty of thought and expression) and the pursuit of happiness." This definition may satisfy contemporary sensibilities: Today democrats are those who cherish the trio of representative institutions, equality of all, and liberty for all. But the language of "democracy" is ours, not that of the protagonists whose views and actions we need to examine. They would see themselves as monarchists and republicans, *Montagnards* and *Girondins*, federalists and antifederalists, *conservadores* and *liberales*, but not democrats and antidemocrats.

Democracy was not made by "democrats." The negative example of Greece made the label foreboding: in Madison's (*Federalist* #55) words, "Had every Athenian citizen been a Socrates, every Athenian assembly would still have been a mob." For many, not just in the United States but in Europe and Latin America as well, the French Revolution confirmed these fears: "democrats" were "Jacobins," whose belief in the unlimited power of the people was lethal to individual liberties. Despotism of one had its mirror image in the tyranny of the many. Most founders of modern representative institutions, even those who rebelled against England, thought that the best system in the world, the ideal to be emulated, was the English one. What they took from the ancient world was not democracy but the idea of a mixed constitution, in which the influence of the people would be tempered and balanced, if no longer by monarchy and aristocracy, at least by the structure of representative institutions. "Democracy" could enter at most as a part of this system, a democratical or popular element of a system that would refine, filter, and check the raw will of the people.

Perhaps it is more enlightening to ask who were not democrats. They certainly included those who believed that laws are given by God or nature, so that they cannot and should not be made by man. But how are we to qualify the view that once a government is chosen, even elected, it is the duty of all to obey it in silence? The three modern components of "democracy" did not necessarily cohere together. As Hansen (2005: 17) observed, "In Classical Athens and again in our times we meet the same juxtaposition of liberty, equality and democracy. But in Montesquieu, in Jaucourt's article about democracy in Diderot's *Encyclopédie* and in other sources as well, democracy was associated with equality, not with liberty. Quite the contrary: democracy was seen as a threat to liberty." Parties, associations, unions – quintessential intermediate bodies of modern democracy – were seen as divisive and thus inimical to the common good of the nation. The role of the people, not just for Madison of the Convention but also for some French revolutionaries and Latin American conservatives, was just to elect the government, not to participate in governance.

If the problem were only the label, we could simply ignore whatever our protagonists thought of themselves. We could decide that "democrats" were those who would have accepted as their own the system we today call "democracy." We could claim that because of their views about Ancient Greece, most early democrats did not want to identify themselves as such, but in fact, that is, by our contemporary criteria, they were democrats. Indeed, we now know that their views about Greek democracy were uninformed and erroneous. Had they been familiar with Perikles's description of the Athenian democracy – "It has the name democracy because government is in the hands not of the few but of the majority. In private disputes all are equal before the law.... Freedom is a feature of our public life" (quoted after Hansen 2005: 1) – they would have recognized it as almost identical to the definition given by the *Britannica*.

We could then proceed genealogically, back from our idea of democracy to its historical origins, yet we would still confront a difficulty. We may all agree that democracy consists of self-government, equality, and liberty, but this consensus quickly breaks down when applied as a criterion to specific persons, bodies of thought, or institutions. When Dahl (1971) argues that in the real world we have only competitive oligarchies, polyarchies, he is appealing to normative ideals that are not shared universally by contemporary democrats. Schumpeter (1942), for one, thought that a competitive oligarchy is all democracy can be. While some people consider any restrictions on majority rule, say judicial review, as antidemocratic, others see them as an essential ingredient of democracy. We face today the same tensions and many of the same divisions as the founders; we are no closer to a consensus about good institutions than they were. For, by what criteria is the United States not a "democracy" but merely a "polyarchy"? Greek, Rousseau's, of the Jacobins? Gargarella (2005), for example, believes that in the nineteenth-century Americas the only true democrats were the "radicals," who believed in unrestricted majority rule, which was to be implemented by the sovereignty of unicameral legislatures elected through universal suffrage. By this criterion, "liberals," among whom he includes Madison, who wanted to weaken the legislature by bicameralism and to constrain it by executive veto, were not democrats. Even in our times, the trio of equality, self-government, and liberty does not easily cohere together: "because participation in self-government, is, like justice, a basic requirement, an end in itself, Jacobin 'repressive tolerance' destroys individual liberty as effectively as a despotism (however tolerant) destroys positive liberty and degrades its subject," so that "there is no necessary connection between individual liberty and democratic rule" (Berlin 2002: 49–50 and 176).

The retrospective criterion would not work because no one could imagine 200 years ago what democracy would become. Whatever were the intensions of the architects of representative institutions, the institutional systems they created did not evolve the way they intended. It was not only because in the long run social and economic transformations rendered the original ideas inoperative – Wills's (1981) defense of Madison is feeble – but, almost immediately, just because the architects did not correctly anticipate the consequences of their blueprints. Having vilified political parties in 1788, Madison went on to create one when he found himself on the losing side only three years later; having barred the people from participating in governance, he found them to be the last resort to control governments; having accepted restrictions of suffrage to those with property, he discovered such restrictions to be unfair and inefficient; having assured himself and others that the Constitution would protect property, he had to admit that property is always in danger when the people have a say in government. And Madison was as smart and as educated as one could be. The "founders," not just in the United States, were doing something truly new and, as they repeatedly bemoaned, they had only distant experiences to rely on for guidance. They could not have anticipated and they did not anticipate what their blueprints would generate. Indeed, they knew they were fallible: This is why they provided that the Constitution could be altered (Schwartzberg 2009). It is obvious that confronted with the reality of contemporary democracies, they could have said only that it would never occur to them that this is what democracy might become.

Few people defined themselves as democrats 200 years ago and those who did are not necessarily those whose actions had consequences for the world in which we live today. Conversely, even if we knew how to read the minds of historical protagonists, they would be simply bewildered if asked for their views about contemporary democracies. Neither method gets us anywhere, yet I think there is a way out of the conundrum: We can ignore their self-identification but we do not need to use our contemporary criteria. We can ask what was the ideal that shaped the establishment of representative institutions *and* guided its evolution into democracy as we see it today, the ideal that motivated actions of historical protagonists throughout the past 200 years, that brought us from representative institutions to "democracy."

As I see it, this ideal was *self-government of the people*. Again, even if etymologically it is nothing but "democracy" – *demokratia = demos* (people) + *kraiten* (rule) – it is important to remember that this ideal was not imported from Ancient Greece.[3] It advanced gradually to become a novel construction that took liberty as the paramount political value and went on to claim that this value can be achieved only if people are governed only by the laws they themselves determine and to which they are equally subject. The "civil constitution," to use Kant's (1881 [1793]: 35) formulation, was to be based on "1. The Liberty of every Member of the Society as a Man, 2. The Equality of every Member of the Society with every other, as a Subject, 3. The Self-Dependency [self-determination] of

---

[3] According to Hansen (2005), the myth that American and French founders were inspired by the Athenian democracy was invented by Hannah Arendt in *On Revolution*.

every Member of the Commonwealth, as a Citizen." The people should be the only sovereign; it should rule itself; all people in plural should be treated as equals; and their lives should be free from undue interference by others, including the government. This ideal was theirs and it is ours. As Skinner (1973: 299) would insist almost two centuries later, democracy is a system in which people rule, not anything else.

1.3 IDEALS, ACTIONS, AND INTERESTS

Obviously, some ideas must precede institutions. Political institutions are always created as a deliberate act, the ultimate of which is the writing of a constitution. Hence, they always materialize ideas. But, Hegel notwithstanding, ideas are too messy for history to be driven by just a single one. One danger we must avoid is assuming that the actions of the historical protagonists were an application of some ready-made, logically consistent blueprints. True, reading Sieyes, Madison, or Bolívar, one finds numerous references to "great thinkers," whether Locke, Montesquieu, Hume, or Rousseau. Moreover, many slogans heard since 200 years ago until today echo these thinkers. Does this mean that founders of representative institutions tried to implement philosophical systems? One could think that causality runs the other way: that protagonists want to do some things for other reasons and use philosophers to justify their positions.[4] Philosophical writings may be, as Palmer (1964) says about Kant, only "The Revolution of the Mind," rather than of practice.[5] If the protagonists appear confused in their thoughts and inconstant in their actions, is it because they do not understand what philosophers had in mind? Is it because they do not comprehend that, as an eminent French historian of Rousseau (Derathé 1964: 48; italics added) claimed, "All the arguments of *The Social Contract* – *this is the part of the book most difficult to understand* – tend to show that the citizen remains free by submitting himself to the general will"? Or is it because Rousseau just did not

---

[4] Here is an anecdote. Not so long ago, I received an e-mail from a former student who worked for a prime minister of a European country. This prime minister decided to launch policies liberalizing divorce, abortion, gay marriage, and euthanasia. The message asked which philosophers could be used to justify such policies.

[5] This is the title of his chapter on Germany. "The criticism to be made of Kant," Palmer (1964: 447) observes, "is that, despite his undoubted knowledge of current events, his philosophy left too impassable a gulf between the ideas of liberty and political action on the one hand, and the domain of empirical knowledge and the actual thinking of individual persons on the other."

make sense? Palmer (1959: 223) notes that John Adams read the *Social Contract* as early as 1765 and ultimately had four copies in his library. However, Palmer goes on, "I suspect that, like others, he found much of it unintelligible or fantastic, and some of it a brilliant expression of his own beliefs."

Even if ideas precede institutions, one should not read the history of actions from the history of thought. As will become abundantly clear, the founders of representative institutions often groped in the dark, seeking inspiration in distant experiences, inventing convoluted arguments, and masking personal ambitions under the guise of abstract ideas, sometimes driven by sheer passion. They often disagreed, so that the institutions they would establish reflected compromises. They were repeatedly surprised by their own creations and with a remarkable alacrity changed their minds, often too late to remedy their mistakes.

To understand the relation between ideas and actions, it is useful to ask what we can observe and what we cannot. We observe what some of the protagonists said and what they did, but we cannot observe what they wanted or thought. Often they said different things, or they said one thing and did another, or at least shouted about what they did not do and whispered about what they did. Consider the first two sentences of the French 1789 Declaration of Rights and Man and Citizen: The first shouts about everyone being equal, the second whispers about treating them as unequal.

Whenever speech and action diverge, we can suspect that interests are at play. Indeed, the skeptical social scientist believes that actions reveal intentions better than pronouncements. Speech is not credible when interests conflict. Take a politician who tells us that we all share common goals: We know that he means his, not necessarily ours.

This introduction serves to identify a central difficulty of the arguments subsequently presented here. I argue two theses.

1. The ideal that ostensibly justified the founding of representative institutions and their gradual evolution into democracy was logically incoherent and practically infeasible.
2. The actions of the founders can be seen as a rationalization of their interests; specifically, the institutions they created protected their privileges.

We do not know, however, that they used speech to rationalize their interests. Morgan (1988: 49–50), who was always skeptical about motives, thought for example that "It would perhaps not be too much to say that representatives invented the sovereignty of the people in order to claim it for themselves." I certainly do not believe that those who established representative institutions knowingly conspired to present their interests as a motor of universal expansion, to use the language of Gramsci (1971). Indeed, there is every reason to think that they truly believed what they said. Even more, those against whom these institutions were directed shared the ideals of their founders and justified their own struggles in terms of these ideals. Working-class leaders justified socialism in terms of equality and self-government: Jean Jaures (1971: 71) thought that "The triumph of socialism will not be a break with the French Revolution but the fulfillment of the French Revolution in new economic conditions," whereas Eduard Bernstein (1961) saw in socialism simply "democracy brought to its logical conclusion." The Declaration of the Rights of Woman and the Female Citizen, written in 1791 by Olympe de Gouges (aka Marie Gouze), simply changed the gender in the 1789 Declaration of the Rights of Man to apply the same principles to women. Leaders of national independence movements appealed to the values of the colonizers: The "Declaration of Independence of [the] Democratic Republic of Vietnam," written by Ho Chi Minh, began with quotes from the U.S. Declaration of Independence and from the French Declaration of Rights. Martin Luther King's dream was "deeply rooted in the American dream": "Now is the time," he demanded, "to make real the promises of democracy."

The conundrum is not easy to solve. We know that founders of representative government spoke of self-government, equality of all, and liberty for all, but established institutions that excluded large segments of the population and protected the status quo from popular will. We know – evidence offered in what follows is abundant – that they feared those whom they excluded and that they wanted the institutions they created to protect property. This is perhaps sufficient to conclude that they acted in self-interest. However, we also know that these ideals – again equality, liberty, and self-government – guided the political life of many peoples during more than 200 years. Perhaps the most plausible way out of this conundrum was offered by Gramsci's (1971: 161, 182) concept of "hegemonic ideology":

The development and expansion of the particular group are conceived of, and presented, as being the motor force of a universal expansion, of a development of all the 'national' energies; in other words, the dominant group is coordinated concretely with the general interests of the subordinate groups, and the life of the State is conceived of as a continuous process of formation and superseding of unstable equilibria (on the juridical plane) between the interests of the fundamental group and those of the subordinate groups – equilibria in which the interests of the dominant social group prevail, but only up to a certain point, i.e., stopping short of narrowly corporate economic interests.

Although he never cited Gramsci and I doubt ever read him, this is how Morgan (1988: 13–14) interpreted the origins of self-government in England and the United States in a masterful essay ironically entitled *Inventing the People.* "Government requires make-believe," Morgan observes. "Make believe that the king is divine, make believe that he can do no wrong or make believe that the voice of the people is the voice of God. Make believe that the people *have* a voice or make believe that the representatives of the people *are* the people." Nevertheless, an ideology is plausible only if it corresponds to something in real-life experience: "In order to be effective, ... a fiction must bear some resemblance to fact." Most of the time we adjust fictions to facts, but at times we must adjust fact to fiction. Fictions can cause facts: "Because fictions are necessary, because we cannot live without them, we often take pains to prevent their collapse by moving facts closer to fit the fiction, by making our world conform more closely to what we want it to be ... the fiction takes command and reshapes reality." This implies, to finish the quotes, that "In the strange commingling of political make-believe and reality the governing few no less than the governed many may find themselves limited – we may even say reformed – by the fictions on which their authority depends."

If we are made to believe that democracy is an implementation of this trio of ideals – self-governments based on equality and supporting liberty – some facts must support this belief. Furthermore, if this is how we think, we must investigate what facts make the ideals credible as well as how ideals inspire facts.

1.4 EQUALITY, PARTICIPATION, REPRESENTATION, AND LIBERTY

In the original ideal of self-government, elaborated by Rousseau (whose influence was extensive) and Kant (whose impact was minimal), people are free because everyone obeys but oneself when the people rules. From its inception, this ideal run into logical, practical, and political problems. It is logically coherent only if everyone agrees about the legal order under which all want to live. The principle that the people in singular rules itself did not easily translate into an institutional system in which people in plural would govern themselves. Whether it could be implemented by representative institutions, in which only some people rule at any time, became a subject of controversies. When the reality of social, economic, and political divisions became apparent, the notion that all people could be represented simultaneously by anyone was no longer tenable. Being governed by teams of politicians who would be selected in periodic elections became the second-best option. The collective power of the people to choose governments through the procedure of elections turned out to give sufficient plausibility to the belief that the will of the people is the ultimate arbiter of rule. As Dunn (1999) observed, no one likes to be ruled, but if ruled we must be at least we can periodically show our distaste by throwing the rascals out.

Given that in a large society not everyone can rule, not even for a short time, so that most of us spend our lives governed by others, and given that people have heterogeneous values, passions, and interests, the second-best to each of us obeying but oneself is a system of collective decision making that best reflects individual preferences and that makes as many of us as free as possible. This is second best because it is constrained by the fact that, given heterogeneous preferences, some people must live at least some of the time under laws they do not like. In turn, a system of collective decision making that best reflects individual preferences and makes as many of us as free as possible must satisfy four conditions: Every participant must be able to exercise equal influence over collective decisions, every participant must have some effective influence over collective decisions, collective decisions must be implemented by those selected to implement them, and the legal order must enable secure cooperation without undue interference.

To identify the limits of democracy, we must investigate whether these conditions can be satisfied, singly and jointly, by any system of institutions.

Here is the preview of the central arguments. Even if the founders of representative institutions spoke in the language of equality, they meant something else, best conceived as anonymity, political oblivion to social distinctions. In spite of lofty pronouncements about all being equal, the equality they had in mind was formal political equality, equal procedural chances to influence collective outcomes and equal treatment by laws. It was not social or economic equality. However, political equality is effectively undermined by economic inequality. In turn, effective political equality is a threat to property. This tension is congenital in democracy, as alive today as it was during the past. The puzzle we are left with is why democracy does not generate more economic equality. In some views, the poor for various reasons do not care about equality. In other explanations, either representative institutions are dominated by the rich whose disproportionate political influence prevents the adopting of egalitarian policies or the supermajoritarian features of these institutions favor the status quo regardless of who dominates them. Nevertheless, there may be exclusively economic or even technological barriers to equality. Equalizing productive assets turns out to be difficult in modern societies, in which land is no longer the most important source of income. Even if capacities to earn incomes were equalized, inequality would resurge in market economies. It may well be that equality is just not a feasible economic equilibrium. We should not expect democracy to do what no system of political institutions conceivably could. Obviously, this does not imply that inequalities could not be reduced in many democracies in which they are flagrant and intolerable. Moreover, because economic inequalities perfidiously infiltrate themselves back into politics, political equality is feasible only to the extent to which access of money to politics is barred by regulation or by political organization of the poorer segments of the population.

The widespread distrust of the raw will of the people led to restrictions of political rights and to institutional checks against people's will. The question that remains is whether political participation can be made more effective in any system of representative institutions in which self-government is exercised through elections. Even if the electoral competitors present clear policy proposals, the choices facing voters are only those that are proposed by someone. Hence, not all conceivable possibilities become subject to choice, and because electoral competition inexorably pushes political parties to offer similar platforms, the choices presented in elections are meager. Moreover, even if voters do face a choice, no one can individually cause a particular alternative to be selected. Nevertheless, even if individuals do not get to choose when they vote and even if their individual votes have no causal effect on the outcomes, the collective decisions that emerge from this process reflect distributions of individual preferences. It is thus puzzling that many people object to collective choices being made in this way. They seem to value being an active chooser independently of the outcomes of the collective choice. This reaction may just stem from an incorrect understanding of the electoral mechanism, but it does not make it any less intense as a deprivation. The nostalgia for effective participation continues to haunt modern democracies.

No rule, however, of collective decision making other than unanimity can render causal efficacy to individual participation. Collective self-government is achieved not when each voter has causal influence on the final result, but when collective choice is a result of aggregating individual wills.

Our institutions are representative. Citizens do not govern. They are governed by others, perhaps different others in turn, but others nevertheless. To assess whether we collectively govern ourselves when we are governed by others, we need to consider two relations: that among different parts of the government and that between citizens and governments. The structure of government is logically prior to its connection with citizens, because that which citizens can demand or expect of governments depends on what governments can and cannot do and what they are able to do depends on the way they are organized. Governments divided into powers may be unable to respond to the will of the majority as expressed in elections, specifically to a mandate for change. Various supermajoritarian or outright antimajoritarian institutional arrangements ostensibly protect so-called minorities. Although these days it is politically correct to use this designation to indicate groups that are for various reasons underprivileged – indeed, we use this label even for a numerical majority, women – we forget that *the* minority it was originally designed to protect and that these arrangements continue to protect are the propertied. Moreover, even if governments can do whatever they are authorized to do in elections, some agency costs are inevitable. Citizens must give governments some latitude in governing. Elections are only periodic and they bundle issues together. Self-government is not implemented by a series of referendums but by periodic elections with broad and often vague mandates. Hence, intense minorities often rise in protest against government decisions – but interpersonal comparisons of intensity are not feasible, so all we can do is to count heads.

Finally, the syllogism according to which a people is free when it rules itself revealed itself to be problematic. Although the concept of liberty was, and continues to be, subject to elaborate philosophical constructions, for the protagonists it meant that the government should enable individuals to cooperate by securing order but not encroach on individual freedom arbitrarily or unnecessarily. Balancing order and noninterference turned out to be difficult, though, particularly in the face of different kinds of threats. This balance is a succession of unstable equilibria, and no design of institutions will settle it once and for all.

Hence, democracy faces limits to the extent of possible economic equality, effective participation, perfect agency, and liberty. But no political system, I believe, can do better. No political system can generate and maintain in modern societies the degree of economic equality that many people in these societies would like to prevail. No political system can make everyone's political participation individually effective. No political system can make governments perfect agents of citizens. Although it is true that order and noninterference do not cohere easily in democracies, no other political system comes even close. Politics, in any form or fashion, has limits in shaping and transforming lives of societies. This is just a fact of life.

I believe that it is important to know these limits, so as not to criticize democracy for not achieving what no political arrangement can achieve. But this is not a call for complacency. Recognizing limits serves to direct our efforts toward these limits; it elucidates directions for reforms that are feasible. Although I am far from certain that I have correctly identified what the limits are and although I realize that many reforms are not undertaken because they threaten specific interests, I believe that knowing both the limits and the possibilities is a useful guide to political action. For in the end, democracy is but a framework within which somewhat equal, somewhat effective, and somewhat free people can struggle peacefully to improve the world according to their different visions, values, and interests.

2

Self-Government of the People

2.1 THE IDEAL OF SELF-GOVERNMENT

The ideal that justified the founding of modern representative institutions was "self-government of the people." The problem to be solved, as posed by Rousseau (1964 [1762]: 182), was to "find a form of association which defends and protects with all the shared force the person and the goods of each associate, and through which each, uniting with all, still obeys but himself, remaining as free as before." Self-government of the people was the solution to this problem. Self-government, in turn, was desirable because it was the best system to advance liberty, understood in a particular way as 'autonomy': We are free when we are bound only by laws we choose. As Dunn (1993: vi) observes, the idea of autonomy is the source of "the power and appeal of democracy." "In sharp contrast to the autocratic alternative," writes another contemporary theorist, "democracy aims to empower all citizens in equal measure. However short of this claim democracies may fall, it is this goal – the goal of autonomy – that characterizes them most centrally in normative and empirical terms" (Lakoff 1996: 155).

As formulated originally, this ideal is neither coherent logically nor feasible practically. When we are governed collectively, each of us cannot obey but oneself. Choosing freely for oneself is not a reasonable criterion for evaluating real democracies. But if the original ideal of self-government cannot be realized, what is the best possible?

Here is a sketch of the answer. The logical premise of the original conception of self-government was that everyone has the same preferences about the legal order under which each and all want to live. This

assumption of homogeneity collapsed in the manifest ubiquity of conflicts over values, interests, or norms. Nevertheless, a weaker notion of
self-government is logically coherent: A collectivity governs itself when
decisions implemented on its behalf reflect the preferences of its members.
Although this understanding is far from new, it is important to specify
the second best: the best self-government possible under the constraint
that some people have to live under laws they do not like because these
laws are preferred by others.

Let me preview the argument in different language. J. S. Mill (1989
[1859]: 7–8) was perhaps the first to observe that all cannot govern at
the same time, a point developed forcefully by Kelsen (1988 [1929]).
Moreover, in the presence of heterogeneity, it matters to all who does
govern. The classical Greek remedy was for everyone to take turns at
ruling and obeying. Rotation, however, cannot be implemented in large
societies because most people would never get to rule. What can be realized is a mechanism through which people who never govern themselves
select their rulers and at different times can select different rulers if they
so wish. Democracy as we know it today is this mechanism.

To provide evidence that the founders of representative government
could not even imagine what democracy would become, this chapter
begins with a history of ideas. Section 1 analyzes the original conception
of self-government. Section 2 highlights the issues inherent in understanding democracy as a mechanism for processing conflicts. Section 3 makes a
brief detour to Athens, showing an alternative to the modern conception
of self-government. With this historical background, I discuss the conditions under which self-government can be said to occur in large societies
with heterogeneous preferences.

2.2   "SELF-GOVERNMENT OF THE PEOPLE"

The ideal of self-government emerged gradually. Here is the briefest possible historical sketch, without any nuances.

1. People, "man" it would be said at the time, cannot live outside
   society, in the "state of nature." Particular thinkers developed different reasons the state of nature would be unfeasible or undesirable: People would physically aggress one another, seeking to take
   away property, or they would forego the benefits of cooperation.
   The state of nature is a state of anarchy and people can live better

under some kind of order. One cannot live outside society, be independent of others; this is not a feasible world. Although the phrase "as before" (*q'aupauravant*) appears repeatedly in Rousseau's comparisons of the state of nature and society, this is a counterfactual reference, serving only as a normative benchmark.

2. Because this natural liberty is infeasible, the only way in which we can be free is living under laws: "Only the force of the State makes the liberty of its members" (Derathé 1964: 48). The only issue is whether one can be free in society: Is there an order in which everyone is free?

3. Order entails compulsion: People are prevented from doing some things they want to do and forced to do some things they do not want to do. The authority that exercises compulsion can be an individual, who is then the guardian of order. This solution, however, raises the issue that Hobbes confronted, namely, who would prevent the sovereign from abusing power. As Dunn (1999) put it, the Hobbesian solution transposes a "horizontal" into a "vertical" danger.

4. An alternative solution is to place authority in the hands of all those over whom this authority is to be exercised: the people itself.

But what could it mean that "the people governs itself"?[1] Note that "the people" always appears in this phrase in the singular, as *le peuple, el pueblo, das Volk, lud,* and so on. "We, the People" is a single entity. This people in the singular is the only authority that can enact laws to which it would be subject. As Montesquieu (1995: 104) observed, it is "a fundamental law in democracies, that the people should have the sole power to enact laws." Democracy, said Rousseau (Letter to D'Alambert, quoted in Derathé 1964: 47) is a state "where the subjects and the sovereign are but the same men considered under different relations." Clearly, not all commands constitute laws; to qualify as laws, commands must satisfy certain substantive criteria, such as those listed by Fuller (1964). Moreover, ruling entails commands other than laws; it is not limited to legislating. Still, if only the people can enact laws, the people is always bound only by laws of its own making. Furthermore, because the laws by which the people is bound are of its own making, the people is free. Hence, at the end of

---

[1] For an enlightening linguistic analysis of reflexive propositions, of the form "I [insert verb] myself," where the politically relevant verbs are "command," "obey," or, more generally "govern," see Descombes (2004).

this cascade of tautologies, the people is free, subject only to those laws it chose, when the people governs itself. In Kant's (1891: 43) rendering, "it is only when all determine all about all that each one in consequence determines about itself."

Yet the people in the singular cannot act. As the Demiurge, the people is an apathetic one. This is why Rousseau (1964 [1762]: 184) needed to make terminological distinctions: "As for those associated, they collectively take the name of the people, and are called in particular Citizens as participants in the sovereign authority and Subjects as submitted to the laws of the State." Kant (1891: 35) made similar distinctions when he spoke of everyone's liberty as a man, equality as a subject, and self-dependency (self-sufficiency, autonomy) as a citizen. Nevertheless, how is the will of the people in the singular to be determined by people in the plural? One is free when one rules oneself, but is one free when the people rules?

Clearly, these questions do not arise if all individuals are in some way identical, if the subjects who choose the order they are to obey are but copies of a species. As Descombes (2004: 337) puts it, "the man as subject is not this or that man, but rather something like the rational faculty which is found among human individuals, everywhere identical." In Kant's view, guided by universal reason, each and all individuals will to live under the same laws, "For Reason itself wills this." And if the same legal order is considered best by all, the decision of each is the same as would be that of all others. Indeed, the fact that others want the same is irrelevant: If others command me to do the same as I command myself, I obey none but myself. Moreover, the procedure for lawmaking is inconsequential: When everyone wants the same, all procedures generate the same decision; each one and any subset of all can dictate to all others with their consent. Finally, this decision evokes spontaneous compliance: If each individual lives under the laws of his or her choice, no one needs to be coerced to follow them.

Hence, the condition under which the people would be free in plural when they rule themselves, collectively autonomous, is that each and all want to live under the same laws. Representative government was born under an ideology that postulated a basic harmony of interests in society.

This is not to say that the founders of representative institutions were blind to conflicts, to the manifest fact that not everyone would agree to everything. Some social divisions were seen as inevitable. As Madison, educated in Hume, observed in *Federalist #10*, "the latent sources of faction are . . . sown in the nature of man." Hume (2002 [1742]) himself thought that divisions based on material interests were less dangerous than those based on principles, particularly religious values, or affection. Not even Sieyes maintained that the consensus must include all issues: "That people unite in the common interest is not to say that they put all their interests on common" (quoted by Pasquino 1998: 48). Condorcet (1986: 22) pointed out that "what is entailed in a law that was not adopted unanimously is submitting people to an opinion which is not theirs or to a decision which they believe to be contrary to their interest." The classical argument admitted that people may disagree about many issues; it claimed only that some values or interests bind them together so strongly that whatever is common overwhelms all the divisions. All that was required was an agreement on some basics or, in Rousseau's (1964 [1762]: 66) words, "some point in which all interests agree."

Yet even those who recognized the inevitability of social divisions saw parties or factions as spurious divisions of a naturally integral body, products of ambitions of politicians, rather than reflections of any prepolitical differences or conflicts.[2] The people were a body, and "No body, corporeal or political, could survive if its members worked at cross-purposes" (Ball 1989: 160). The analogy with the body originated in the late medieval period and was widely utilized until recently. Even when the contractual perspective replaced the organic one, parties to a covenant or contract were seen as parts of a whole, rather than any kind of divisions. Proponents of representative government thought that because the people were naturally united, it could be divided only artificially. As Hofstadter (1969: 12) reports, eighteenth-century thinkers "often postulated that society should be pervaded by concord and governed by a consensus that approached, if it did not attain, unanimity. Party, and the malicious and mendacious spirit it encouraged, were believed only to create social conflicts that would not otherwise occur." "The spirit of party," George Washington (2002: 48) sermonized in his 1796 Farewell Address, "serves to distract the public councils and enfeeble the public administration. It agitates the community with ill-founded jealousies and false alarms, kindles the animosity of one part against another, foments occasionally riots and insurrections. It opens the door to foreign influence and corruption." His successor, John Adams, remarked, "There is nothing I dread so much as a division of the republic into two great parties, each arranged under its

---

[2] Rosenblum (2008, Part I) distinguishes two traditions of antipartyism: holyism, which assumes a harmony of interests, and pluralist antipartyism, which recognizes divisions but sees them as nefarious. She provides extentive evidence of antipartisan views.

leader, and concerting measures in opposition to each other" (quoted in Dunn 2004: 39). Ironically, one solution to partisan divisions could be a single party, uniting everyone in the pursuit of common good. According to Hofstadter (1969: 23), the main proponent of this solution was James Monroe: "It is party conflict that is evil, Monroe postulated, but a single party may be laudable and useful..., if it can make itself universal and strong enough to embody the common interest and to choke party strife." However unity was to be attained, unity had to prevail.

Partisan divisions had to be moderated and mitigated by a proper design of representative institutions. "If separate interests be not checked, and not be directed to the public," Hume predicted, "we ought to look for nothing but faction, disorder, and tyranny from such government." Among the virtues of the United States Constitution that Madison vaunted in the *Federalist #10*, "none deserves to be more accurately developed than the tendency to break and control the violence of factions." Madison recognized that differences of passions and interests are ubiquitous and inevitable; moreover, their most common and durable source is the "various and unequal distribution of property." Such differences, however, must not enter into the realm of politics. Nevertheless, the cost of prohibiting them would be the loss of liberty. Thus, Madison concluded that "the causes of faction cannot be removed; and that relief is only to be sought in the means of controlling its effects." Even if the etymology of these two words is different (Ball 1989: 139), "factions" of the time were exactly what we would understand today as "parties."[3] "By a faction," Madison defines, "I understand a number of citizens, whether amounting to a majority or minority of the whole, who are united and actuated by some common impulse of passion, or of interest, adverse to the rights of other citizens, or to the permanent and aggregate interests of the community." Factions would be controlled, Madison asserts (still in *Federalist #10*), by discussion among representatives as well as by the fact that in sufficiently large districts each representative would respond to heterogeneous interests. Indeed, the role of the legislatures is to

to refine and enlarge the public views, by passing them through the medium of a chosen body of citizens, whose wisdom may best discern the true interest of their country, and whose patriotism and love of justice will be least likely to sacrifice it to temporary or partial considerations. Under such a regulation, it may well

---

[3] "Faction," however, had a more clearly offensive connotation: as Bolingbroke would say, "Faction is to party what the superlative is to the positive: party is a political evil, and faction is the worst of all parties" (cited in Hofstadter 1969: 10).

happen that the public voice, pronounced by the representatives of the people, will be more consonant to the public good than if pronounced by the people themselves, convened for the purpose.

The French were less concerned about liberty. The last decree of the French Constituent Assembly of 1791 stated that "No society, club, association of citizens can have, in any form, a political existence, nor exercise any kind of inspection over the act of constituted powers and legal authorities; under no pretext can they appear under a collective name, whether to form petitions or deputations, participate in public ceremonies, or whatever other goal" (quoted in Rosanvallon 2004: 59). This principle seems to have traveled: the 1830 Constitution of Uruguay also made it illegal for citizens to organize into associations (López-Alves 2000: 55).

The hostility to parties was so profound that they were banned in German principalities in 1842; in some countries it was illegal to refer to parties in the parliament until 1914; and mass parties became fully legal in France only in 1901. When Burke defended parties in 1770, he reverted to what everyone else considered a wishful view: "Party is a body of men united for promoting by their joint endeavours the national interest upon some principle in which they are all agreed" (2002: 40).[4] Henry Peter, Lord Brougham (2002: 52), referred in 1839 to party government as "this most anomalous state of things – this arrangement of political affairs which systematically excludes at least one half of the great men of each age from their country's service, and devotes both classes infinitely more to maintaining a conflict with one another than to furthering the general good." "Party government" was a negative term, connoting conflicts motivated by personal ambitions of politicians, "obsession with winning power by winning elections,"[5] and the pursuit of particularistic interests – altogether a rather unsavory spectacle. It required a remedy in the form of some neutral, moderating power, such as the Emperor in the 1824 Brazilian Constitution or the President in the Weimar Constitution.[6] Yet, as Schmitt (1993) observes, even this solution was devoured by partisan

---

[4] Moreover, Hofstadter (1969: 34) observes, this view found only a faint echo in the United States.

[5] This quote is from the German President Richard von Weizsäker, in Scarrow (2002: 1).

[6] The connection between the emergence of parties and the need for a moderating power was the theme of Henry Saint-John, Viscount Bolingbroke (2002: 29), in 1738: "To espouse no party but to govern like the common father of his people, is so essential to the character of a Patriot King that he who does otherwise forfeits the title." Washington, in the Farewell Address, thought that parties have virtues under monarchy, where the king can arbitrate between them, but not under democracy.

politics; in the end, presidents were elected by parties. When this solution failed, constitutional review by independent courts emerged to constrain party government (Pasquino 1998: 153).

Although representative government meant that people have the right to organize in order to remove the incumbent government through elections, the proper role of the people in between elections remained, and continues to remain, ambiguous. Madison observed that what distinguished the American from the ancient republics "lies in the total exclusion of the people, in their collective capacity from any share in the government" (*Federalist #63*). He seems to have meant it literally, that the people should leave governing to their representatives "as a defense against their own temporary errors and delusions." According to Hofstadter (1969: 9), "When [the Founders] began their work, they spoke a great deal – indeed they spoke almost incessantly – about freedom, and they understood that freedom requires some latitude for opposition. But they were far from clear how opposition should make itself felt, for they also valued social unity or harmony, and they had not arrived at the view that opposition, manifested in organized popular parties, could sustain freedom without fatally shattering such harmony." Lavaux (1998: 140), in turn, observes that "The conceptions of democracies that emerged from the tradition of the *Social Contract* do not necessarily treat the role of the minority as that of the opposition. Democracy conceived as identity of the rulers and the ruled does not leave room for recognizing the right of opposition." The notion that people can freely oppose the government elected by a majority emerged only gradually and painfully everywhere, the United States included. After all – Hofstadter (1969: 7) is right – "The normal view of governments about organized opposition is that it is intrinsically subversive and illegitimate."[7]

2.3 SELF-GOVERNMENT IN THE PRESENCE OF HETEROGENEITY

2.3.1 Democracy as a Method of Processing Conflicts

Already J. S. Mill (1859) observed that all citizens cannot rule simultaneously. Following Kelsen (1988: 27), this observation became the point of

---

[7] Sukarno, the first president of Indonesia, thought that parliamentary democracy was a Western import because it "incorporates the concept of an active opposition, and it is precisely the addition of this concept that has given rise to the difficulties we have experiences in the last eleven years" (cited in Goh Cheng Teik 1972: 231).

departure of democratic theory: "It is not possible for all individuals who are compelled and ruled by the norms of the state to participate in their creation, which is the necessary form of exercise of power; this seems so evident that the democratic ideologists most often do not suspect what abyss they conceal when they make the two 'people' [in singular and in plural] one." People must be represented and they can be represented only through political parties, which "group men of the same opinion to assure them real influence over the management of public affairs" (Kelsen 1988: 28) or which are groups "whose members propose to act in concert in the competitive struggle for political power" (Schumpeter 1942: 283) or "a team of men seeking to control the governing apparatus by gaining office in a duly constituted election" (Downs 1957: 25). Isolated individuals cannot have any influence over the formation of general will; they exist politically only through parties (Kelsen 1988: 29).

No other aspect of democratic theory experienced a turnabout as sharp as political parties. Consider Madison himself. As soon as he found himself in opposition to Hamilton's policies, by the spring of 1791, he undertook with Jefferson a trip through New York and Vermont with no purpose other than to create a party.[8] Although he still believed that, ideally, if economic differences could be reduced, parties would not be necessary, he came to recognize that "the great art of politicians lies in making one party a check on another" (quoted in Dunn 2004: 53). Soon he used a label, "Republican," to identify its programmatic orientation. Toward the end of his life, at some time between 1821 and 1829, Madison would arrive at the conclusion that "No free Country has ever been without parties, which are a natural offspring of Freedom" (In Ketcham 1986: 153).

The first partisan divisions emerged in England in 1679–80.[9] In Sweden, two parties were organized to function not only in the Estates but also between elections as of 1740 (Metcalf 1977). Polarization over the policy toward France led to the rise of parties in the United States in 1794, even if the Federalist Party dissipated after the defeat of 1800 and a two-party system crystallized only a quarter of a century later. In France parties became recognizable in 1828. In some Latin American countries,

---

[8] This account is based on Dunn (2004: 47–61).
[9] Laslett (1988: 31) considers the 1681 "Instructions to the Knights of the Country – for their Conduct in Parliament," perhaps written by Locke, as the first party document in history.

notably Colombia and Uruguay, parties emerged from the wars of independence even before the formation of the state (López-Alves 2000).

By 1929 Kelsen (1988: 29) would observe that "Modern democracy rests entirely on political parties." Several post-1945 constitutions recognized parties as institutions essential to democracy (Lavaux 1998: 67–8).[10] Moreover, parties developed the capacity to discipline the behavior of their members in legislatures, so that individual representatives could no longer exercise their own reason. Indeed, in some countries representatives are legally compelled to resign their mandate if they change parties: The law recognizes that they serve only as party members.

Parties, in turn, have followers and leaders, who become representatives through elections. Representatives will for the people. "Parliamentarism," says Kelsen (1988: 38), "is the formation of the directive will of the State by a collegial organ elected by the people.... The will of the State generated by the Parliament is not the will of the people." Schumpeter (1942: 269) echoes the thought: "Suppose we reverse the roles of these two elements and make the deciding of issues by the electorate secondary to the election of the men who are to do the deciding." Although in the classical theory "the democratic method is that institutional arrangement for arriving at political decisions... by making the people decide issues through the election of individuals who are to assemble in order to carry out its will," in fact the democratic method is one in which the individuals who are to assemble to will for the people are selected through elections (1942: 250).

Thus far these views do not diverge as far from the classical conception as Schumpeter would have it. Although they would be uncomfortable with the emphasis on interests and parties, Madison or Sieyes would have agreed that the role of representatives is to determine for the people, and sometimes against the people, what is good for them. But here comes the crucial break with the classical tradition: Kelsen, Schumpeter, Bobbio, Dahl, and Downs all agree that nobody and no body can represent the will of all the people. In sharp contradistinction to the classical view, these theorists maintain that political parties represent distinct interests. The theory of democracy based on the assumption of the common good is

---

[10] The Italian Constitution of 1947 was the first to mention the role of parties in "the determination of national policy" (Article 2). The Bonn Constitution of 1949 (Article 21) and the Spanish one of 1978 render to parties a constitutional status. The Swedish Constitution of 1974 mentions the preeminent role of parties in the formation of the democratic will.

just incoherent. As Shklar (1979: 14) put it, in an article entitled "Let Us Not Be Hypocritical," "A people is not just a political entity, as was once hoped. Parties, organized campaigns, and leaders make up the reality, if not the promise, of electoral regimes."

Kelsen (1988: 25–6) was perhaps the first to systematically challenge the theory of self-government based on the assumption of consensus: "Divided by national, religious and economic differences, the people presents itself to the view of a sociologist more as a multiplicity of distinct groups than as a coherent mass of one piece." He rejected what Schumpeter would dub "the classical conception" with an equal vigor: "Moreover, the ideal of a general interest superior to and transcending interests of groups, thus parties, the ideal of solidarity of interests of all members of the collectivity without distinction of religion, of nationality, of class, etc. is a metaphysical, more exactly, a metapolitical illusion, habitually expressed by speaking, in an extremely obscure terminology, of an 'organic' collective or 'organic' structure" (Kelsen 1988: 32–3).

Schumpeter (1942: 250 ff.) offered a systematic critique of the concept of the common good or general will by making four points: (1) "There is no such thing as a uniquely determined common good that all people could agree on or be made to agree on by the force of rational argument." (2) The individual preferences which the utilitarians adopted to justify their conception of common good are not autonomous but shaped by persuasion, "not a genuine but a manufactured will." (3) Even if a common will would emerge from the democratic process,[11] it need not have the rational sanction of necessarily identifying the common good. Given the pathologies of mass psychology, nothing guarantees that people would recognize what is good for them. (4) Even if we could know the common good, there would still be controversies about how to implement it.

If no body, parliament or government, can represent all the people, is democracy just a method for imposing the will of some, who happen to constitute a numerical majority, on others? Schumpeter (1942: 272–3) does pose the question but quickly asserts the positive answer. "Evidently," he observes, "the will of the majority is the will of the majority and not the will of 'the people'." Then he mentions that some authors – he must have had in mind Kelsen (1988 [1929]: 60–3) – tried to solve the problem by various plans for proportional representation. He finds this

---

[11] The difficulty of identifying the common will was recognized by Arrow (1951) only nine years after Schumpeter published his text.

system unworkable, because "it may prevent democracy from producing efficient governments and thus prove a danger in times of stress." "The principle of democracy," Schumpeter insists, "merely means the reins of government should be handed to those who command more support than do any of the competing individuals or teams."

Kelsen (1988: 34) did offer a solution: a compromise among parties. He argued that "the general will, if it should not express the interest of a single and unique group, can be only a result of such oppositions, a compromise between opposing interests. The formation of the people in political parties is in fact an organization necessary to realize such compromises, so that the general will could move in the middle." "The application of the majority principle," Kelsen (1988: 65) maintained, "contains quasinatural limits. Majority and minority must understand each other if they are to agree." However, here he encounters a problem so thorny that it requires Freudian psychology, the "unconscious," to solve: Why would "compromise," in fact concessions made by the majority to the minority, be specific to democracy? He claims – erroneously so in the light of recent research (Gandhi 2008) – that autocracies do not compromise.[12] The only reason Kelsen could adduce was psychological: "Democracy and autocracy thus distinguish themselves by a psychological difference in their political state" (1988: 64). But if this solution – preserving political rule by making concessions – is not exclusive to democracy, a central value Kelsen claims for democracy vanishes.

Bobbio (1989: 116), attributing this view to Max Weber, observes that the normal procedure for making decisions under democracy is one in which collective decisions are the fruit of negotiation and agreements between groups that represent social forces (unions) and political forces (parties) rather than an assembly where majority voting operates. Furthermore, when party leaders negotiate, the role of voters is reduced to a minimum. All that voters can do is to ratify agreements "reached in other places by the process of negotiation."

Compromise among party leaders, subject to periodic ratification by voters, is as much as Kelsen or Bobbio can salvage from the classical conception of self-government. Self-government now means the government of parties in the parliament. Parties do not pursue the common good but

---

[12] The difference between these two types of regimes is not that compromises occur only under democracy but that autocracies can be, and many are, ruled by a minority. Dictators, however, also combine repression with cooptation to maintain their rule (Gandhi and Przeworski 2006).

search for compromises among conflicting interests. Bargaining replaces deliberation. The outcomes are to a large extent independent of results of elections. The specificity of democracy is reduced to the requirement that from time to time these bargains must be approved by voters. Nonetheless, all voters can do is either approve the deals negotiated by party leaders or throw the rascals out – in the language of the recent Argentine outburst against the political class, "fuera todos!," everyone out. And then?

In what follows, I offer an alternative view. Even if at each time a government can represent only some people, it represents as many as possible. If majorities so wish, governments can change, so that most people are represented some of the time. Although the people does not govern itself, it can be governed by different others in turn.

2.3.2 Self-Government and Rotation in Office

To understand the modern conception of self-government, it is enlightening to take a detour to classical Greece. The following is based on Hansen (1991). For Artistotle, the mechanism connecting democracy and liberty was that everyone "would rule and be ruled in turn." Here is his crucial passage (quoted in Hansen 1991: 74):

A basic principle of the democratic constitution is liberty. That is commonly said, and those who say it imply that only in this constitution do men share in liberty; for that, they say, is what every democracy aims at. Now, one aspect of liberty is being ruled and ruling in turn.... Another element is to live as you like.... So this is the second defining principle of democracy, and from it has come the ideal of not being ruled, not by anybody if possible, or at least only in turn.

The difference between the Greek and the modern conceptions of self-government is striking. Commenting on a passage by Castoriadis – "I give here the term human being, anthropos, the sense . . . of a being that is autonomous. One can say as well, remembering Aristotle, a being capable of ruling and being ruled" – Descombes (2004: 327) observes, "It is remarkable that Castoriadis did not say, as would only naturally a partisan of autonomy in the modern sense, 'a being capable of ruling himself.' . . . The good citizen is someone who is as capable to command as to obey." In Manin's (1997: 28) rendering, "democratic freedom consisted not in obeying only oneself but in obeying today someone in whose place one would be tomorrow."

The institutional feature that implemented taking turns in Athens was rotation in office: a combination of selection by lot with short terms and restrictions on reeligibility. Thus 6,000 jurors were picked by lot at the beginning of each year and from those as many as needed were picked by lot on a given day. About 540 magistrates, who had to prepare decisions of the Council and implement them, were picked by lot for a year and could not hold the office more than once (or at most a few times). Members of the Council of 500 were chosen by lot for one year from among those who presented themselves and could hold the office at most twice in their life, but not in consecutive years.[13] Finally, the ceremonial office of the *epistates*, who held the seal of Athens and the keys of the treasuries and represented Athens in relation to other states, could be held for only one night and one day in one's life. Here is Hansen's (1991: 313) summary of these arrangements:

> The rule that a man could be a councillor no more than twice in a lifetime means that every second citizen above thirty . . . served at least once as a member of the Council; and three quarters of all councillors in any one year had to serve for a night and a day as *epistates ton prytaneon* (and never again). Simple calculation leads to this astonishing result: every fourth adult male Athenian citizen could say. "I have been for twenty-four hours President of Athens" – but no Athenian citizen could ever boast having been so for more than twenty-four hours.

Rotation could not have become the institutional form of taking turns in modern democracies because of their large size. The 1776 Constitution of Pennsylvania, under which legislators, sheriffs, coroners, tax assessors, and justices of the peace were elected for one year and executive councillors for three, all with limitations on reeligibility, came closest to the ideal of rotation in the modern era. Nonetheless, even if we assume that no one ever served twice, at most one person in thirteen could serve ever.[14]

One can contrast Athenian and the modern democracy in several ways. The standard distinction is that Greek democracy was direct, whereas the modern one is representative. Manin (1997) highlights the method

---

[13] According to Finley (1983: 74), in any decade between one fourth and one third of citizens over the age of thirty would have been Council members and fewer that 3 percent served a second term.

[14] I assume that 1,000 people were elected. The population of Pennsylvania was 434,373 in 1790 and I use 400,000 for 1776. I also assume that adult life lasted thirty years.

  In the United States, there were 511,039 popularly elected local officials in 1992 (www.census.gov), 7,382 state legislators, and 535 federal legislators, for a total of 518,956. If everyone served only one year and could not serve ever again, about one in seven citizens would ever rule and only during one year (if adult life lasts fifty years).

for selection to public offices: in Athens it was predominantly by lot, whereas elections characterize modern democracies. However, the power of lot stemmed not from "simple political equality" in the sense of Beitz (1989), an equal procedural chance, but from short terms in office and prohibitions of reeligibility, rotation. After all, we could use lot to choose even a hereditary monarch. The sharpest contrast, in my view, is that the Athenian democracy ensured that most citizens would rule and be ruled in turn, while nothing of the sort would enter the minds of modern democrats. Even short terms in office and restrictions on reelection, wherever they were introduced, were intended to prevent entrenchment by the incumbents, rather than to give everyone a chance to rule. For the Greeks – Rousseau (1964 [1762]) had it right – "democracy was a state in which there are more citizens who are magistrates than ordinary citizens who are not." Although Paine (1989: 170) described the American system of government as "representation ingrafted upon Democracy," the graft transformed the entire body. All the elaborate constructions about the common good, ideal preferences, and collective will mask the basic fact that nothing in the modern conception of democracy precludes the possibility that some people could rule always and others never.[15] George Washington could say, "I have been for eight years President of the United States" and almost no one else could say that they were president even for a day.

2.4 SECOND-BEST SELF-GOVERNMENT

The original conception of self-government was based on an assumption that rendered it incoherent and infeasible, namely that everyone has the same preference for the legal order under which all would want to live. The classical Greek conception did not assume homogeneity but it was implemented by a mechanism that is not feasible in large collectivities. To define the ideal of self-government in large societies with heterogeneous preferences, therefore, we need to find a second-best option, which is still a system of collective decision making that best reflects individual preferences and that makes as many of us as free as possible. It is a

---

[15] Indeed, Sieyes justified representation by claiming that the people would want those who make laws to have specialized knowledge. Having observed that, in modern society, individuals must have specialized skills, he concluded that "The common interest, the improvement of the state of society itself cries out for us to make Government a special profession (cited after Manin 1997: 3; a more extensive discussion of Sieyes's view is in Pasquino 1998).

second best because it is constrained by the fact that, given heterogeneous preferences, some people must live at least some of the time under laws they do not like.

In turn, a system of collective decision making that best reflects individual preferences and makes as many of us as free as possible must satisfy four conditions: every participant must have equal influence over collective decisions (equality); every participant must have some effective influence over collective decisions (participation); collective decisions must be implemented by those selected to implement them (representation); and the legal order must enable secure cooperation without undue interference (liberty).

In analyzing these conditions we are aided by two theorems of social choice theory. May's (1952) theorem states that simple-majority rule is the only rule of collective decision making that satisfies four axioms: equality, neutrality, responsiveness, and decisiveness. Hence, if these axioms are desirable, so is this rule. Moreover, the normative importance of these axioms extends beyond simple-majority rule, because this rule implies in turn that as many people as possible live under a legal order they prefer (Kelsen 1929; Rae 1969). Hence, if these axioms are satisfied, collective decisions reflect individual preferences and as many people as possible live under laws they like. Social choice theory, however, is mute about the conditions for equality to be real and for participation to be effective, about the agency problems inherent in the fact that we are governed by others, and about the scope of issues that should be decided collectively.

2.4.1 Two Theorems

Consider first May's (1952) four axioms.

Equality–Anonymity. Equality means that *all* individuals have an equal weight in influencing the decision of the collectivity. Anonymity requires a collective decision to remain the same if *any* two individuals interchange their preferences. If anonymity is to apply to all possible pairs of individuals ("open domain"), then it can be satisfied only if everyone has an equal weight. Hence, equality and anonymity are equivalent over open domain.[16] Note, however, that equality must be effective, not only formal.

---

[16] David Austen-Smith alerted me to the importance of the open domain assumption.

Neutrality. The essence of the neutrality condition is that no choice should be favored independently of individual preferences. This condition is often formulated as saying that decisions should not depend on the names attached to alternatives. If a majority prefers "S" to "A" and their labels are reversed, then as long as preferences remain the same "A" should prevail. This condition may seem innocuous but it is not, for its target is the status quo. Say the law authorizing the death penalty is the status quo, abolishing it is the alternative, and a majority prefers the death penalty. Now suppose that the labels are reversed. Neutrality requires that the death penalty should prevail whether or not it is the status quo. Note that it may well be that changing the status quo alters people's preferences, which seems to be the case with regard to the death penalty. If collective decisions change when preferences change, then neutrality is not violated. It is violated only if decisions change as a consequence of relabelling when preferences remain the same.

Decisiveness. A collective decision rule is decisive if, having applied it, the community knows what to do. Somewhat more carefully, it is decisive if it picks one among all the feasible choices for each combination of individual preferences. This axiom is a can of worms and it is discussed at greater length below.

Responsiveness. Technically, this is the most complicated condition, and it comes in variants (see McGann 2006: 18). To keep things simple, think that a change of (at least) one individual preference either maintains the same collective preference or it breaks the tie in the direction preferred by the pivotal voter ("positive responsiveness," according to Austen-Smith and Banks 2000: 87). This condition, however, applies to committees, so agency problems have to be considered if it is to be applied in a representative framework.

These axioms imply two theorems.

Majority Rule. May's theorem is fairly obvious and well known, so it does not need to be restated. Just note that this theorem applies when there are only two choices and voters either prefer one of them or are indifferent between them. Because a tie is theoretically possible, some kind of a tie-breaking procedure is required, but this point is trivial when the number of decision makers is large.

May's is not the only justification of simple-majority rule. A brief historical excursion elucidates what is entailed.[17]

According to the classical conception, the role of representatives was to find the true common interest of all. As Schumpeter (1942: 250) aptly characterized it, "The eighteenth century philosophy of democracy held that... there exists a Common Good, the obvious beacon light of policy.... There is no excuse for not seeing it and in fact no explanation for the presence of persons who do not see it except ignorance – which can be removed – stupidity and anti-social interest." But how were they to know if and when they found it? What should be, to use the language of computer science, the "stopping signal" for their deliberations?

Objective truth is subjectively convincing, at least to people endowed with reason. Thus, Milton proclaimed, "Let [Truth] and Falsehood grapple; who ever knew Truth put to the worse in a free and open encounter."[18] Locke believed that "the truth would do well enough if she were once left to shift for herself." Cato wrote "Truth has so many Advantages above Error, that she wants only to be shewn, to gain admiration and Esteem." Jefferson asserted that "Truth is great and will prevail if left to herself." Because truth was manifest, everyone should be able to recognize it. Hence, the obvious sign that the truth is found is unanimity. Indeed, this criterion was widely used in early medieval times. As recently as in 1962, Buchanan and Tullock assumed that deliberation would lead to unanimity if not for the pressure of time. Even today, this is the assumption of some theories of political deliberation. Endowed with reason, recognizing everyone as equal, and susceptible to moral appeals, participants in the deliberative process do not need to "aggregate" their preferences through voting because they arrive at the same decision. Thus, according to Cohen (1989: 33), "deliberation aims to arrive at a rationally motivated consensus – to find reasons that are persuasive to all."

Yet "consensus" is not the same as unanimity (Urfalino 2007). As a signal that a decision has been reached, consensus occurs when no one objects against the presumptive decision – but silence need not indicate agreement, only recognition that further opposition would be futile. If unanimity cannot be reached, however, truth is in doubt. As Simmel

---

[17] Konopczyński (1918), in his classical treatise on the origins of majority rule, emphasizes that this rule was nowhere decreed, it did not result from imitation, and it was not subject to sustained arguments. It seems to have emerged spontaneously, independently in different countries.

[18] This and the subsequent quotes are from Holmes (1995: 169–70).

(1950: 241) observed, "a mere majority decision probably does not yet contain the full truth because, if it did, it ought to have succeeded in uniting *all* votes." Disagreement may indicate that truth is not manifest, that any decision may be erroneous. Hence, Condorcet (1986) required unanimity in situations when ascertaining the truth was a matter of life and death, although he was willing to accept less consensus in other situations. A hung jury, that is, a body that cannot reach unanimity even after all possible deliberation, does not provide certain guidance as to how each and all of us ought to act. If some want us to do one thing and others another, what ought we do in common?

Note Schumpeter's caveats: Unanimity may be not reached even when the beacon light is obvious, because of ignorance, stupidity, or antisocial interests. How can one tell whether it is not reached because the truth is not manifest or because of these illegitimate reasons? One solution is to distinguish persons and their reasons. Both the early German legal theories and the canon law held that in addition to numbers (*numerus*), we can distinguish authority (*auctorita*), merit (*meritus*), and intensity (*zelum*). In the early medieval English theory, these would become rank, repute, and judgment. Decisions should be based on opinions that are not only more numerous but also more valid, *major et sanior*.

Yet even if not all opinions are of the same quality, an overwhelming numerical evidence is sufficient to recognize that the decision is based on all the relevant dimensions. Thus, according to Heinberg (1926), different supermajorities were used by the thirteenth-century Italian communes: While Genoa typically demanded unanimity, Brescia, Ivrea, and Bologna required two-thirds, and several other cities four-sevenths. In turn, although still in 1159 the election of the pope Alexander III by twenty-four out of twenty-seven votes provoked a schism, the rule of two thirds was subsequently adopted by the Church for the election of popes.

All these accounts assume that the rule sought was one that would make decisions persuasive to reason, that would establish their epistemic validity as the reading of the common interest of a collectivity. Nevertheless, rules for collective decision making must also be operative in situations in which there is no interest in common, when interests only divide.[19] Unanimous decisions not only indicate that the truth is established; they are also self-implementing. If everyone agrees what is best for

---

[19] A fascinating example is offered by the use of majority voting during the sixteenth century to decide whether a community should remain Catholic or become Protestant. See Christin (1997).

each and all of us, each and all of us will follow the course of action that has been decided. Short of unanimity, though, compliance becomes problematic. Thus, the early German tribes did not feel obligated to follow decisions for which they did not vote. Sixteenth-century English nobles did not consider that they should pay taxes either when they voted against raising them or when they were absent when the decision was made. However, when collective bodies make decisions, they do not make them only for those who agree. As Simmel (1950 [1908]: 240) observed, "The significance, therefore, of voting, of voting to the result of which the minority, too, agrees to yield – is the idea that the unity of the whole must, under all circumstances, remain master over the antagonism of conviction and interest." Why would a minority comply with decisions of a majority?

Thus another line of historical research interprets the majority rule as a device for avoiding violent conflict by taking a reading of the physical strength. According to Bryce (1921: 25–6; italics added), Herodotus used the concept of democracy "in its old and strict sense, as denoting a government in which the will of the majority of qualified citizens rules, . . . *so that physical force of the citizens coincides (broadly speaking) with their voting power.*" According to von Gierke, German tribes used this rule but with no implication that the decision of the numerical majority would legally or morally bind the numerical minority. Only if the numerical majority could physically enforce its will did it prevail. Condorcet (1986: 11) as well, while interpreting voting in modern times as a reading of reason, observed that in the ancient, brutal times, "for the good of peace and general utility, it was necessary to place authority where the force was." This was also the view of Simmel (1950: 241–2), who reasoned that "because the voting individuals are considered to be equals, the majority has the physical power to coerce the minority. . . . The voting serves the purpose of avoiding the immediate contest of forces and finding out its potential result by counting votes, so that the minority can convince itself that its actual resistance would be of no avail."

Whether majorities indicated the true common interest or because disobeying would be futile, majority rule was thought to be at best an expedient substitute for consensus. Divisions were a sign of a malady, either incomplete knowledge or particularistic interests. The contribution of May's theorem was to justify simple-majority rule in terms of properties that we may find normatively attractive independently of the consequences of applying the rule, whether for truth or for civil peace. Simple-majority rule is not the only collective decision-making rule that makes collective decisions reflect individual preferences. If, however, self-government means that all should have the same influence over these decisions and if no alternative should be favored independently of individual preferences, then this is the rule that implements self-government.

Autonomy. Rae's (1969) theorem, in turn, asserts that simple-majority rule maximizes the number of people who live under the laws they like. It is noteworthy that the idea was presaged already in Kelsen's 1929 essay. In his words (1988: 19), "There is only one idea which leads in a reasonable way to the majoritarian principle: the idea that, if not all individuals, at least the largest possible number of them should be free, said differently that the social order should be in contradiction with the will of the smallest number of people possible." Indeed, in another passage, Kelsen (1988: 58) formulated the relation between simple-majority rule and autonomy almost as a theorem:

> When the number of individual wills with which the societal will is in agreement is larger than the number of those with which it is in contradiction – and this is the case, we have seen, when the majoritarian principle is applied – the maximum of liberty – understood as autonomy – possible is reached.

Kelsen's reasoning goes as follows. Suppose that there is a status quo social order, as there always is. There are n people. Now, if the rule for changing the status quo is unanimity, $n - 1$ may want to alter it and cannot. Hence, $n - 1$ will live under an order not to their liking. Assume now the rule is that the status quo is altered if at least $n/2 + 2$ people support a change. Then $n/2 + 1$ still suffer under a status quo they do not like. In turn, assume that the qualifying number is $n/2 - 1$. Then the status quo can be altered, leaving $n - (n/2 - 1) = n/2 + 1$ people unhappy. However, under simple-majority rule the decisive number is $n/2 + 1$, which leaves at most $n - (n/2 + 1) = n/2 - 1$ dissatisfied. Hence, majority rule minimizes the proportion of people who are unhappy about the laws under which they live.

Rae conceptualized the problem from the point of view of an individual who wants to select a collective decision-making rule that would maximize the probability that she or he would be on the winning side as often as possible given uncertainty about the preferences of everyone else. Because simple-majority rule "is the one decision-rule that precludes the possibility that more people would be outvoted by less people," it constitutes the solution to the original problem (1969: 52). Rae seemed to have been unaware of Kelsen's argument and used a different language.

What for Kelsen was "autonomy," for Rae is "political individualism." The intuition, though, is the same: The virtue Rae (1969: 42) claims for simple-majority rule is that it "will optimize the correspondence between individual values and collective policies."[20]

Simple-majority rule maximizes autonomy because it is responsive to the contingency that individuals change preferences: The incumbent party can be dethroned and the status quo can be altered if enough individuals change their preferences. Self-government must allow partisan alternation in office. To make this, perhaps redundantly, clear, consider the role of alternation in maximizing autonomy. Suppose that the society faces two alternative legal orders, A and B, advocated respectively by parties A and B. Let $v(t)$ be the proportion of citizens who support A at time t, and suppose that $v(t) = 1/2 + \varepsilon(t)$ while $v(t + 1) = 1/2 - \varepsilon(t + 1)$, where $\varepsilon(t)$, $\varepsilon(t + 1) > 0$. If there were no alternation at $t + 1$, the extent of autonomy over two electoral periods would have been $[1/2 + \varepsilon(t)] + [1/2 - \varepsilon(t + 1)] = 1 + \varepsilon(t) - \varepsilon(t + 1)$, while with alternation it would have been $[1/2 + \varepsilon(t)] + [1/2 + \varepsilon(t + 1)] = 1 + \varepsilon(t) + \varepsilon(t + 1)$. Conversely, suppose that alternation occurs even if $v(t) = v(t + 1) = 1/2 + \varepsilon > 1/2$. Then the extent of autonomy would have been $(1/2 + \varepsilon) + (1/2 - \varepsilon) = 1 < 1 + 2\varepsilon$, which would have been the case without alternation. All this much is obvious but important, because it shows that autonomy is maximized if partisan control alternates according to current majorities.

In contrast to rotation, however, the mere possibility of alternation does not guarantee that different people would rule in turn. The Greeks ensured that everyone would have an equal chance to rule by using lot and arranged that the chance would materialize by keeping the terms in office short. Representative government offers no such assurances. Some people may have to wait indefinitely. Indeed, in an electorate in which grandchildren inherit the preferences of their forefathers, a perfectly representative party would remain in office for ever. This possibility haunts democracy in ethnically divided societies. For alternation to be possible, that is, for the chances of victory of particular alternatives to be uncertain, either individual preferences must be changing or the

---

20 Note that Kelsen uses the language of "social order" or "societal will," while Rae speaks of "collective policies." It is not clear whether these terms are intended to cover only the laws a collectivity adopts or also other aspects of political decisions, including the composition of the government.

incumbents must err in representing them.[21] Even then, people who are unlucky enough to have unpopular preferences will never see them implemented. Simple-majority rule nevertheless maximizes the probability of partisan alternation in office. The winner can say to the loser, "Change the mind of the smallest possible number of people, and you will prevail."

2.4.2 A Caveat

The most banal definition of democracy is one according to which decisions implemented by governments reflect, correspond to, respond, or bear some other relation of proximity to preferences of citizens. The metric of proximity also underlies the conception of self-government proposed here. However, any conception of this kind, considered "populist" by Riker (1972), hurls itself against the theorem of Arrow (1951), which in our context implies that the very language of proximity between individual preferences and collective decisions is meaningless.

As has been observed innumerable times, Arrow's theorem has radical implications for our understanding of democracy. Suppose we were to abandon the language of proximity. How could we distinguish democracy from other political arrangements? If we identify it solely by the institutional procedures – competitive elections – how are we to evaluate it? Freedom still remains as a potential criterion, but no longer freedom understood as autonomy, or living under laws of one's choosing. The metric of autonomy goes together with the metric of proximity. Pareto efficiency is too weak to serve as a criterion: A dictator would be worse off if he were to live under democracy, while other people may be better off, so that these two regimes cannot be compared by this criterion. Civil peace might be another candidate but, without freedom, peace can be maintained by the threat of force, and many dictatorships are peaceful. In the end, all we could use as criteria are some indices of material welfare: economic growth, income inequality, infant mortality, and the like. Our normative apparatus would be greatly impoverished.

The implications of Arrow's theorem are so unpalatable that there have been numerous attempts to get around it (a representative one is

---

[21] Following Miller (1983), there is now a line of argument that claims that policies change as a virtuous consequence of cycling. This seems to me to be a misinterpretation of Arrow's theorem. This theorem asserts nothing about the occurrence of cycling; it says only that collective decisions are indeterminate (Austen-Smith and Banks 2000: 184). Cycling may or may not occur and I am not persuaded by McGann (2006) that it often does.

by Mackie 2004). Arrow's theorem is based on assumptions, axioms, and these axioms can be questioned. The axiom of unrestricted domain – people can hold any kind of (transitive) preference – is vulnerable to the observation that societies structure individual preferences and thus restrict their variety. When the domain of preferences is restricted in some particular ways, decisiveness is restored and with it the metric of proximity. For example, if we confront only two choices, majority rule is decisive and the proximity metric is valid: The choice supported by the majority is closer than the one supported by a minority. The same is true if all the choices can be arranged along one dimension (more or less of something) and preferences are single peaked (Black 1958; Downs 1957). There are also good arguments for abandoning Arrow's axiom of the independence of irrelevant alternatives. Finally, one can attack the theorem by pointing out that individuals confront the same difficulty as collectivities yet, in the end, individuals order their preferences, which is Arrow's point of departure. For example, Bird (2000) argues that deciding what one wants to do is not any less problematic at the individual level, yet we assume that individuals know what they want.

The alternative I pursue is to relax and reinterpret the axiom of decisiveness. Since social choice theory is highly technical – and I am not an expert – we are on slippery ground. But here is the argument, couched in intuitive terms.

There are three voters who decide on one among five choices. Three girls are given money by their parents to buy one flavor of ice cream. The girls are $\{i, j, k\}$ and the flavors $\{D, C, S, T, V\}$, for dulce de leche, chocolate, strawberry, tea, and vanilla. Suppose first that they all like chocolate above anything else. Then any procedure and any rule will generate the same decision, which will be chocolate. Indeed, if any one of them takes command and orders what they should buy, no one will object. Even dictatorship picks up the most preferred choice when preferences are identical. Now assume, though, that the preferences are as follows ($\succ$ stands for "strictly prefers"):

Decider	Prefers
i	$C \succ S \succ D \succ T \succ V$
j	$D \succ T \succ S \succ V \succ C$
k	$C \succ D \succ V \succ S \succ M$

They decide by voting on two flavors at a time and using a simple-majority rule (Condorcet tournament). One can easily see that chocolate still beats all the other choices by a vote of 2:1 and that it cannot be beaten by any other choice by a majority rule. Chocolate is thus the Condorcet winner.

Note that the decision will be different if we use a different procedure. Suppose each decider gives 5 points to her first choice, 4 to the second, and so on, and that the collective decision is the choice that obtains the most points (Borda count). It turns out that dulce de leche gets 12 points, while Chocolate only 11.

Which of these procedures is better has been the subject of polemics that originated in the second half of the eighteenth century, and these are not the only ways to reveal ordinal preferences. Nonetheless, we have enough of an apparatus to enter into our problem. Suppose that the preference profiles are as follows:

Decider	Prefers
i	$C \succ S \succ V \succ T \succ D$
j	$S \succ V \succ C \succ D \succ T$
k	$V \succ C \succ S \succ D \succ T$

These preferences illustrate the Condorcet paradox, of which Arrow's theorem is a generalization. As one can see, now chocolate defeats strawberry, strawberry defeats vanilla, and vanilla defeats chocolate by pairwise majority vote. Hence, this procedure is not decisive. Moreover, the first three choice are equally close to individual preferences, so the proximity metric does not work. The Borda count does not do better: Chocolate, strawberry, and vanilla all get 12 points. We still do not know what the collectivity would decide. Arrow's theorem says that this situation is possible under all nondictatorial decision rules of collective decision making.

Let us therefore relax the decisiveness criterion. Note that although neither procedure uniquely identifies the collective decision, both at least lead to the conclusion that this collectivity prefers any element in $\{C, S, V\}$ to any element in $\{T, D\}$. Democracy now looks better than dictatorship by the proximity metric: It ensures that the collective choice will an element in the first set, while dictators may have a proclivity for dulce de leche or tea. Now, with at least as many decision makers as choices, there is some probability, increasing in both numbers (Ordeshook 1986), that any nondictatorial collective decision-making rule will be indecisive. But this means that there is also some probability that it is at least weakly decisive, in the sense illustrated by the example. In the language of proximity, any collective decision in the "top cycle" $\{C, S, V\}$ is closer to individual preferences than would be any other choice, so that any decision-making rule that is sure to pick an element of the top cycle is superior to any that may fail to do so.

One can go further. Think now that the procedure of decision making is sequential and that it uses a so-called closed rule, meaning that a choice that was once proposed and defeated cannot be proposed again. Decisions are still made by simple-majority rule. Then the outcome in $\{C, S, V\}$ will be uniquely determined by the sequence of proposals. If V is first paired with S and then S with C, then the winner will be C; if S is first paired with C and then C with V, then it will be V, and so on. In this way, whoever sets the agenda can orchestrate the pairings in such a way as to get her or his first choice as the choice of the collectivity (McKelvey 1976). Now we have a unique decision. This decision may seem arbitrary, accidental. But it is not accidental who gets to set the agendas in democracies: We elect presidents, prime ministers, chairs of parliamentary committees, or floor leaders. Moreover, if we do not like the outcomes they orchestrate, we can elect someone else.

This argument can be and has been contested by arguments that it constitutes *regressus ad infinitum*. After all, the same intransitivities can arise when we choose procedures by which decisions are made and, if they are just holders of particular preference profiles, presidents or prime ministers. Nevertheless, these choices may still be weakly decisive, so the same counterargument applies. Moreover, they are more likely to be dichotomous, and then simple-majority rule is decisive.

The fact is that voters vote and elect, and that legislatures adopt laws. These laws constitute collective decisions. The decisions may have been different, but they are what they are. Ordinary citizens do not say "Oh! But given the preferences of the individuals the decision may have been different." It takes a Riker (1972) to claim that this fact undermines the validity or the legitimacy of the results generated by the democratic process. The issue is only whether we can tell that one decision is closer to individual preferences than would have been another. The answer is that we do know that no other decision would have been closer, and that some, in the extreme all, other decisions may have been farther. Hence, the proximity metric does weakly order all the collective decisions.

2.4.3 Beyond Social Choice Theory

May's axioms are satisfied when everyone has equal influence over collective decisions, no choice is favored ex ante, and the collective decision is responsive to individual preferences. Moreover, when this is true, the resulting decision maximizes the number of people who are free in the sense of living under laws they prefer. Unfortunately, neither these axioms, nor social choice theory in general, provide sufficient conditions for second-best self-government as defined above. Social choice theory has nothing to say about the conditions under which effective equality of influence over collective decisions obtains or about the conditions under which individual participation in the process of deciding is causally effective. Moreover, the axioms of social choice concern decision making by committees, while self-government must be analyzed within a context of institutions that are representative, in which the implementation of collective decisions is a prerogative of specialized agents, the government. Finally, the axiom of decisiveness says nothing about the scope of collective decision making, about the extent to which private lives need to be regulated by laws at all. Hence, to understand self-government and its limits, we must venture beyond social choice theory. We do this best by considering the four conditions of second-best self-government – again, equality, participation, representation, and liberty – one at a time. Because these conditions are complex, each is the subject of a separate chapter.

3

A Brief History of Representative Institutions

3.1 FROM REPRESENTATIVE INSTITUTIONS TO DEMOCRACY

Before delving into the analysis, it should be helpful to have at least a brief historical background. What follows in this chapter are some stylized facts, without any attempt at explanations. Additional facts are provided in the subsequent chapters, where they are most relevant. This chapter begins with an overall glance and then enters into some details.

Modern representative institutions are those that combine lower houses of legislatures elected on the basis of individual suffrage (even if restricted but as distinct from estate or corporate representation),[1] separation of executive from legislative functions,[2] the power of legislatures to convoke themselves (even if they could be dissolved), and the placement of taxing power in legislatures. While recent research dug up a variety of legislative assemblies in various parts of Europe already in the late medieval period and, indeed, quite a few in other places around the world, systems of representative institutions as defined here first emerged in England[3] and in Poland, where they can be dated discretely to 1493 (Jędruch 1998). The War of Independence in the United States resulted

---

[1] The Swedish legislatures of the "Age of Liberty," from 1719 to 1772 (Roberts 2002) and, again, from 1809 to 1866 (Verney 1957) were based on estate representation.
[2] Several European republics in Italy, the Low Countries, and Switzerland were governed by elected collective bodies, but these bodies combined the legislative and the executive functions.
[3] The inclusion of England is somewhat problematic because franchise was a privilege of localities rather than of individuals. Not until the reform of 1832 was franchise standardized on an individual basis.

in the first appearance of such institutions in the Western Hemisphere. They were first established in France in 1789 and in Spain in 1812. After Poland lost independence in 1795, England, the United States, France, and Spain became the paragons of institutional engineering for countries in Latin America that became independent after 1810 and in Europe, beginning with Norway in 1814.

Once established, these institutions did not always last. In many countries representative institutions collapsed, in some repeatedly, either because the incumbent government decided to rule without observing the institutional rules, or because the losers would not obey the verdict of elections, or because some political forces that did not find a place for themselves in the institutional arrangements acted to destroy them. While representative institutions were established for all kinds of reasons idiosyncratic to the periods and countries, rather than as a systematic result of social or economic development, they were more likely to survive if countries were more developed economically.

Given that in many countries the history of representative institutions was punctuated by frequent reversals, their evolution was often discontinuous. There are, however, some general patterns. For almost a century after representative institutions were first established, conflicts over suffrage were organized along class lines. The lower classes struggled to gain a place within them, encountering resistance from the incumbent holders of political rights. Even if it took a long time, poor men conquered their place in the framework of representative institutions. The political rights of women came later and in most countries followed a different dynamic. While in the United Kingdom and the United States the extension of suffrage to women entailed a fair dose of protagonism on their part, in most countries these rights were extended without much ado as a consequence of partisan logic. Until well into the second half of the nineteenth century, whatever issues that may have divided propertied men were not sufficient for partisan considerations to prevail over the fear of the distributional consequences that would ensue from incorporating the poor into representative institutions. Once poor men became enfranchised, though, politics became organized by political parties. In pursuit of their economic and social goals, parties sought to enhance their electoral positions, treating the issue of female suffrage as an instrument of electoral competition. When current majorities thought they would benefit electorally from the votes of women, they granted women the right to vote.

Conceding rights did not mean conceding power. When the poor were allowed to vote, institutional devices regulated their participation. Lists of official candidates, indirect elections, open voting, practices of registration, electoral systems, design of districts, and outright fraud were just some devices used to influence who participates and with what consequences. In their combination, the ideas and institutional devices affect the relation between voting and electing and thus both the incentives to avail oneself of one's rights and the effects of exercising them. Because elections operate according to rules and rules have consequences, elections are inextricably manipulable. And they were manipulated. Electoral defeats of incumbents have been startlingly rare: Until recently only about one election in six resulted in partisan alternations in office.

The development of representative institutions followed different paths in the countries that preserved monarchies and in those that freed themselves from distant monarchs or deposed local ones. The best design of representative institutions – the separation of functions, their allocation to different powers of government, mutual checks and balances among these powers – was not obvious to the original founders. Some designs had faults that quickly became apparent: They granted too much power either to the legislature or to the executive. Moreover, they were instituted without considering that politics would become partisan and that parties can destroy even the best schemes of separation.

In the end, even if most grudgingly, with all the twists and turns, over the past 200 years representative institutions evolved toward what we now call "democracy." Again, the evolution toward democracy has not been linear. While during the nineteenth century the main issues of conflict were the extent of suffrage and the relation between the executive and the legislative powers, wherever and whenever representative institutions existed at all, they tended to allow some opposition, some political pluralism. In turn, the main line of political conflicts since the 1920s was no longer suffrage but the very possibility of contesting political power through elections. Many newly independent countries emulated the technological innovation of V. I. Lenin, namely, political institutions controlled by a single party. Yet most single-party regimes died at the end of the previous century, so that today only a few autocracies still populate the world. In most countries formal political rights are almost universal; political life is organized by political parties; elections are competitive, giving the opposition a reasonable chance to win; and both governments and oppositions observe at least the basic rules of democracy.

3.2 THE RISE OF REPRESENTATIVE INSTITUTIONS

The representative institutions considered here are those that combine elected lower houses of legislatures, the separation of executive from legislative powers, the power of legislatures to convoke themselves, and the placement of taxing power in legislatures. Such systems of representative institutions first emerged in England and in Poland, which, however, disappeared as a country in 1795. The war of independence in the United States resulted in the appearance of such institutions in the Western Hemisphere. In Europe, they were first formed in France in 1789, followed by Spain in 1812, Norway in 1814, Netherlands in 1815, Switzerland in 1815, and Portugal in 1820.[4] Three European countries that became independent before 1848 joined this list almost immediately: Belgium in 1830, Luxembourg in 1841, and Greece in 1844. The revolutionary wave of 1848 resulted in experiments with representative government in Denmark and Piemonte, where it lasted, and in Germany and the Austrian-Hungarian Empire, where it turned out to be ephemeral. Other European countries joined this list before the First World War as they became independent or at least autonomous: Romania in 1864, Bulgaria in 1879, and Finland in 1906. Representative institutions emerged with unification in the German Reich in 1867 and in Italy in 1861, and they were reestablished in the Austrian Empire in 1867. Finally, the first parliament opened in Russia in 1906. In Latin America, all countries established representative institutions within a few years after independence, beginning with Colombia in 1810, Paraguay and Venezuela in 1811, and Chile in 1818. In other parts of the world, the Ottoman Empire unsuccessfully experimented with representative institutions in 1876–7 and then reestablished them in 1908, while Iran had its first elected legislature as of 1906. Representative institutions also functioned in several colonies that enjoyed self-rule: In Barbados and Jamaica they were already in place at the end of the eighteenth century, and in Canada they were in place as of 1867. Most countries that became independent after 1918 established at least nominally representative institutions (nominally because, after 1960, many of them did not allow any partisan opposition).

Figure 3.1 shows the proportion of countries and dependent territories that had representative institutions, as just defined, by year. This proportion increased almost secularly until the 1930s, when some parliaments

---

[4] They also existed for a short period after 1796 in the Batavian Republic. Note that Sweden, which adopted a new constitution in 1809, had an estate-based legislature until 1866.

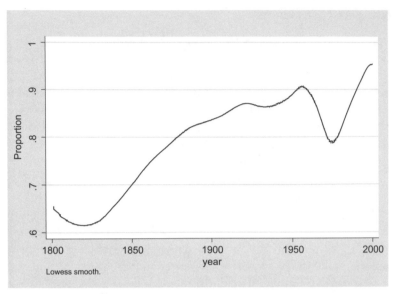

FIGURE 3.1 Proportion of countries with legislatures.

were closed by fascist governments, with a big dip that followed the massive wave of independence in Africa as well as the advent of the last wave of military regimes in Latin America. Note that the legislatures portrayed here include those that were elected only in part and those elected in noncompetitive elections, as long as these legislatures had a nominal power to approve taxation.

3.3 SUFFRAGE

When representative institutions were first established, political rights were everywhere restricted to wealthy men. The road to universal suffrage took a long time to traverse. Still by 1900, only seventeen countries enfranchised all men while only one country enfranchised women. We had to wait until the second half of the twentieth century, more than 150 years after representative institutions were first established, for universal suffrage to become an irresistible norm.

While some early constitutions made male suffrage nearly universal, during most of the nineteenth century the right to vote was confined to adult men who owned property, earned some amount of income, or paid some amount of taxes. Two countries – Liberia in 1839[5] and Greece in

[5] Liberia was a private settlement of American slaves, a Commonwealth, in 1839.

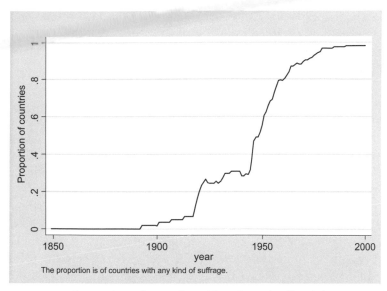

The proportion is of countries with any kind of suffrage.

FIGURE 3.2 Proportion of countries with universal suffrage, by year.

1844 – extended the right to vote to all adult men in their first suffrage laws.[6] Beginning with France in 1792,[7] the first suffrage qualifications were also relatively extensive in nineteen countries that gave the right to vote to all independent men. The operative category that qualified for suffrage in Spanish America was *vecino* (literally "neighbor")[8], defined by phrases such as "Having a property, or exercising some profession, or a skill with a public title, or having an occupation in some useful pursuit, without subjection to another as a servant or day worker" (Peru in 1823) or "exercising some useful occupation or having known means of subsistence" (Costa Rica in 1824). As several essays in Sabato (2000) emphasize, this was a sociological, not a legal, concept: a *vecino* was simply

---

[6] The 1821 electoral law of Buenos Aires introduced universal suffrage but only for free men. About 12 percent of the population was not free (Ternavaso 1995: 66–7).

[7] The law of 1792 required direct tax payment equivalent to three days of local wages. Universal male suffrage was introduced in the Constitution of 1793 (Article 4) but this Constitution never went into effect and no elections were held under it. The Constitution of 1795, which replaced it, required in turn payment of a direct tax contribution (Article 8) or participation in at least one military campaign (Article 9). Moreover, it excluded domestic servants and persons convicted of bankruptcy (Article 13). See the documents in Serge Aberdam et al. (2006) and a discussion in Crook (2002).

[8] The equivalent term in early North America was "inhabitant," defined in New Jersey in 1766 as a Freeholder, Tenant for years, or Householder in Township or Precinct. See Klinghoffer and Elkis (1992: 190 n)

someone who had a standing in a local community. Moreover, because eligibility for voting was determined by local authorities, the application of these criteria was informal and loose. As Canedo (1998: 188–9) recounts, if Pedro was known to be a good person by members of the local electoral table, he was a *vecino*. In these countries, the nationalization of citizenship (about which see Annino 1995, 1998), which transformed it from a social to a legal concept, meant replacing these vague criteria by specific income or tax thresholds, sometimes combined with the literacy requirement, which were more restrictive. Thus of the nineteen countries in which the first qualifications gave the right to vote to all independent men, suffrage was subsequently restricted in sixteen. Because Liberia also restricted franchise in 1847 and because all other countries that introduced suffrage before 1848 conditioned the right to vote on property, income, or literacy, Greece, Mexico (which extended suffrage to all men in 1847), and El Salvador (which maintained the *vecino* suffrage) were the only countries with broad male suffrage as of 1847. Except for a few landowners in the Austrian Empire, no women could vote in national elections before 1893.

These original restrictions were either gradually or abruptly relaxed as time went on, with some further reversals. In several countries, "Conservatives," to use the Spanish terminology, repeatedly fought with "Liberals" over suffrage, with the result that franchise qualifications oscillated according to their political power. France is the best known example of a country that changed from income qualifications to universal male suffrage, back to income qualifications, to income and literacy restrictions, back to income, to universal male suffrage, back to income, and back to universal male, to make suffrage universal for both sexes only in 1945. The history of Spanish suffrage was not any less convoluted (Bahamonde and Martinez 1998), as was the history of several Latin American countries, notably Guatemala, which had ten different suffrage rules, plus periods without elections.

The qualifications for suffrage can be classified into several categories[9]:

    0. No suffrage rules.

---

[9] These are not the only criteria that were ever applied. In addition to these categories, additional criteria served to exclude some ethnic groups, inhabitants of some territories, adherents of some religions, political sympathizers of some parties or ideologies, slaves, military personnel, and priests or nuns. Sometimes several disqualifying criteria were used simultaneously.

For men,

1. Estate representation,
2. Property requirement,
3. Property (or income or tax payment above some threshold or exercise of some professions) *and* literacy,
4. Property (or income or tax payment above some threshold or exercise of some professions) but not literacy,
5. Literacy (or literacy *or* income),
6. "Independent,"
7. All above some age, perhaps with residence requirements, except for those legally disqualified ("manhood").

For women, the first digit characterizes male qualifications. The second digit is as follows:

0. If no women can vote,
1. If qualifications applying to women are stricter than those applying to men (higher age, only if no male household head, only relatives of military, etc.),
2. If women are qualified on the same basis as men.

Note that these franchise codes do not distinguish numerical thresholds, only the quality of the restrictions. The reason is that increasing incomes as well as inflation extended the electorate even without legal changes.[10]

The prevalence of *regime censitaire* during the nineteenth century is manifest. Among the countries and dependent territories where only men could vote, requirements of property, income, or literacy were by far most frequent still around 1900 and more frequent than universal male ("manhood" in Figure 3.3) suffrage until the end of World War II.

---

[10] For example, the annual income requirement in Imperial Brazil was 100 *milreis* in 1824, which was raised to 200 in 1846. Graham (2003: 360) reports that because of inflation everyone except for beggars and vagabonds, even servants, earned enough to satisfy this criterion.

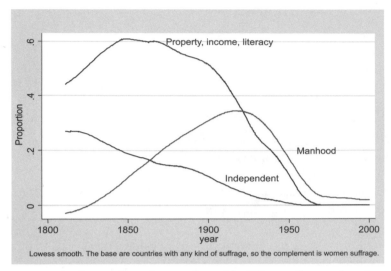

FIGURE 3.3 Proportion of countries with different forms of male suffrage, 1810–2000.

The first country in which women could vote on the same basis as men was New Zealand in 1893,[11] followed by Australia in 1901, Finland in 1907, and Norway in 1913. In Norway as of 1907, Iceland as of 1915, Canada as of 1917, and the United Kingdom as of 1918, women gained the right to vote on a basis narrower than that of men. Still as of 1950, only one-half of the countries with any kind of suffrage enfranchised women on the same basis as men.

Given these different types of suffrage qualifications, we can identify suffrage reforms, that is, the instances when these qualifications differed during successive years. Moreover, we can distinguish extensions by the groups that were enfranchised as their result. Those extensions in which only the first digit increased are by class; those in which only the second digit increased are by gender; and those in which both digits increased are by both class and gender. Given these distinctions, there were 185 extensions by class (of which 155 only to men), 70 by gender, and 93 by both class and gender.

[11] Not counting the Isle of Man, which in spite of its name, allowed propertied women to vote in 1866. Among places where suffrage was regulated at a subnational level, the territory of Wyoming was the first to institute universal suffrage in 1869. In some countries women could vote earlier in municipal elections: in Sweden unmarried women could participate as of 1863 and in the rural communes of Finland as of 1868 (Törnudd 1968: 30).

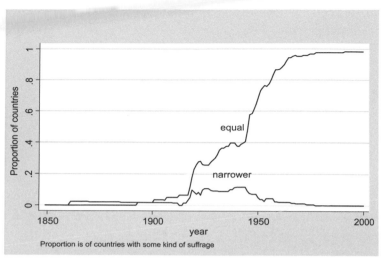

FIGURE 3.4 Proportion of countries with female suffrage, narrower and equal to male suffrage, 1850–2000.

These extensions occurred during different periods. Until 1914, suffrage was extended along class line in 112 instances, while only four extensions to women took place during this period and only two to both. After this date, suffrage was more frequently extended either to women alone or to poorer men and to women.

3.4 ELECTORAL PARTICIPATION

Few people voted in the middle of the eighteenth century. Even where they were formally supposed to be elected, public offices were routinely inherited or filled by appointments. Only Poland, Great Britain, and some British American colonies enjoyed fully elective lower houses of legislatures before 1788, when the first national Congress was elected in the newly formed United States of America. Revolutionary France and the short-lived Republic of Batavia (the Netherlands) were the only countries to join this list before 1800. Spain experienced its first legislative election in 1813, Norway in 1814, Portugal in 1820, and the newly independent Greece in 1823. At least eight new Latin American countries joined this list between 1821 and 1830,[12] while Belgium and Luxembourg followed

---

[12] The actual number is almost certainly larger. While we do not have a record for legislative elections during this period in several Latin American countries, we know that they held

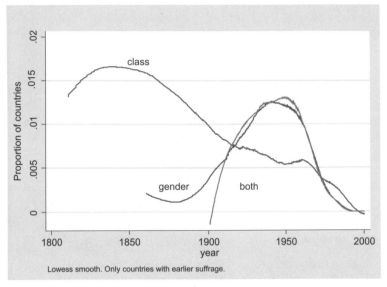

FIGURE 3.5 The timing of different types of extensions.

in 1831. The revolutionary years of 1848–9 expanded this list by seven new entrants. With four Latin American countries holding first legislative elections in the meantime, by 1850 at least thirty-one independent countries or dependent territories had an experience of voting in at least one legislative election. By 1900, this number was at least forty-three. Most countries that emerged from World War I had elected legislatures at least during a part of the interwar period, when several dependent territories also held their first elections.

Hence, as time went on, the number of people who in any year voted in legislative elections increased vertiginously. From about 1 million in 1820, their numbers increased to at least 2.5 million in 1850, to at least 21 million in 1900, to 125 million in 1950, and to 730 million in 1996. From a handful in 1750, the multitude of voters erupted to hundreds of millions.

presidential elections and that presidents were indirectly elected by legislatures. Ecuador held a presidential election in 1830 and Nicaragua 1825, but we have no record of legislative elections. In turn, legislative elections may have occurred before 1830 in El Salvador, which held its first presidential election in 1824 (we can date the first legislative election only to 1842), and Peru, which had a presidential election in 1814 (but we have a record for legislative elections only as of 1845). Note that elections to constituent assemblies that were not intended to have ordinary legislative powers are not counted here.

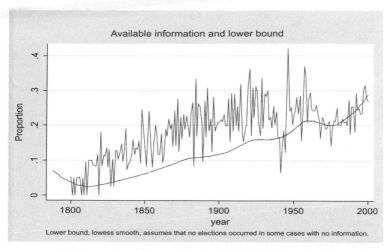

FIGURE 3.6 Proportion of countries that held legislative elections, 1800–2000.

Figure 3.6 shows the proportion of countries and dependent territories that held national legislative elections in each year between 1800 and 2000. The upper curve is based on the available information. This information is upward biased for the early period. The reason is that this series takes as the base the number of countries for which information is available and most likely no elections occurred in the cases for which there is no information. The lower bound series, in turn, is downward biased since it is based on the assumption that no election took place whenever no information is available. The true series would probably track the lower bound with somewhat higher values before 1900.

Even if this observation sometimes evokes surprise among ethnocentric Europeans, it bears emphasis that Latin American countries tried elections earlier than Europe.[13] To some extent this timing is due to the fact that several parts of Latin America participated in the 1809 election to the *Junta Central*, thus launching the idea of representative institutions at the time when many European countries were involved in the Napoleonic wars and elections were still rare.[14] A more general reason, however,

[13] Annino (1996: 10) observed that "the Latin American case presents an extraordinary precocity in the international context. . . . If we look at the Euroatlantic space as a whole, it is evident that Latin America finds itself in a situation of a vanguard." For a discussion of early consitutions in Latin America, see Gargarella (2005).

[14] Palacios and Moraga (2003: 147) emphasize the impact of these elections: "Limited as they were, the elections of 1809 of American representatives to the *Junta Central* were a central moment in the birth of modern political systems in Iberoamerica."

TABLE 3.1: *Timing of the First National Legislative Elections*

	Latin America		Western Europe	
Before	N	Cum. Prop.	N	Cum. Prop.
1820	4	21.1	6	37.5
1830	12	63.2	7	43.8
1850	17	89.5	14	87.5
1870	18	94.7	16	100
Total	19	100	16	100

Note: Panama became independent only in 1904.

was that Latin American wars of independence were at the same time directed against monarchical rule, while most European countries experienced a gradual devolution of power from monarchs to parliaments (see Table 3.1).

If we think in quantitative terms of electoral participation as the ratio of actual voters to the population,[15] we can decompose it by the following tautology:

$$\text{participation} \equiv \frac{\text{voters}}{\text{population}} = \frac{\text{eligible}}{\text{population}} \times \frac{\text{voters}}{\text{eligible}},$$

where the entire tautology is conditional on an election occurring at all. "Participation" is then the ratio of voters to the population, "eligibility" is the ratio of the number of people legally qualified to vote to the population, and "turnout" is the ratio of actual to eligible voters. In this language,

$$\text{participation} = \text{eligibility} \times \text{turnout}.$$

Figure 3.7 shows the trends of the average proportion of the population that did vote (participation), the proportion that had the right to vote (eligibility), and the proportion among those allowed who actually cast votes (turnout) in national legislative elections.

To provide a descriptive background, Figure 3.8 shows the range of turnout under each franchise category. As we see, the composition of the electorate seems to have had no effect on turnout, implying that changes in participation were mainly due to extensions of eligibility.

During the entire period, participation increased at the average by 1.01 percentage points between any two successive elections for which

---

[15] Using the total population as the base introduces a bias that is due to the aging of the population. Data on age composition, however, are scarce.

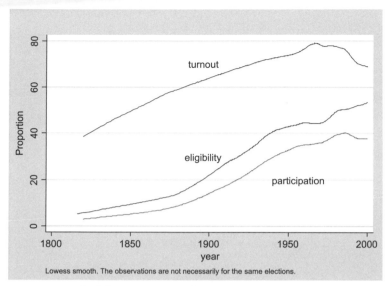

FIGURE 3.7 Eligibility, turnout, and participation, 1815–2000.

data are available.[16] Eligibility increased at the average of 1.48, while turnout of the eligible declined by 0.16 percentage points. Decomposing the change in participation shows that the average increase in participation was due exclusively to increases in eligibility: Of the average increase in participation, 1.01, 1.10 is due to eligibility and −0.09 to turnout.[17] Unfortunately, these averages are not very informative, since eligibility and turnout evolved differently during different periods. Figure 3.9 shows the decomposition of average changes in participation by year.

Eligibility was increasing at an accelerated rate until the massive wave of decolonization around 1960, when suffrage became almost universal in most countries, while the contribution of turnout was negative until about 1900, positive from 1900 until 1978, and then sharply negative.[18]

[16] Note that the periods may span episodes during which the government was not elected but not periods during which there were intervening elections for which no data are available.

[17] Let P_t stand for participation, E_t for eligibility, and T_t for turnout: $P_t = E_t T_t$. Let Δ stand for the forward difference. Since $P_t = E_t T_t$, $\Delta P_t = \Delta T_t \times E_t + T_t \times \Delta E_t + \Delta E_t \times \Delta T_t$ or $\Delta P_t = T_t \times \Delta E_t + \Delta T_t \times E_{t+1}$. The first product on the right-hand side is the part due to increases in eligibility; the second is due to increases of turnout.

[18] An analysis of splines shows that the difference between periods is maximized by taking 1978 as the dividing year. The difference, either of intercepts or slopes, is not significant for any plausible breaking point before 1978, but both the intercept and the slope are different for the pre- and post-1978 periods.

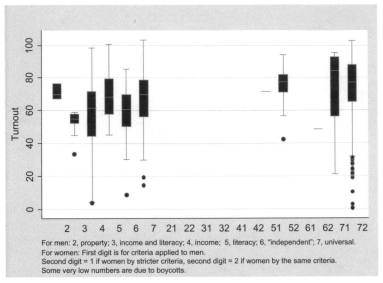

FIGURE 3.8 Turnout by franchise qualifications.

Moreover, the post 1978 decline of turnout seems to have been world-wide. The average decline of turnout was 0.76 percentage points between 107 successive elections in Western Europe, 0.68 between 150 elections in the OECD countries (where OECD stands for the Organisation for Economic Co-operation and Development; Western Europe plus

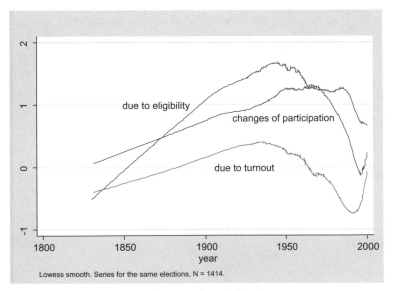

FIGURE 3.9 Decomposing changes of participation.

TABLE 3.2: *Decomposing Participation by Period*

Participation	Pre-1915	1915–1977	1978–2000	Total
Change of participation	0.54	1.82	0.34	1.01
Due to eligibility	0.46	1.19	1.18	1.10
Due to turnout	0.09	0.63	−0.84	−0.09
N	163	676	575	1414

Australia, Canada, Japan, New Zealand, and the United States), and 0.69 between 438 elections in the non-OECD countries, including a decline of 0.44 between 102 elections in Latin America (see Table 3.2).

Thus, even when the turnout of eligible persons was increasing, the growth of participation was largely due to the rules that determined who can avail himself or herself of the right to vote rather than to individual decisions.

3.5 LEGISLATIVE–EXECUTIVE RELATIONS

The ideal of self-government was to be implemented by representative institutions. But what kind of representative institutions would best implement this ideal? While the optimal design of representative institutions was subject to learned debates by the founders, the actual institutions differed more because of the historical circumstances under which they were established than because of divergent ideas.

Except for the Swiss communes and the Italian and Batavian republics, European countries were monarchies before 1789. Powers of the monarchs were limited by constitutional provisions only in Poland, where each newly elected king had to agree to specific limitations (*pacta conventa*; see Jędruch 1998), in England after 1688, and in Sweden during the so-called Age of Liberty, from 1719 to 1772 (Roberts 2002). Other monarchs ruled absolutely, or at least were not constrained formally. The French Revolution, which temporarily abolished monarchy, found constitutional echoes throughout the continent. Beginning again with Sweden in 1809 and then Norway in 1814, several European monarchies became constitutionalized, including in Restoration France. Nevertheless, the relations between the executive, nominally headed by the monarchs, and the parliaments, which had the power of the purse but no formal say about the composition of a king's ministries, were inherently conflictive and thus unstable. The emergence of parliamentary systems, in which governments serve at the discretion of majorities in the parliament, was a gradual process, subject to reversals. Moreover, the practice emerged in most countries before it was enshrined in law, while in some countries the principle was legalized without being applied.

The rise of parliamentarism did not follow the same trajectory in all countries. It was gradual, almost imperceptible, in Great Britain,[19] which is often taken to be the prototypical case, as well as in Belgium, Denmark, Norway, the Netherlands, and Sweden. It was punctuated by revolutionary events in France, where it finally prevailed in 1877, under republican government. It did not advance much in Prussia, later in Germany (Schmitt 1993: 478–83), and in Austria, where it also had to wait for monarchies to be abolished. In the end, though, wherever the monarchy was preserved, Thiers's precocious characterization of parliamentary monarchy prevailed: "The king reigns and does not govern."

In turn, beginning with the United States, the countries that freed themselves from distant monarchs or overthrew local ones faced an unprecedented problem of having to organize government from scratch. They had no idea how to do it: The examples were few and most of them uninspiring, the theoretical blueprints too abstract to guide practice.

They ended with what we call today "presidentialism," but this choice was a punt. The fact that it survived two centuries does not make it less of an accident; it only shows the power of inertia or, to use a more respectable language, "path dependence." The striking fact is that the French, who overthrew their king, and the Americans, who revolted against distant ones, had no idea what to put in his place. The Articles of Confederation did not create any executive power; they only gave the Congress the authority to "appoint such other committees and civil officers as may be necessary for managing the general affairs of the united states under their direction" (Article IX). No individual chief executive was provided for in the constitutions of Pennsylvania and New Hampshire of 1776, while Delaware, South Carolina, and New Hampshire did designate a single head and called him "president" in 1784. Nonetheless, South Carolina in 1778, Pennsylvania in 1790, and Delaware and New Hampshire in 1792 changed the title to "governor." Hence within sixteen years New Hampshire went from having no chief executive, to having a president, and then having a governor. As late as on April 16, 1787, trying to convince Washington of the need for a new constitution that

---

[19] For a penetrating analysis of the evolution of views about the British parliamentary system, see Vile (1998: Chapter 8).

would include "A National Executive," Madison had nothing concrete to propose: "I have scarcely ventured," he had to admit, "as yet to form any opinion either of the manner in which it ought to be constituted or of the authorities with which it ought to be clothed" (Madison to Washington, in Ketcham 1986: 34). At the Convention,[20] as late as on June 4, James Mason observed that "We have not yet been able to define the Powers of the Executive." The first draft of the Constitution (of August 6) still provided for a President to be elected by the Legislature for seven years with a prohibition on reelegibility. The provisions that became final were formulated only on September 4, thirteen days before the Constitution was signed.

What is surprising, albeit in omniscient retrospect, is that the framers did not analytically distinguish the two functions traditionally performed by monarchs, namely, that of the head of state and of the head of the government. After all, one could think that people obsessed with preventing tyranny might have wanted to somehow separate these functions. They were distinguished by Constant in 1821 (cited in Pasquino 1998: 136): "There are two powers in the monarchical power, the ministerial power and the royal power. . . . The royal power is above, a neutral authority, which moderates the frictions and restores balance. . . . Royal power intervenes only to terminate all dangerous conflicts and to preserve imperiled harmony." Constant's idea was implemented in the 1824 Constitution of Brazil, which declared in Part V, entitled "Of the Moderating Power," that "The moderating power is the key of all political organization; it is delegated exclusively to the emperor as the superior leader of the nation and its first representative" (cited in Schmitt 1993: 432). Nevertheless, it took almost 100 years before the idea of a nongoverning president would be constitutionalized in France in 1875 and even more before the invention of semipresidential systems.

Monarch, collective executive, or president were the three examples available to other Americans, when first Haiti in 1804 and then Venezuela in 1811 proclaimed independence. In several countries the first form of the executive was collective, with either a joint or rotating exercise of office. Triumvirates governed Argentina from 1811 to 1814 and Venezuela in 1811–12. Venezuela, as well as Paraguay, also briefly adopted a rotating Supreme Executive Power. However, the French collective executive was

---

[20] All the references to the Convention are based on documents collected in Ketcham (1986).

by then extinct and the French experience did not serve as a reference to Latin American founders.[21] Philadelphia was prominent in their minds: The intermediary was General Francisco Miranda, who participated in the United States War of Independence and who became the central figure in proclaiming the Constitution of the United Provinces of Venezuela in 1811.[22] Also prominent was the Spanish liberal Constitution of Càdiz, adopted in 1812, which preserved monarchy but severely limited its powers.

The sentiments for a monarchical solution intermittently sprung up in most Latin American countries. In the National Assembly of Tucuman, Argentina (1816), General Belgrano put forward *una monarquia temperada*, a project of a king native to the Americas – a monarch of Incan descent rather than that of European lineage. General San Martin also favored a monarchical solution (López-Alves 2000: 179). Sentiments for monarchy under an Italian or British prince were present in Uruguay. In the end, only Brazil adopted this solution until it became a republic in 1889. In Mexico the first emperor, Agustin de Iturbide, lasted two years, with a brief return of monarchy between 1862 and 1867. The reasons, according to Rippy (1965: 89), were that "the royalties of Europe and the monarchists of America had difficulty in reaching an agreement, the United States was opposed to American kings, the princesses were difficult to find, and the people were not disposed to tolerate them." In turn, Diniz (1984: 155) argues that presidentialism prevailed in Latin America because it "was much closer to oligarchical interests than to democratic ideals."

---

[21] There is no doubt that French thought was influential among Latin Americans. As for actual experience, the issue is less clear. Palmer (1964), whom one learns to trust, claims its impact was negligible. Soriano (1969: 34), however, claims that Bolivar was influenced by the French constitutions.
    The identification problems are two. First, while several countries were originally ruled by a collective body, these may have sprang up from the local *cabildos* rather from imitating the French pattern. Second, declarations of rights could have been and were derived from the French Declaration as well as from the U.S. Bill of Rights.

[22] Note, however, that against the view of Miranda the 1811 Constitution provided for a rotation of power among members of a trimuvirate, rather than a single executive (Soriano 1969: 21). One year later the Congress granted extraordinary powers to Miranda, named first *generalissimo* and then *dictador*. Miranda may have been the first person to bear the title of "dictator" in the modern era, but this denomination was still based on the Roman concept of dictatorship. In 1808–9, Miranda wrote an *Esquise de Gouvernement fédéral*, a blueprint in which he justified an exceptional dictatorship by invoking the experience of Rome (Aguilar 2000: 169).

Presidentialism did prevail – in time all Latin American political systems, democratic or autocratic, civilian or military, would be led by presidents[23] – but this alternative became complicated from the onset by Bolívar's itch to keep the position for life.[24] While *El Libertador* did not dare claim royalty, he let it be known that his ideal was the English constitutional monarchy and that he was eager to become a monarch for life even under the title of the president (*Discurso de Angostura* 1819).[25] "The President of the Republic," orated Bolívar in 1825 to the Bolivian constituent assembly, "is in our Constitution like the Sun which, firm in its center, gives life to the Universe. This supreme Authority must be perpetual, because in the systems without hierarchies it is necessary more than in others to have a fixed point around which revolve the legislators and the citizens" (Bolívar 1969: 130). Bolívar's monarchical ambition installed in Latin Americans a fear that would subside only at the end of the twentieth century and that became institutionalized in term limits, the "Gordian knot" of Latin American politics (De Luca 1998: 155). Only one constitution, authored by Bolívar himself, which lasted two years from 1826 in Bolivia and even less in Peru, granted a life term to the president.

While these solutions were focal, they did not preclude inventiveness. The plan for provisional government elaborated by Francisco Miranda in the 1790s called for an executive chosen by the parliament, whose title would have been *el Inca* (Palacio and Moraga 2003: 102). The first two leaders of Chilean assumed the title of the "Supreme Director of the Nation," although from then on they would be presidents. Miranda's first title was *Generalíssimo*. Most creative was Dr. José Gaspár Rodriguez de Francia who, having become one of two consuls who were to alternate

---

[23] The very term has weak roots in the Spanish colonial tradition. *La Presidencia* was an administrative unit below the vice-royalty and it was headed by a president, who as a member of the *Audiencia* had jurisdictional faculties.

[24] On Bolívar's ambition as the original sin of Latin America, see Garcia Marquez, *The General in His Labyrnth*. Bolívar's 1827 letter to Sucre turned out to be prophetic. "It will be said," Bolívar predicted, "that I have liberated the New World, but it will not be said that I have perfected stability and wellbeing (*dicha*) of the nations that compose it" (cited in Soriano 1969: 38).

[25] This is a fascinating text. Bolívar first argues against following the U.S. example of presidents elected for terms by invoking Montesquieu to the effect that institutions should reflect local conditions – but then he goes on to observe that the country that best succeeded in combining power, prosperity, and stability is England. Then he is ready to make his move: You will get a hereditary Senate, to be elected by the present Congress from among you, to whom the Republic owns its existence, and I will become the British hereditary monarch under the title of President.

every four months in 1813, then a dictator appointed for three years, in 1816 proclaimed himself *El Dictador Perpetuo* of Paraguay and ruled it until 1840 as *El Supremo*.[26] While this story may sound anecdotal, Francia's innovation was both radical and durable, deserving to be placed on par with Lenin's invention of a one-party state. It was radical because the only model of dictatorship known at the time was the Roman one, and in this model dictatorship was a power that was delegated, exceptional, and limited in duration. "Perpetual Dictator" was an oxymoron in the language of the time.[27] Moreover, the last attempt to make dictatorship permanent, almost twenty centuries earlier, did not bode well for Dr. Francia's fate. Nonetheless, this invention turned out to be durable: Francia set the precedent for such illustrious gentlemen as Mussolini, Hitler, Franco, Kim Il Sung, Khadafi, and Castro.[28] Paradoxically, this precedent was rarely followed in Latin America.

Most countries that emerged from the respective colonial powers inherited their institutions, but when one-party regimes emerged in Africa after independence, many of them shifted from parliamentary to presidential systems. While the separation of the functions of the head of state and the head of government emerged gradually in those European countries that preserved monarchy, the programmatic idea of distinguishing them appeared for the first time only in the Weimar Constitution of 1919. Having to choose between the U.S. presidential and the French parliamentary model of the republic, Germans opted for a compromise between the two: On the one hand, the cabinet and every single minister depended on the confidence of the Reichstag; on the other hand, the president was elected by the people and he appointed the head of the government (Schmitt 1993: 497).[29] Austria, Finland, Czechoslovakia, Estonia, and the Spanish Republic from 1931 followed suit between the wars.

---

[26] Francia is the protagonist of a richly documented historical novel by Augusto Roa Bastos, *Yo el supremo*. I could not find there, however, any surprise at the notion of a perpetual dictator.

[27] When Bolívar wanted to resign from his first of three dictatorships, for example, he was asked to keep the office in the following terms: "Remain, your Excellency, as a Dictator, improve your efforts at saving the Fatherland, and once you have done it, then restore full exercise of sovereignty by proposing a Democratic Government." On Bolívar and dictatorship, see Aguilar (2000: Chapter V).

[28] I do not include Stalin since in the light of the marxist theory the "dictatorship of the proletariat," which he personified, was supposed to have been a transitional phase. Moreover, according to the 1936 Soviet Constitution, he served terms.

[29] Schmitt considers the presidency to rest on "the monarchical principle" but he also emphasizes that the idea of direct democracy contributed to the introduction of the directly and independently elected president.

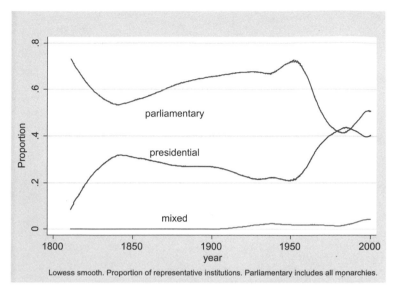

Lowess smooth. Proportion of representative institutions. Parliamentary includes all monarchies.

FIGURE 3.10 Types of representative institutions, 1810–2000.

This experiment did not end well and by 1946 there were only three "mixed" or "semipresidential" systems in the world: Austria, Finland (which abandoned it in 1999), and Iceland. But between 1946 and 2002, thirty-two additional countries opted for mixed systems during at least some periods (Cheibub 2007: 45).

Figure 3.10 portrays the relative frequencies of these arrangements over time. Note, however, that the picture is only approximate because it includes as parliamentary all monarchies with functioning legislatures, independent of whether or not the principle of government responsibility to the parliament was operative.

4

Equality

4.1 INTRODUCTION

For a collectivity to govern itself, all of its members must be able to exercise equal influence over its decisions. No individual or group can be favored because of some traits they have.

This condition is not as obvious as it may appear.[1] Note first that the definition of equality does not assume a duty to participate. Nevertheless, it does require that (1) all members must have an effectively equal opportunity to participate and (2) if they participate, their preferences must have the same weight. "Effectively equal opportunity" is not the same as "the right to." I am weary of the language of rights: An effectively equal opportunity entails not just rights but also conditions, some minimal material and intellectual conditions, "decent wages and reading." Furthermore, even if everyone has the minimal conditions, individual conditions may still be unequal. Hence, for political influence to be equal in an unequal society, the inequality of conditions cannot be transformable into inequality of influence.

Thus defined, equality is not equivalent to anonymity.[2] Anonymity means only that democratic citizens are not distinguished *qua* citizens

---

[1] I thank Joshua Cohen for pushing me to clarify.

[2] As we have seen, social choice theory treats equality and anonymity, sometimes also so-called symmetry, as equivalent. However, the very fact that this condition is identified by three different words shows ambiguity. May labels the condition "symmetry" and renders it as follows: "The second condition is that each individual be treated the same as for his influence on the outcome is concerned. . . . This condition might well be termed anonymity. . . . A more usual label is *equality*" (1952: 681; italics in the original). Rae (1969: 42, ft. 8) says that anonymity and equality are "closely related," and in another

by any traits, including the traits that reveal them as unequal. One can say "a wealthy man" or a "handsome man," but not a wealthy or handsome citizen. All individual qualities are left at the doorstep of democratic politics; they are irrelevant for the status of citizens. But this means only that anonymity is a veil over the inequality that exists in society.

Democratic citizens are not equal but only anonymous. In spite of its egalitarian pedigree, equality could not and does not characterize democracy. Even the one sense in which equality can be said to characterize democracy – equality before the law – derives from anonymity: The law has to treat all citizens equally because as citizens they are indistinguishable. Moreover, even the norm of anonymity was circumvented in early representative systems by an elaborate intellectual construction that justified restrictions of suffrage. The argument held that the role of representatives is to promote the good of all, yet the intellectual capacity to recognize the common good and the moral qualities necessary to pursue it are not universal. These traits can be recognized by using some indicators, such as wealth, age, or gender. Hence, relying on such indicators to restrict suffrage does not violate democratic norms. The logic of the argument is unimpeachable, but the assumptions are questionable and have been questioned.

To ignore distinctions is not to obliterate them. Democracy was a political, not a social, revolution. Furthermore, in spite of almost universally shared expectations – fears for some and hopes for others – democracy turned out to be compatible with varying, and sometimes large, degrees of economic inequality. Democracies function in economic systems in which most resources are distributed by markets and markets perpetually (re)generate inequality. No political system, democracy included, can generate and maintain perfect equality in the socioeconomic realm. Redistributing incomes is just difficult. Indeed, the entire political language of "redistribution" is anachronistic, harking back to the days in which the most important productive asset was land. Land is divisible and it can be exploited by family units. No other productive input can be easily redistributed. Hence, there may be purely technological barriers to economic equality. Because no political system can overcome these barriers, we should not blame democracy for not achieving what no system of political institutions can achieve.

article he also refers to this condition as "symmetry" (Rae 1975: 1271). Dahl (1989: 139) treats anonymity as equivalent to equality.

Yet socioeconomic inequality has ways of infiltrating itself into the political realm. If the traits that are being ignored differentially affect the capacity to exercise political rights or if they weigh unequally the political influence of unequal individuals, the condition of political equality is violated.

These arguments are developed below.

4.2 PEDIGREE: ARISTOCRACY AND DEMOCRACY

How did "democracy" reappear on the historical horizon and what did it mean to its proponents and opponents?

Because the emergence of democracy in the modern era is the topic of Palmer's (1959, 1964) monumental treatise, no more than a brief summary is necessary. Palmer's main point is that democracy was not a revolution against an existing system but a reaction against the increasing power of aristocracy. It was aristocracy that undermined monarchy; democracy followed in its footsteps. Palmer argues the following. (1) By the early eighteenth century, the aristocratic system of government was institutionalized in assemblies of various forms, the participation in which was reserved to legally qualified groups (constituted bodies) that always included hereditary nobility but in different places (countries, regions, principalities, cantons, city republics) also clergy, selected categories of burgers, and in Sweden even peasants. In all cases these bodies were politically dominated by hereditary nobility. (2) In the course of the century, these estate-based bodies increased their political influence. (3) At the same time, access to nobility, however it was defined in different places, became increasingly closed; nobility turned into aristocracy. (4) The resulting aristocratic system suffered from several tensions, prominently one between birth and competence. (5) Politically crucial conflict was due to the exclusion from privilege of those who possessed all the qualifications to participate – wealth, talent, bearing – except for birth. In Sieyes's (1970 [1789]: 29) words, "the people were told 'whatever are your services, whatever your talents, you will go only until here; you will not depass others'." (6) Democracy emerged as a demand for access to these bodies, not as a movement against monarchy.

Hence, by the end of the eighteenth century, "democracy" was a slogan directed against legal recognition of inherited distinctions of political status. Democrats were those who agitated against aristocrats or aristocracy. As Dunn (2003: 10) observes, "democracy was a reaction, above all, not to monarchy, let alone tyranny, but to another relatively concrete social category, initially all too well entrenched, but no longer plausibly aligned with social, economic, or even political or military, functions – the nobility or aristocracy. . . . Democrat was a label in and for political combat; and what that combat was directed against was aristocrats, or at the very least aristocracy." Thus, in 1794 a young Englishman described himself as "being of that odious class of men called democrats because he disapproved of hereditary distinctions and privileged orders of every species" (Palmer 1964: 10). "Could any further proof be required of the republican complexion of this system," wrote Madison in *The Federalist #39*, "the most decisive might be found in its absolute prohibition of titles of nobility." In France, the Constituent Assembly decided that aristocratic privilege was in conflict with the very principle of popular sovereignty (Fontana 1993: 119). The Batavian (Dutch) Republic, established in 1796, required voters to swear an oath to the belief that all hereditary offices and dignities were illegal. In Chile, General O'Higgins, the first Director of the State, abolished in 1818 all outward and visible signs of aristocracy (Collier and Sater 1996: 42).

Here, though, is a puzzle. Although democrats fought against aristocracy, either as a system of government (the original meaning of the word) or as a legal status, this struggle did not have to result in abolishing other distinctions. One distinction could have been replaced by another. The flagrant case is the Polish Constitution of May 3, 1791, which was directed against aristocrats, defined as large landowners, magnates, under the slogan of equality for the gentry at large (*szlachta*, which constituted about 10 percent of the population),[3] while preserving the legal distinction of the latter. Social traits that could serve as basis for legal distinctions were many: property owners and laborers, burgers and peasants, inhabitants of different localities,[4] clergy and army,[5] whites and blacks. Nevertheless, democrats turned against these distinctions as well. "All the privileges," Sieyes (1970: 3) declared,"are thus by the nature of things unjust, despicable and contradictory to the supreme goal

---

[3] The slogan was *Szlachcic na zagrodzie równy wojewodzie*, loosely translated as "A gentry man in a cottage equals a lord."

[4] Palmer (1964) emphasizes that while the French tried to eradicate all subnational differences, Americans recognized them. The division of France into departments was intended according to Rosanvallon (2004: 34) to create a purely functional division, which would not refer to any social, political, or cultural reality. Hence, democrats were centralizers in France but decentralizers in the United States.

[5] They did enjoy special status, *fueros*, in the Cádiz Constitution of 1812 and several Latin American constitutions afterward.

of all political society." From aristocracy, the enemy became any kind of distinction. Thus, in faraway Brazil, the four mulattoes who were hanged and quartered after the failure of the Citade da Bahia Republicana in 1798 were accused of "desiring the imaginary advantages of a Democratic Republic in which all should be equal... without difference of color or condition" (Palmer 1964: 513). The French Revolution emancipated Protestants and Jews and freed slaves, not only Catholic peasants.

Rosanvallon (2004: 121) claims that "The imperative of equality, required to make everyone a subject of law and a full citizen, implies in effect considering men stripped of their particularistic determinants. All their differences and all their distinctions should be placed at a distance." But where did the imperative of equality come from? Thinking in the rational choice terms of modern political science, one would suspect that democrats instrumentally turned against all social distinctions just to mobilize the masses against aristocracy. Finer (1934: 85), for example, accuses Montesquieu of "deliberately juxtaposing the Citizen to all the powers that be, either the King or the aristocracy: it was a convenient, a striking and useful antithesis; nothing could be better calculated to win the support of every man." Some facts support this hypothesis: In Poland, Tadeusz Kościuszko made vague promises to peasants to induce them join the anti-Russian insurrection in 1794; the members of the French Convention flagrantly played to the gallery filled by the ordinary people of Paris; Simon Bolívar made interracial appeals to recruit for the war against Spain. Yet it is also easy to believe that democrats truly believed that all men are equal as the Declaration of Independence declared or that men are born equal as the Declaration of the Rights of Man and Citizen would have it. The idea of innate equality certainly preceded the actual political conflicts. It could be found already in Locke's *Second Treatise* (1988 [1689–90]) as the principle that "equal Right that every Man hath, to his Natural Freedom, without being subjected to the Will or Authority of any other Man." We do not have a theory of action in which people are moved by logic, in which they do things because they cannot tolerate logical contradictions. Nonetheless, if one is willing to accept that people can be moved by fictions, democrats would have turned against other distinctions by the sheer logic of their ideology: Aristocrats are not distinct because all men are born equal; because all men are born equal, they cannot be treated differently. Abolishing all distinctions would then be a logical outcome of the struggle against aristocracy.

The fact is that democrats turned against all distinctions. The only attribute of democratic subjects is that they have none as such. The democratic citizen is simply without qualities.[6] Not equal, not homogeneous, just anonymous. As Rousseau (1964 [1762]: 129) said, "the sovereign [the people united] knows only the body of the nation and does not distinguish any of those who compose it." Because citizens are indistinguishable, there is nothing by which law could possibly distinguish them. The democratic citizen is simply an individual outside society.

4.3 DEMOCRACY AND EQUALITY

In spite of its egalitarian pedigree, there is no sense in which equality could or does characterize democracy. "One should not let oneself be trapped by words," Pasquino (1998: 149–50) warns, "the 'society without qualities' is not a society of equals; it is simply a society in which privileges do not have a juridical-institutional status or recognition."

Consider the different meanings in which equality appeared in democratic ideology. Why are people equal? They could be because God or nature made them so, because society makes them so, or because the law makes them so. Equality can be innate or generated by spontaneous social transformations, but it can also be instituted by law. Democratic equality may be a reflection of equality preexisting in the nonpolitical realm or it may be imposed by laws.

To return to the Declarations, their point of departure was the innate equality of human beings. Democratic equality is but a reflection of a natural equality. However, the implications of a preexisting equality are indeterminate. As Schmitt (1993: 364) observed, "From the fact that all men are men it is not possible to deduce anything specific either about morality or about religion or about politics or about economics." Even if people are born equal, they may distinguish themselves by their merits and their merits may be recognized by others. More, to maintain order, some people must at each moment exercise authority over others. As Kelsen (1988: 17) put it, "From the idea that we are all equal, ideally equal, one can deduce that no one should command another. But experience teaches

---

[6] Pasquino (1996: 31) claims that this conception was introduced by Hobbes in the context of religious distinctions: "In the face of this type of conflict [religious], political order to Hobbes is founded on an ovelapping consensus and is based on an anatomy of the city as a society without qualities."

that if we want to remain equal in reality, it is necessary on the contrary that we let ourselves be commanded."

Moreover, even if all human beings are born only as such, society generates differences among them. Indeed, if their parents are unequal, they become unequal at the moment they are born. To make them equal again, recourse to laws is necessary. Montesquieu (1995: 261) thus observed that "In the state of nature, men are born equal but they do not know how to remain so. Society makes them lose equality and they do not return to be equal other than by laws."

Yet must society make people unequal? Rosanvallon (1995: 149) documents that when the term "democracy" came into widespread usage in France after 1814, it connoted modern egalitarian society, not the political regimes associated with the classical Greek or Roman republics but what Tocqueville would refer to as equality of conditions. The tendency toward social equality was inevitable. Taking a theme of Marquis d'Argenson, Tocqueville (1961: 41) observed that "The gradual development of equality of conditions... is universal, it is durable, it escapes human intervention every day; every event, like every man, furthers its development."[7]

Whether modern societies must become more equal is a complex question. What matters here is that not everyone was willing to rely on the spontaneous evolution of society to generate political equality. Robespierre thought that "Equality of wealth is a chimera" (quoted in Palmer 1964: 109). Madison (*Federalist #10*) listed all kinds of social differences and gradations, assuming they were there to stay. Most democrats believed against Tocqueville that citizenship creates equality, rather than that equals become citizens. Pasquino (1998: 109) summarizes this belief: "Citizens are not simply equal before the law, in the sense in which the law does not recognize either special rights or privileges, but they become equal by the grace of law and by law itself."

Democrats adhered to what Beitz (1989: 4) calls a simple conception of political equality, namely, the requirement that democratic institutions should provide citizens with equal procedural opportunities to influence political decisions (or equal power over outcomes). Criticizing this notion, he points out that equality of the abstract leverage that procedures provide to each participant does not imply equality of the actual influence over the outcomes: The latter depends also on the distribution of

---

[7] In a beautiful pastiche about a visit by Tocqueville to Mexico, Aguilar Rivera (1999) imagines how he would have reacted to an extremely inegalitarian New World society.

the enabling resources. Education was one instrument that would equip people to exercise their citizenship rights. Several early constitutions (of the Italian republics between 1796 and 1799, the Cádiz Constitution of 1812) established systems of universal and free, although not compulsory, education. In the meantime, most solved the problem by restricting political rights to those who were in condition to exercise them. When suffrage became universal and democracy found roots in poorer countries, however, the problem reappeared with a vengeance: Masses of people acquired equal procedural opportunities without enjoying the conditions necessary to exploit them. The absence of the effective capacity to exercise formal political rights remains at the heart of criticisms of really existing democracies. Can people be politically equal if they are socially unequal?

But political equality is vulnerable not just to social inequality but also to specifically political distinctions. Democracy, according to Schmitt (1993: 372), is "the identity of the dominating and the dominated, of the government and the governed, of he who commands and he who obeys." The issue is whether the very faculty of governing does not create a distinction, a political class. "Political aristocracy" was seen as much of a danger as social aristocracy. The Antifederalists feared that if the rulers were other than the ruled, "Corruption and tyranny would be rampant as they have always been when those who exercised power felt little connection with the people. This would be true, moreover, for elected representatives, as well as for kings and nobles and bishops" (in Ketcham 1986: 18). Hence, democrats were preoccupied with duration of terms (as short as six months in New Jersey), term limits, restrictions on representatives to determine their own salaries, and censuring procedures.

These, however, are palliatives. The distinction between the representatives and the represented is inherent in the representative system: Parliaments seat representatives, not the people. The very method of choosing representatives through elections, rather than by lot, is based on the belief that all people are not equally qualified to rule. Elections, Manin (1997) argues, are based on the assumption that the qualities necessary to govern are not universally shared and that people want to be governed by their betters. These qualities need not be associated with distinctions of birth, so that elections are not "aristocratic" in the eighteenth-century sense. Elections are, however, a method for selecting one's betters and, as Manin amply documents, they are and were seen as a way of recognizing a natural aristocracy of talent, reason, or whatever else voters would see as the index of the ability to govern.

Moreover, to be represented, people must be organized – and organization demands a permanent apparatus, a salaried bureaucracy, a propaganda machine. Hence, Michels (1962: 270) bemoaned, some militants become parliamentarians, party bureaucrats, newspaper editors, managers of the party's insurance companies, directors of the party's funeral parlors, and even *Parteibudiger* – party bar keepers. As a disillusioned French communist would write many years later, "The working class is lost in administering its imaginary bastions. Comrades disguised as notables occupy themselves with municipal garbage dumps and school cafeterias. Or are these notables disguised as comrades? I no longer know" (Konopnicki 1979: 53).

To summarize, the idea that political equality reflects some preexisting state, either of nature or society, is untenable on both logical and empirical grounds. Logically, equality preexisting in other realms does not imply political equality. Empirically, even if all human beings were born equal, they become unequal in society, and even if societies experienced an inevitable tendency toward equality, the existing inequalities were and are sufficient to call for political remedies. In turn, political equality instituted by law is effectively undermined by social inequality. Political equality is equality in the eyes of the state, but not in the direct relation between persons. In no meaning, then, is equality the correct way to characterize democracy. If the founders used the language of equality, it was to justify something else, better described as oblivion to social distinctions, or anonymity.

4.4 DO SUFFRAGE RESTRICTIONS VIOLATE DEMOCRATIC IDEOLOGY?

There is one fact that appears to undermine anonymity: restrictions of suffrage. Indeed, the French Declaration of 1789 qualified its recognition of equality in the sentence that immediately followed: "Men are born equal and remain free and equal in rights. Social distinctions may be founded only upon the general good." Nonetheless, even if the arguments were convoluted, franchise restrictions were not portrayed as inegalitarian by their proponents.

Consider the justification of such distinctions by Montesquieu (1995: 155), who started from the principle that "All inequality under democracy should be derived from the nature of democracy and from the very principle of democracy." His example was that people who must work to live are not prepared for public office or would have to neglect their functions. As barristers of Paris put it on the eve of the Revolution, "Whatever respect one might wish to show for the rights of humanity in general, there is no denying the existence of a class of men who, by virtue of their education and the type of work to which their poverty had condemned them, is . . . incapable at the moment of participating fully in public affairs" (quoted in Crook 2002: 13). "In such cases," Montesquieu went on, "equality among citizens can be lifted in a democracy for the good of democracy. But it is only apparent equality which is lifted." The generic argument was as follows: (1) Representation is acting in the best interest of all. (2) To determine the best interest of all, one needs reason. (3) Reason has social determinants: not having to work for a living ("disinterest"), or not being employed or otherwise dependent on others ("independence"). As a Chilean statesman put it in 1865, to exercise political rights it is necessary "to have the intelligence to recognize the truth and the good, the will to want it, and the freedom to execute it" (quoted in Maza Valenzuela 1995: 153). In turn, the claim that only apparent equality is being violated was built in three steps: (1) Acting in the best common interest considers everyone equally, so that everyone is equally represented.[8] (2) The only quality that is being distinguished is the capacity to recognize and pursue the common good. (3) No one is barred from acquiring this quality, so that suffrage is potentially open to all.

The last two points are crucial. Legal distinctions of social status are valid only as indicators of the ability to govern and there are no barriers of any kind to prevent people from acquiring this ability and thus being relevantly indicated. The Polish Constitution of May 3, 1791 illuminates the distinction between the democratic *regime censitaire* and nondemocratic regime of legal distinctions. The Constitution asserts in Paragraph VI that "deputies to the local parliaments . . . should be considered as "representatives of the *entire nation*" (italics in the original). However, to become a deputy to local parliaments (*seymiki*, which in turn elected deputies to the national legislature, the *seym*) one had to be a member of a legally defined group, the gentry (*szlachta*). In turn, only members of the hereditary gentry could own land entitling them to political rights.[9] Hence, this was not a *regime censitaire* in the sense just defined: (1) it barred access

---

[8] Condorcet (1986 [1788]: 212) went as far as to claim that "The propertied have the same interest as the non-propertied in all aspects of the legislation: they only have a greater interest in civil laws and laws relating to taxation. There is, therefore, no danger in making them depositories and preservers of interests of the rest of the society."

[9] While according to the law on towns of April 18, 1791 burgers in all cities were to enjoy all the protections of the gentry (most importantly habeas corpus, which dated in Poland

to politics to everyone who was not a member of a legally recognized group, the landed gentry, and (2) it barred access to the landed gentry.

In fact, the Polish justification for privileging gentry was not reason but "Respect for the memory of our forefathers as founders of free government" (Article II). Simon Bolívar (1969: 19) used the same principle in 1819 when he offered positions of hereditary senators "to the liberators of Venezuela, . . . to whom the Republic owns its existence." His celebrated speech, known as the *Discurso de Angostura*, merits attention because its combination of appeals to reason with acceptance of inequality became the hallmark of antidemocratic postures in Spanish America. Bolívar observed that most people do not know their true interests and went on to argue that "Everything cannot be left to the adventure of elections: the People errs easily." His solution was the institution of a hereditary Senate: future senators "Would learn the arts, sciences, and letters which adorn the spirit of a public man; from infancy would know to what Providence destined them." He had the gumption to claim that "The creation of a hereditary Senate would in no way violate political equality."[10]

In contrast, although the English suffrage reform of 1832 restricted suffrage by criteria of income, Seymour (1915) was right to emphasize that the crucial consequence of the reform was to open to everyone a possibility of gaining political rights by acquiring wealth. Guizot famously retorted to objections against the census criterion by exclaiming, "Get rich!" (quoted in Crook 2002: 32). According to the argument in favor of *suffrage censitaire*, political inequality was justified by the inequality of social conditions but social advancement was not barred by any laws. Hence, the claim was that political inequality did not violate the norm of universalism.

Restrictions of political rights based on religion were sometimes also couched in a universalistic language, but the appeal was not to reason but to common values. From Rousseau and Kant to J. S. Mill, everyone believed that a polity could function only if it was based on common interests, norms, or values. In Latin America the cement holding societies together was to be Catholicism: Of the 103 Latin American constitutions studied by Loveman (1993: 371), 83 proclaimed Catholicism as the official religion and 55 prohibited worship of other religions. Although

---

to 1433), could occupy public positions (except for Bishops), and could own and buy land adjacent to cities, they could not participate in the local parliaments (Kowecki 1991).

[10] I put it this way because Bolívar's motives were suspect: He was trying to soften the future senators for granting him hereditary presidency.

many arguments for restricting political rights to Catholics were openly directed against the principle of popular sovereignty – it is not for the people to change what God willed – quite a few were pragmatic. For example, in 1853 the Mexican thinker Lucas Alamán maintained that "Catholic religion deserves support by the state, even if we do not consider it as divine, because it constitutes the only common tie that connects all Mexicans, when all others are broken" (quoted in Gargarella 2005: 93, who provides other examples).

Restrictions on female suffrage present the most difficult issue. While early proponents of female suffrage observed that reason is not distributed along gender lines, the main argument against giving the right to vote to women was that, like children, they were not independent, had no will of their own. Women were already represented by the men in their households and their interests were to be protected through a tutelary, rather than an electoral, connection. Thus the justifying criterion was dependence, not gender. Indeed, when a study in England in the 1880s discovered that almost one-half of adult women lived in households in which there was no adult man, this justification collapsed, and only pure prejudice retarded extending suffrage to women.

Yet why were women not independent in the same way as some men were? Where women could not own property, they were legally barred from qualifying for suffrage, so this would violate the democratic ideology. But where they could and did own property in their own name, why would property ownership not be a sufficient indicator? Condorcet (1986 [1785]: 293), who defended property qualifications, thought it should be: "The reason for which it is believed that they [women] should be excluded from public function, reasons that albeit are easy to destroy, cannot be a motive for depriving them of a right which would be so simple to exercise [voting], and which men have not because of their sex, but because of their quality of being reasonable and sensible, which they have in common with women." And Chilean suffragettes claimed that "Wives and mothers, widows and daughters, we all have time and money to devote to the happiness of Chile" (quoted in Maza Valenzuela 1995: 156).

Because this is an issue about which it is easy to fall into anachronisms, let me process it through an example. Suppose that it is in the best interest of each and all people to evacuate a coastal town if a hurricane is impending and not to evacuate it if the danger is remote. A correct decision is good for everyone: all men, women, and children. The correct decision can be reached only by people who can interpret weather forecasts. This excludes children, so the decision should be made by parents in the best interest of children. I suspect that – with some quibbles about where to draw the age line – most people today would accept this reasoning; all contemporary constitutions do. But why should only men participate in making this decision? If the reason is that women are barred from taking meteorology courses in school, then we are back to 1791 Poland. Suppose instead that they do take such courses. Now the argument must be that even if they had the same capacity to exercise reason, women would always follow the views of their male protectors, independently of their own opinions. This is then another sociological assumption, in addition to those that tied reason to property, income, or education.

Now, Schumpeter (1942: 244) argued that if any distinction is accepted, then the principle of making such distinctions must be as well: "The salient point is that, given appropriate views on those and similar subjects, disqualifications on ground of economic status, religion and sex will enter into the same class with disqualifications which all of us consider compatible with democracy." Nevertheless, each distinction is based on a specific assumption – for example, that 12-year-olds are not prepared to vote – tying it to the capacity to exercise reason. Moreover, some such assumptions were driven by only thinly veiled self-interest. Today we would and do reject most such assumptions, although not those based on age or legally certified sanity.

To put it analytically, inequality does not violate self-government if (1) preferences of those excluded are identical to those who have the right to influence collective decisions and (2) those who are chosen to decide are distinctly qualified to do so. Theories of representation differ in whether they take as the input of collective decisions the actual or ideal preferences, the latter being restricted by some normative requirements, such as they be other-regarding, consider common good, and so on.[11] Obviously, this distinction disappears if all people naturally hold such ideal preferences. If they do not, the burden is placed on institutions, either to promote such preferences by educating citizens – a common theme from Montesquieu to Mill – or to treat such preferences in some privileged manner, by restricting suffrage or weighting votes. As Beitz (1989: 35) observes, the latter solution – defended by Mill in 1857 – is not unfair if those without such ideal preferences or without the conditions to develop such preferences are willing to accept it. Moreover, although inegalitarian, such a system can be justified in universalistic terms if everyone can acquire such preferences or the conditions to acquire them.

---

[11] For a recent discussion of this distinction, see Ferejohn (1995) and Sunstein (1995).

Whatever one thinks of this logic, the outcome was that birth was replaced by wealth, aristocracy by oligarchy. Still only a select few were to rule in the best interest of all. The society was to be divided into "the rich, the few, the rulers and the poor, the many, the ruled": which a Connecticut representative, Samuel Dana, thought was quite proper (quoted in Dunn 2004: 23). The drafter of the French Constitution of 1795, Boissy d'Anglas, declared that "We must be ruled by the best... a country governed by property-owners is within the social order, that which is dominated by non-property owners is in a state of nature" (quoted in Crook 2002: 46). The consensus in mid-nineteenth-century Colombia was that "We want enlightened democracy, a democracy in which intelligence and property direct the destinies of the people; we do not want a barbarian democracy in which the proletarianism and ignorance drown the seeds of happiness and bring the society to confusion and disorder" (Gutiérrez Sanin 2003: 185). The right to make laws belongs to the most intelligent, to the aristocracy of knowledge, created by nature, a Peruvian constitutionalist, Bartolomé Herrera, so declared in 1846 (Sobrevilla 2002: 196). The Peruvian theorist José María Pando maintained that a "perpetual aristocracy... is an imperative necessity"; the Venezuelan Andrés Bello wanted rulers to constitute a body of wise men (*un cuerpo de sabios*); while the Spanish conservative thinker Donoso Cortés juxtaposed the sovereignty of the wise to sovereignty of the people (Gargarella 2005: 120). Still by 1867, Walter Bagehot (1963: 277) would warn that

It must be remembered that a political combination of the lower classes, as such and for their own objects, is an evil of the first magnitude; that a permanent combination of them would make them (now that many of them have the suffrage) supreme in the country; and that their supremacy, in the state they now are, means the supremacy of ignorance over instruction and of numbers over knowledge.

Justifications of colonialism were couched in the same terms. Ever since the early Spanish conquests, colonial domination was justified by the claim that the uncivilized peoples required "by their own nature and in their own interests, to be placed under the authority of civilized and virtuous princes or nations" (Juan Gines de Sepulveda, quoted in Young 1994: 59). Cecil Rhodes portrayed colonialism as serving universal interests: "the more of the world we inhabit, the better it is for the human race" (in Young 1994: 89).

It was perhaps not a full circle but a circle it was, and it left a legacy that gave rise to conflicts that in many countries lasted over 100 years. These new distinctions were soon perceived as evidence that democracy did not fulfill its own ideals. Neither the poor nor women thought that their best interests were being represented by propertied men. They would struggle for suffrage, and suffrage was a dangerous weapon.

4.5 DEMOCRACY AND PROPERTY

In a society that is unequal, political equality, if it is effective, opens the possibility that the majority would by law equalize property or the benefits of its use. This is a central theme in the history of democracy, as alive and controversial today as it was at the inception of representative government. Because, as distinct from liberty or happiness, property – the kind of property that can be used to generate incomes – always was and continues to be held by a minority, the right to property would have to hurl itself against the interest of majorities. Hence, a tension between democracy and property was predictable, and indeed it was predicted.

To sketch the history of this tension, one must begin with the Levellers, who are identified by Wootton (1993: 71) as the first democrats who thought in terms of representative government within a nation-state. Although they persistently and vehemently denied it, Levellers were feared by their opponents as wanting to make everyone equal by redistributing land.[12] In Harrington's (1977: 460) words, "By levelling, they who use the word seem to understand: when a people rising invades the lands and estates of the richer sort, and divides them equally among themselves." Some among them – those calling themselves True Levellers or Diggers – did set a commune on common land.

The demand for economic equality appeared during the French Revolution in Babeuf's Plebeian Manifesto of 1795. Until then, while the revolutionary government confiscated the lands of the Church and of the emigrant nobility, those were not redistributed to peasants but sold to rich commoners (Fontana 1993: 122). Babeuf did not want to equalize property, but to abolish it: "We do not propose to divide up property, because no equal division would ever last. We propose to abolish private property altogether." Claiming that stomachs are equal, Babeuf wanted every man to place his product in a common pool and receive from it an equal share. Hence, no one could take advantage of greater wealth or ability. He motivated his communist program by the principle of *le bonheur commun*,

---

[12] Demands for a redistribution of land were made intermittently in Latin America, most notably by Hidalgo and Morelos in Mexico in 1810 and Artigas in Uruguay (then Banda Oriental) in 1813.

which must lead to the "*communauté*, comfort for all, education for all, equality, liberty and happiness for all" (citations are from Palmer 1964: 240–1). His demand for economic equality was based on moral principles. Babeuf claimed that both legal and economic equality were only the natural outcome of the Enlightenment and both within the spirit of the French Revolution. Why should the fact or the postulate that all men are born equal justify political equality but not an economic one? Why should reasons be treated as equal but stomachs not? If logic does not dictate this distinction, one can suspect that only interests did. Does not economic compulsion to sell one's services to another bind as much as the political subjugation to the command of another? Rousseau (1964 [1762]: 154), at least, thought that "no Citizen should be so opulent as to be able to buy another, and none so poor as to be constrained to sell himself."

But one can also think not on moral but on purely positive grounds that democracy, via political equality, must lead to economic equality. Indeed, at some moment, political and economic equality became connected by a syllogism: Universal suffrage, combined with majority rule, grants political power to the majority. Because the majority is always poor, it will confiscate the riches. The syllogism was perhaps first enunciated by Henry Ireton in the franchise debate at Putney in 1647: "It [universal male suffrage] may come to destroy property thus. You may have such men chosen, or at least the major part of them, as have no local or permanent interest. Why may not these men vote against all property?" (quoted in Sharp 1998: 113–14). It was echoed by a French conservative polemicist, J. Mallet du Pan, who insisted in 1796 that legal equality must lead to equality of wealth: "Do you wish a republic of equals amid the inequalities which the public services, inheritances, marriage, industry and commerce have introduced into society? You will have to overthrow property" (quoted in Palmer 1964: 230).

Note that, contrary to frequent misquoting, of which I am guilty as well,[13] Madison (*Federalist #10*) thought that this consequence applied to direct but not to representative democracies. Having identified a "pure Democracy" as a system of direct rule, Madison continues that "*such* Democracies have ever been spectacles of turbulence and contention; have ever been found incompatible with personal security or the rights of property; and have in general been as short in their lives as they have been violent in their deaths" (italics added). However, "A Republic, by

---

[13] The misquoting consists of skipping the "such" in the citation by Madison here. See, for example, Hanson (1985: 57) or Przeworski and Limongi (1993: 51–69).

which I mean a Government in which the scheme of representation takes place, opens a different prospect and promises the cure for which we are seeking." Still, he seems to have been less sanguine some decades later: "the danger to the holders of property can not be disguised, if they are undefended against a majority without property. Bodies of men are not less swayed by interest than individuals.... Hence, the liability of the rights of property."[14]

Once coined, this syllogism has dominated the fears and the hopes attached to democracy ever since. Conservatives agreed with socialists[15] that democracy, specifically universal suffrage, must undermine property. The self-serving nature of the convoluted arguments for restricting suffrage to the propertied became apparent: Suffrage was dangerous because it would threaten property. The Scottish philosopher James Mackintosh predicted in 1818 that "if the laborious classes gain franchise, a permanent animosity between opinion and property must be the consequence" (Collini, Winch, and Burrow 1983: 98). David Ricardo was prepared to extend suffrage only to "that part of them which cannot be supposed to have an interest in overturning the right to property" (Collini, Winch, and Burrow 1983: 107). Thomas Macaulay (1900: 263) in the 1842 speech on the Chartists vividly summarized the danger presented by universal suffrage:

> The essence of the Charter is universal suffrage. If you withhold that, it matters not very much what else you grant. If you grant that, it matters not at all what else you withhold. If you grant that, the country is lost.... My firm conviction is that, in our country, universal suffrage is incompatible, not only with this or that form of government, and with everything for the sake of which government exists; that it is incompatible with property and that it is consequently incompatible with civilization.

Nine years later, from the other extreme of the political spectrum, Karl Marx (1952: 62) expressed the same conviction that private property and universal suffrage are incompatible:

> The classes whose social slavery the constitution is to perpetuate, proletariat, peasantry, petty bourgeoisie, it puts in possession of political power through universal suffrage. And from the class whose old social power it sanctions, the bourgeoisie, it withdraws the political guarantees of this power. It forces the political rule of the bourgeoisie into democratic conditions, which at every moment jeopardize

---

[14] Note that this was written at some time between 1821 and 1829, in Ketcham (1986: 152).

[15] According to Rosanvallon (2004), this particular word appeared in France in 1834.

the very foundations of bourgeois society. From the one it demands that they should not go forward from political to social emancipation; from the others they should not go back from social to political restoration.

According to Marx, democracy inevitably "unchains the class struggle": The poor use democracy to expropriate the riches; the rich are threatened and subvert democracy by "abdicating" political power to the permanently organized armed forces. The combination of democracy and capitalism is thus an inherently unstable form of organization of society, "only the political form of revolution of bourgeois society and not its conservative form of life" (1934 [1852]: 18), "only a spasmodic, exceptional state of things . . . impossible as the normal form of society" (1971 [1872]: 198).

The "fundamental contradiction of the Republican constitution" identified by Marx would not materialize if either property ownership would expand spontaneously or the dispossessed for some reasons abstained from using their political rights to confiscate property.[16] On the other hand, Maier (1975: 127) notes, "if the observer feared that social leveling would continue toward proletarianization, then the advance of democracy must appear an alarming trend. For this would suggest . . . that all democracy must in effect tend towards social democracy. That is, the advent of popular government and expanded electorate would ineluctably lead to programmes for further social equalization and redistribution on wealth." Indeed, the idea that democracy in the political realm must logically lead to social and economic equality became the cornerstone of Social Democracy. As Beitz (1989: xvi) observes, historically a main goal of democratic movements has been to seek redress in the political sphere for the effects of inequalities in the economy and society.

Socialists entered into elections with ultimate goals. The Hague Congress of the First International proclaimed, "the organization of the proletariat into a political party is necessary to insure the victory of social revolution and its ultimate goal – the abolition of classes." The first Swedish socialist program specified that "Social Democracy differs from other parties in that it aspires to completely transform the economic organization of the bourgeois society and bring about the social liberation of the working class" (Tingsten 1973: 118–19). Even the most reformist

---

[16] James Mill, for one, challenged the opponents "to produce an instance, so much as one instance, from the first page of history to the last, of the people of any country showing hostility to the general laws of property, or manifesting a desire for its subversion" (cited in Collini, Winch, and Barrow 1983: 104).

among socialists, Alexandre Millerand, admonished that "whoever does not admit the necessary and progressive replacement of capitalist property by social property is not a socialist" (quoted in Ensor 1908: 51). Nonetheless, on the road to these ultimate goals, socialists saw numerous measures that would reduce social and economic inequalities. The Parti Socialiste Français, led by Jean Jaures, proclaimed at its Tours Congress of 1902, "The Socialist Party, rejecting the policy of all or nothing, has a program of reforms whose realization it pursues forthwith," and listed fifty-four specific measures (Ensor 1908: 345 ff.). Swedish Social Democrats in 1897 demanded direct taxation, development of state and municipal productive activities, public credit, legislation concerning work conditions, old age, sickness, and accident insurance, as well as purely political rights (Tingsten 1973: 119–20).

The question that haunted Social Democrats was whether, as Hjalmar Branting posed it in 1886, "the upper class [would] respect popular will even if it demanded the abolition of its privileges" (Tingsten 1973: 361). Were there limits to popular sovereignty, as exercised by electoral majorities? Would revolution not be necessary, as August Bebel feared in 1905 (quoted in Schorske 1955: 43), "as a purely defensive measure, designed to safeguard the exercise of power legitimately acquired through the ballot"? Yet there is a prior question they did not consider. Can any political arrangement generate economic equality? Can equality be established by laws, even if the upper class does concede to the abolition of its privileges? Or is some extent of economic inequality inevitable even if everyone would want to abolish it? Did Social Democrats fail or did they accomplish all that was within reach?

4.6 DEMOCRACY AND INCOME DISTRIBUTION

According to Dunn (2003: 22), democracy surprisingly turned from a revolutionary project into a conservative one:

Where the political force of the idea of democracy came from in this new epoch was its combination of formal social equality with a practical order founded on the protection and reproduction of an increasingly dynamic system of economic inequality. . . . No one at all in 1750 either did or could have seen democracy as a natural name or an apt institutional form for the effective protection of productive wealth. But today we know better. In the teeth of ex ante perceived probability, that is exactly what representative democracy has in the long run proved.

Should we share his surprise?

My argument has been that the sin was original. Although democracy in the second part of the eighteenth century was a revolutionary idea, the revolution it offered was strictly political. In my reading, in its inception democracy was a project simply blind to economic inequality, regardless of how revolutionary it may have been politically. Morally based arguments for redistribution or abolishment of property were marginal and ephemeral. Moreover, by restricting suffrage, representative institutions replaced aristocracy with oligarchy.

Nonetheless, the coexistence of universal suffrage with unequal distribution of property is hard to fathom. The syllogism according to which the poor would use their majority status to expropriate the rich was almost universally accepted – and it still makes logical sense today. Just consider the favorite toy of political economists, the median voter model (Meltzer and Richards 1981): Each individual is characterized by an endowment of labor or capital and all individuals can be ranked from the richest to the poorest. Individuals vote on the rate of tax to be imposed on incomes. The revenues generated by this tax are either equally distributed to all individuals or spent on equally valued public goods, so that the tax rate uniquely determines the extent of redistribution. Once the tax rate is decided, individuals maximize utility by deciding in a decentralized way how much of their endowments to supply to production. The median voter theorem asserts that there exists unique majority-rule equilibrium, that this equilibrium is the choice of the voter with the median preference, and that the voter with the median preference is the one with median income. Furthermore, when the distribution of incomes is skewed to the right, that is, if the median income is lower than the mean, as it is in all countries for which data exist, majority-rule equilibrium is associated with a high degree of equality of post-fisc (tax and transfer) incomes, tempered only by the deadweight losses of redistribution.

Moreover, the demand for social and economic equality persists. Although elites see democracy in institutional terms, mass publics, at least in Eastern Europe and Latin America, conceive of it in terms of "social and economic equality." In Chile, 59 percent of respondents expected that democracy would attenuate social inequalities (Alaminos 1991), while in Eastern Europe the proportion associating democracy with social equality ranged from 61 percent in Czechoslovakia to 88 percent in Bulgaria (Bruszt and Simon 1991). People do expect that democracy would breed social and economic equality. Hence, the coexistence of democracy and inequality continues to be puzzling.

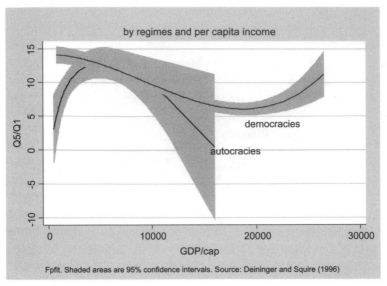

FIGURE 4.1 Ratio of incomes of the top to the bottom 20 percent.

Consider first some facts.

First, if we dichotomize political regimes as democracies and autocracies, we discover that the extent of inequality, measured by the ratio of incomes of the top to the bottom 20 percent of income recipients, differs little between them at each level of per capita income (See Figure 4.1 and Table 4.1).[17] Note that some democracies appear in countries with high income levels for which there are no autocracies. The upward-sloping part of wealthy democracies is due to the United States, which is unusually unequal given its level of development.[18]

Statistical analyses show that the estimates of the average difference between regimes are small and not robust.

Second, income distributions appear to be amazingly stable over time. The strongest evidence, albeit for a relatively short period, comes from Li, Squire, and Zou (1997), who report that about 90 percent of the total variance in Gini coefficients is explained by the variation across countries,

---

[17] Democracies here are regimes in which there are elections with some opposition, from the ACLP database. Autocracies are simply not democracies. The data are from Deininger and Squire (1996); they cover, with a highly varying number of observations per country, the post-1960 period. Major oil exporters are not included.

[18] The United States is the most unequal country, in terms of real disposable income, among twenty-four high-income democracies studied by Brandolini and Smeeding (2008, Table 2.1).

TABLE 4.1: *Differences Between Autocracy and Democracy in the Ratio of the Top to the Bottom Quintile of Income Recipients*

Variable	Autocracy	Democracy	Difference
n	93	238	
Observed	10.50	9.19	1.31
Match			3.84
2SLS			−1.25
Heckman 2	11.27	10.75	0.52
Heckman 1			−1.38

Note: The results are based on different selection estimators. Observed, the observed means; Match, based on Imbens *nn* match with one match; 2SLS, the instrumental variables estimator; Heckman 2, Heckman's estimator with separate regressions for the two regimes; Heckman 1, a pooled estimator with interaction terms. Selection models are based on per capita income and past experiences with democracy. Outcome regressions use per capita income and its square.

while few countries show any time trends. Earned incomes show almost no variation during the twentieth century (Piketty 2003).

Third, increases in inequality appear to be much more rapid than declines. Particularly after 1982, some increases in inequality have been dramatic. In Poland, where distribution was quite egalitarian under communism, the ratio of the median to the mean income (a convenient way to characterize log-normal income distributions) was 0.82 in 1986, while in Mexico in 1989 it was 0.59. By 1995 this ratio in Poland was 0.62, almost the same as in highly unequal Mexico. In the United States, income inequality hovered around a constant level until about 1970 and then increased sharply (Bartels 2008: 35). In turn, longer time series show that while income shares of top recipients declined in some democratic countries, redistribution was quite limited.[19] It seems that no country rapidly equalized market incomes without some kind of cataclysm: destruction of large property as a result of foreign occupation (Japanese in Korea, Soviet in Eastern Europe), revolutions (Soviet Union), wars, or massive emigration of the poor (Norway, Sweden).

---

[19] These assertions are not contradictory: the main reason for this decline was that wars and major economic crises destroyed large fortunes and they could not be accumulated again because of progressive income tax. For long-term dynamics of top income shares, see the articles in Atkinson and Piketty (2007).

Because the issue is burning, explanations abound.[20] I can only list generic varieties.

One class of explanations maintains that, for a variety of reasons, the poor do not want to equalize property, incomes, or even opportunities. The reasons come in several variants.

1. False consciousness, due to a lack of understanding of the distinction between productive and nonproductive property.
2. Ideological domination, due to the ownership of the media by the propertied (Anderson 1977).
3. Divisions among the poor, due to religion or race (Frank 2004; Roemer 2001).
4. Expectations of the poor that they would become rich (Benabou and Ok 2001).
5. Poor information about the effects of particular policies, even among people holding egalitarian norms (Bartels 2008).
6. The belief that inequality is just because it is a consequence of effort, rather than luck (Piketty 1995).

Another variety of explanations claims that even if a majority holds egalitarian norms, formal political rights are ineffective against private property. Some distinctions are again relevant.

1. Wealthy people occupy positions of political power, which they use to successfully defend themselves from redistribution (Lindblom 1977; Miliband 1970). The "power elite" is the same as the economic elite.
2. Independent of their class composition, governments of all partisan stripes must anticipate the trade-off between redistribution and growth. Redistributing productive property or even incomes is costly to the poor. Confronting the perspective of losing their property or not being able to enjoy its fruits, property owners save and invest less, thus reducing the future wealth and future income of everyone. This "structural dependence on capital" imposes a limit on redistribution, even for those governments that want to equalize incomes (Przeworski and Wallerstein 1988).

None of these explanations remains unscathed when exposed to counterarguments and to evidence. Personally, I am not taken by the

---

[20] Several of these explanations appear in Bartel's (2008) book, where, however, the story is much more complex and nuanced than this schematic list would suggest.

claim that the poor would not want to live better, even if it were at the expense of the rich. In turn, the relation between redistribution and growth is controversial theoretically and the empirical evidence is inconclusive (Banerjee and Dufflo 2003). Some forms of redistribution – those that take the form of subsidies to education or to investment by those who are credit constrained – are obviously growth enhancing. A pure redistribution of consumption, however, may retard growth.

Yet this entire way of thinking confronts an awkward fact that many governments were elected with the support of the poor, wanted to equalize incomes, and tried to do so. Hence, to the extent to which they failed, it must have been for reasons other than not wanting or not trying. Because we are now approaching the limits of democracy, the argument has to be developed with some care.

Note first that there are different ways to equalize incomes. One is to tax market incomes and either finance consumption of the poor or spend the revenues on equally valued public consumption goods. This is what many governments do, to varying degrees; redistribution is more extensive under left-wing governments (for references and discussion, see Beramendi and Anderson 2008). Redistribution via taxes and transfers ("the fisc"), however, does not reduce the underlying inequality of the capacity to earn incomes. It finances private or public consumption with little effect on income-earning potentials. Hence, this form of redistribution has to be undertaken over and over again, year after year, just to alleviate the inequality of earned incomes. Because it is costly, either in terms of incentives or merely administrative expenditures, it is an urgent, not a permanent, solution.

The second mechanism to equalize income is through an equalization of income-earning potentials. Because incomes are generated by efforts applied to productive assets – whether land, physical capital, education, or skills – to equalize the capacities to earn incomes, we must think in terms of distribution of these assets.

But what assets can be equalized in modern societies? When the idea of equal property first appeared, productive assets meant land. Land is relatively easy to redistribute. It is enough to take it from some and give it to others. Hence, agrarian reforms were frequent in the history of the world: There were at least 175 land reforms entailing redistribution between 1946 and 2000 alone. Today, however, the distribution of land plays a relatively minor role in generating income inequality. In turn, other assets resist such a simple operation.

First, communists redistributed industrial capital by placing it in the hands of the state and promising that uninvested profits would be equally distributed to households. Although this system generated a fair degree of equality, for reasons that cannot be discussed here, it turned out to be dynamically inefficient: It inhibited innovation and technical progress.

Second, and alternatively, one could redistribute titles to property in the form of shares. This form of redistribution, however, has problems of its own. One is that, as the Czech privatization experience shows, they could be and likely would be quickly reconcentrated. People who are otherwise poorer would sell them to those who are wealthier. Another problem is that the dispersion of ownership lowers the incentives of shareholders to monitor managers. Although some solutions to this problem have been proposed, they do not seem to be very effective.

Third, many countries equalized human capital by investing in education. Nevertheless, people exposed to the same educational system acquire different income-earning capacities as a function of their social and economic background. Moreover, because people are born with different talents and because the use of these talents is socially beneficial, we would want to educate talented people more.

Fourth and finally, income-earning capacities can be generated by policies that are narrowly targeted on increasing the productivity of the poor ("pro-poor growth"), such as relaxing credit constraints, training for specific skills, subsidizing the necessary infrastructure, focusing on diseases to which poor people are most vulnerable, and so on. Such policies, however, require a high level of administrative competence to diagnose the needs and to target the policies.

Thus, equalizing productive assets seems to be difficult for purely technological, not just political or economic, reasons.

Moreover, even if productive assets were equalized, perfect equality cannot be sustained in a market economy. Asking "How laws establish equality in a democracy?" – the title of Chapter 5 of Book 5 – Montesquieu (1995: 151–5) takes as his point of departure equality of land. He then goes on:

If, when the legislator makes such a division, he does not give laws to maintain it, he only makes a passing constitution; inequality will enter from the side the laws do not defend, and the republic will be lost. Therefore, although real equality would be the soul of the state, it is so difficult to establish that an extreme rigor in this respect is not always convenient. It is sufficient, to reduce differences to some point, after which, it is for particular laws to equalize, to put it this way, the inequalities, by the charges they impose on the rich and the relief they accord to the poor.

Remember that Babeuf believed that the redistribution of property would not solve the problem of inequality, "since no equal division would ever last." Suppose productive assets had been equalized. Individuals would still have different and unobservable abilities to transform productive assets into incomes. Moreover, they are subject to the vicissitudes of luck. Assume that particular individuals (or projects they undertake) are subject to slightly different rates of return: Some lose at the rate of -0.02 per annum and some gain at the rate of 0.02. After twenty-five years, the individual who generates a 2 percent return will be 2.7 times wealthier than the individual who loses 2 percent per year, and after fifty years (say from the age of 18 to 68) this multiple will be 7.4.[21] Hence, even if productive assets were to be equalized, inequality would creep back in.[22]

The issue – discussed in the next chapter – is to what extent the redistributive choices are tightly circumscribed because the logic of electoral competition pushes political parties to offer and pursue similar policies and to what extent there is just little governments can do. The question is important because it affects our judgment of democracy. Suppose that economic inequality could be diminished below the levels prevailing in developed democracies without reducing the future incomes and that it is not being diminished only because of the institutional features of democracy, however one thinks about them. Obviously, judging this trade-off would depend on other values we would have to give up when we opt for equality. There is, however, no such trade-off. Some degree of economic inequality is just inevitable. Democracy is impotent against it, but so is every other conceivable political arrangement. Think of Brazil: During the past two centuries it was a colony, an independent monarchy, an oligarchical republic, a populist military dictatorship, a democracy with a weak presidency, a right-wing military dictatorship, and a democracy with a strong presidency. Nevertheless, to the best of our knowledge, income distribution did not budge. Even the communists, who were out to *uravnit* (equalize) everything, and who did equalize assets in the form of public ownership, had to tolerate the inequality arising from different talents and motivations. The quest for equality has limits.

This is not a call for quiescence. Unless governments continually combat inequality, unless they maintain an active role in protecting the poor

---

[21] The assumption that the annual rates of return are correlated for each individual over time reflects the fact that people differ in unobserved traits that affect their capacity to use productive assets.

[22] For different versions of this argument, see Mookherjee and Ray (2003) and Benhabib and Bisin (2008).

and in transferring productive resources to those whose income-earning capacity is low, inequality has a tendency to rise. As the neoliberal experiment has shown, when governments fail to play this role, the rise of inequality can be quite rapid. Moreover, the extent of economic inequality is simply appalling in several democracies. Among contemporary democracies, the ratio of income shares of the top to the bottom quintile, which is perhaps the most intuitive measure of inequality, ranges from less than 6 in Finland, Belgium, Spain, and South Korea to about 33 in Brazil and Peru. Even the ratio of 6 is still very large: It means that in a country with a per capita income of $15,000 (about average for these countries in 2002, counted in 1995 purchasing power parity, or PPP, dollars), a member of the top quintile would have an income of $27,000, while a member of the bottom quintile would have an income of $4,500. Most survey respondents in Spain and South Korea see such inequality as excessive. Moreover, the difference between many Latin American democracies and the more equal European ones is enormous. Even if democracy hurls itself against limits, many democracies are far away from these limits.

4.7 CLOSING THE CIRCLE

Democracy is a mechanism that treats all participants equally. Nevertheless, when unequal individuals are treated equally, their influence over collective decisions is still unequal. Imagine a game of basketball. There are two teams, perfectly universalistic rules, and an impartial referee to administer them. However, one team consists of players who are seven feet tall and the other of people who barely exceed five. The outcome of the game is predetermined. The rules of the game treat everyone equally, but this only means that the outcome of the game depends on the resources participants bring to it.

In a scathing critique of "bourgeois rights," Marx (1844) characterized this duality between universalistic rules and unequal resources as follows:

The state abolishes, in its own way, distinctions of birth, social rank, education, occupation, when it declares that birth, social rank, education, occupation, are nonpolitical distinctions, when it proclaims, without regard to these distinctions, that every member of the nation is an equal participant in national sovereignty.... Nevertheless the state allows private property, education, occupation to act in their way – i.e., as private property, as education, as occupation, and to exert the influence of their special nature.

This duality has been repeatedly diagnosed ever since. The chairman of the Drafting Committee of the Indian 1950 Constitution, B. R. Ambedkar (quoted in Guha 2008: 133), saw the future Indian republic as entering a "life of contradictions":

In politics we will be recognizing the principle of one man one vote and one vote one value. In our social and economic life, we shall, by reason of our social and economic structure, continue to deny the principle of one man one value. How long shall we continue to live this life of contradictions? How long shall we continue to deny equality in our social and economic life? If we continue to deny it for long, we will do so only by putting our political democracy in peril.

How does socioeconomic inequality become transformed into political inequality? Cannot the impact of socioeconomic inequality be mitigated by regulatory measures or by political organization of the poor?

Unfortunately, our knowledge of the role of nonpolitical resources – and I concentrate narrowly on money – in shaping political outcomes is scant. A general conclusion of surveys conducted in twenty-two countries by the National Democratic Institute for International Affairs (Bryan and Baer 2005: 3) is that "Little is known about the details of money in political parties or in campaigns. Political party financing patterns are extremely opaque." To a large extent this lack of knowledge is due to the nature of the phenomenon: Legally or not, money infiltrates itself into politics in ways that are intended to be opaque. Moreover, the mechanisms through which financial resources affect policies are difficult to identify even when the information is available.

Schematically, one may think that money biases the outcomes of the democratic process if (1) poor people are less likely to vote, (2) political contributions affect the platforms offered by parties, (3) campaign funds affect individual voting decisions, (4) political contributions affect the legislative process, or (5) bribes influence bureaucratic or judicial decisions. I consider these channels in turn.

Outside the United States, class – income or education – differences in electoral turnout are small. Recalculating the data reported by Anduiza (1999: 102) for fourteen Western European countries shows that the average difference between the turnout of the top and bottom income quartiles is only 6 percent. The largest difference, in France, is 16.4 percent. According to Norris's (2002: 93–4) analysis of pooled data from twenty-two countries, the difference in turnout between the highest and the lowest quintile is 9.6, but this sample includes the United States. Norris's (2004: 174) data for thirty-one countries in 1996, including again the United States, shows this difference to be 8 percent. Moving outside Europe and its wealthy offshoots to poorer countries shows again that income has little impact on turnout. Yadav (2002) found that members of the scheduled casts and registered tribes voted at higher rates than people who were better off in India during the 1990s; this finding is confirmed by Krishna (2008) within North Indian villages. Using data from Afrobarometer for fifteen African countries, Bratton (2008) found that the poor were somewhat more likely to vote than the nonpoor. Booth and Seligson (2008) report that in a pooled analysis of six Central American countries plus Mexico and Colombia, turnout was not related to income. The United States is a clear outlier: According to Verba, Schlozman, and Brady (1995: 190), 86 percent of those with incomes of $75,000 or higher turned out at the polls but only one-half of those with incomes under $15,000 did.

The impact of education seems to vary more across countries. Bratton (2008) as well as Booth and Seligson (2008) find that educated people are somewhat more likely to vote in their respective regions. Norris (2002: 93–4) estimates the difference of turnout between college graduates and high school dropouts to be 9.5 percent, while her sample of thirty-one countries in 1996 shows a difference of 14 percent (2004: 175). Norris, however, emphasizes that education has no effect on turnout in Western Europe. Anduiza's (1999: 99) data show the difference between the turnout of people with "high" and "low" education to be only 2.3 percent in fifteen European countries, with six countries in which people with low education turn out at higher rates than the most educated ones. The highest difference in favor of highly educated persons is in Switzerland, which is an outlier at 19.2 percent. The data of Goodrich and Nagler (2006) show the average difference between the top and bottom quartiles of education to be 8.3 percent in fifteen countries not including the United States, with Switzerland again the outlier at 22.7 percent. They also show the difference for the United States: It is 39.6 percent.

Altogether, therefore, it seems that poorer people do not vote at distinctly lower rates than wealthier ones. Now, it may be true that many very poor people vote in exchange for clientilistic favors for wealthier candidates, who, once elected, pursue their own interests rather than those of their constituencies (Bratton 2008; Gallego 2009). Hence, high turnout of the poor need not mean that money does not matter. Indeed, one-half of campaign expenditures in twenty-two countries studied by Bryan and Baer (2005: 13) was derived from "personal funds," wherever these came from, and one may suspect that these expenditures were not disinterested. The fact remains, though, that outside the United States the relation between class and turnout is very weak.

The effects of political contributions on party platforms, individual voting decisions, and legislative process are difficult to identify. Consider different, not mutually exclusive, possibilities: (1) Special interest groups, or lobbies, use political contributions to influence party platforms. If an interest group succeeds in persuading all major parties to adopt programs to its liking, then it does not care which party wins and it does not need to make campaign contributions designed to influence voters. Moreover, if a lobby manages to establish a long-term relation with a party, then it does not need to buy legislative votes each time an issue on the agenda affects its interests. (2) Candidates have different preferences with regard to policies. Special interests guess who favors what. They contribute to the candidates whose positions would lead them to adopt policies favorable to the special interests. Campaign money buys votes. While in office, the elected candidates pursue policies they prefer, thus advancing the interests of some special interests. (3) Special interests buy legislation on the "spot market," that is, they make contributions to legislators in exchange for their vote on particular pieces of legislation.

Grossman and Helpman (2001) attempted to distinguish the role of money in buying platforms and buying votes in the U.S. context. In their model, parties maximize the probability of winning a majority of seats, while special interest groups maximize the welfare of their members. Voters, note, come in two kinds: Strategic voters maximize expected utility while impressionable voters are favorably influenced by campaign advertising. Special interests can make campaign contributions, politicians choose policies, and voters vote, but not necessarily in this order because contributions can play a twofold role. They can be used early in the campaign to induce parties to announce platforms that are to the liking of special interests or they can be used once the platforms have been announced to sway voters to vote for the party closer to the special interest. If there is only one interest group, the conclusions are as follows: (1) To influence their platforms, the group contributes to both parties, giving more to the party that is the ex ante favorite to win. (2a) If the resulting platforms are the same, the special interest is indifferent as to which party would win and contributes no more. (2b) If the resulting platforms differ, then the group contributes additional funds to tilt the election in favor of the front-runner. "Overall," Grossman and Helpman conclude (2001: 339), "the contributions bias the policy outcome away from the public interest both by influencing the parties' positions and perhaps by tilting the election odds." The electoral motive – contributions designed to tilt elections in favor of the party whose announced position is more to the liking of the special interest – is even weaker when several interest groups compete for influence because each group can ride free on the contributions of other groups. In the end, platforms reflect contributions and deviate from the welfare of the average voter. Parties act as if they were maximizing a weighted average of campaign contributions and of the aggregate welfare of strategic voters.

Empirical studies of the impact of money are limited almost exclusively to the United States and generate divergent results, often showing that money has little effect (Stratman 2005). The difficulty of these studies is to identify the direction of causality in two relations: First, do parties (candidates) win because they spend more money, or do they have more money to spend because they are expected to win? Second, do legislators vote for special interests because they receive contributions, or do they receive contributions because they are perceived as having preferences coincidental with interests of special interests? In the end, we know that winners spend more money on campaigns than losers and that legislators tend to vote in favor of groups from which they receive contributions, but the mechanisms that generate these correlations remain opaque.

Regulation differs importantly across countries with regard to transparency, public financing, and private financing. Pierre, Svåsand, and Widfeldt (2000) report that as of 1989, the proportion of state subsidies in the total income of Western European political parties ranged from 25.1 percent in Austria to 84.2 in Finland. According to IDEA (www.idea.int/parties/finance), out of 116 countries for which this information was available as of 2002, 75 have some kind of regulation of political financing while 41 have none. Furthermore, 59 countries have provisions for disclosure of contributions to political parties while 52 do not. Most countries allow private contributions, even from government contractors (86 do; 27 do not). In turn, in 83 countries there is some scheme of direct public financing of political parties while in 61 there was none, and in 81 countries the parties receive free television time during electoral campaigns while in 34 they do not. Another source (http:\\aceproject.org) reports that 156 countries allow private funding and 28 do not, while 106 provide direct and 110 indirect public funding and 46 provide none. Note that none of the arguments against public financing – that it makes parties dependent on the state, that it petrifies the party system, and that it induces apathy in mobilizing members – seems to hold at least in the Western European context (Pierre, Svåsand, and Widfeldt 2000).

To my best knowledge, there are no comparative studies of the effect of these regulatory regimes on the policy outcomes, although there are claims that campaign finance plays little role in some countries, notably the Netherlands, Denmark, or Sweden, while it is large in Italy, the United Kingdom, and the United States (Prat 1999). Moreover, regulation is not the only way to equalize the political influence of economically unequal groups. The political playing field seems to be more equal in countries in which the poor have been organized by political parties associated with powerful trade unions.

Corruption scandals abound: Suitcases filled with cash are found in a prime minister's office, government contracts are awarded to firms co-owned by government ministers, insider trades are rampant, political parties are found to have bank accounts in Switzerland, local governments operate systematic bribe schedules on developers, the list goes on and on. Moreover, such scandals are by no means limited to less developed countries or to young democracies; these examples are drawn from Germany, Spain, France, Italy, and Belgium. Nevertheless, reducing the political role of money to instances of corruption is deeply misleading and politically misguided. Conceptualized as "corruption," the influence of money becomes something anomalous, out of the ordinary. We are told that when special interests bribe legislators or governments, democracy is corrupted – and then nothing needs to be said when special interests make legal political contributions. The British learned late in the eighteenth century that "influence" is nothing but a euphemism for "corruption," but contemporary political science chose to ignore this lesson. In order to exist and to participate in elections, political parties need money; because election results matter for private interests, they understandably seek to befriend parties and influence results of elections: The logic of political competition is inexorable. That the same acts are legal in some countries and illegal in other systems – U.S. political financing practices would constitute corruption in several democracies – is in the end of secondary importance. The corruption of politics by money is a structural feature of democracy in economically unequal societies.

Given the scarcity of systematic knowledge and the difficulties in distinguishing different mechanisms of access of money to politics, the conclusion has to be speculative. Although access of money to politics can be to some extent regulated, money has endless ways to infiltrate itself into politics. While regulation can reduce the extent to which political inequality reflects economic inequality, the influence of private property, education, or occupation cannot be completely eliminated. Regulation can to some extent equalize the playing field, but regulation designed to favor the current losers is not likely to be adopted by the current winners, those who are in power. Moreover, regulation can generate perverse effects. Stratman (2005: 140), for example, points out that if money has little effect on the vote for incumbents but a larger effect on the vote for challengers, limitations on campaign spending would favor incumbents. In turn, if marginal differences in campaign spending have a large effect on vote shares, spending limitations would favor undetected cheaters.

Perfect political equality is not feasible in economically unequal societies. Democracies cannot fail, however, in their commitment to political equality. Even if some dose of political inequality may be inevitable, even if we do not quite understand how economic resources affect political outcomes, the corrupting influence of money is the scourge of democracy.

5

Choice and Participation

5.1 INTRODUCTION

Self-government is exercised through elections. The collective decision-making process operates indirectly: Citizens choose parties or candidates, authorizing them to make decisions on behalf of the collectivity.

Even when electoral competitors present clear policy proposals, to which I refer as "platforms," the alternatives from which voters can choose are only those that are proposed. Not all conceivable and not even all feasible options become subject to collective choice. The choices presented to voters in elections do not include the ideal points, the alternatives they like most, of all citizens. The number of options is necessarily limited, so that if voters are sufficiently heterogeneous in what they would like most to occur, some may find that their preferences are far away from the closest platform that is being proposed. Moreover, electoral competition inexorably pushes political parties, at least those that want to and have a chance to win, to offer similar platforms. The result is that the alternatives presented in elections are meager: Choices are few and the range of decisions they offer is paltry. Indeed, if elections were truly described by the model that serves as the workhorse of electoral analysis – the median voter model in which two parties converge to the same platform – individual voters would have no choice at all.

Now, one may think that if voters do not get a chance to choose, they do not decide anything. Bobbio (1987: 25), at least, includes in his minimal definition of democracy the condition that "those called upon to take decisions, or to elect those who are to take decisions, must be offered some real alternatives." Dunn (2000: 146–7) also emphasizes the importance of choice: "the state at this point is more plausibly seen as a structure through which the minimally participant citizen body . . . select from the meagre options presented to them those they hope will best serve their several interests. In that selection, the meagreness of the range of options is always important and sometimes absolutely decisive." Nevertheless, even if individual voters are not offered any choice at the moment of the election, the collectivity decides. Consider again the median voter model, in which two parties fully informed about voters compete in an election that focuses on a single issue, say the tax rate. Even if they represent diametrically opposed interests, to have a chance to win the parties must please the decisive voter. Hence, both parties offer the same platform, proposing to do what the decisive voter wants them to do (Downs 1957, Roemer 2001). The decisive voter, though, is not a dictator; she is decisive only contingent on the preferences of everyone else. Even if voters are offered no choice, the decision reached by the collectivity reflects the distribution of individual preferences. Had this distribution been different, so would have been the collective decision resulting from the election.

Hence, even if individuals do not get to choose when they vote, the absence of choice does not invalidate self-government. In fact, a choice has been made. The parties read the preferences of all citizens and compared the numerical support for each of them[1] – except that once the parties calculated which among the alternatives is the majority winner, at the moment of the election they can say to voters, "This is what the majority of us wants. We, citizens, have chosen and this is what our choice is."

Yet many people seem to object to collective choices being made in this way. They want to be presented with distinct choices and to be able to cast their votes, selecting among them. How general is this dissatisfaction is impossible to tell. At least some voices loudly bemoan the meagerness of choice. They seem to value choosing, independently of the outcomes. This reaction may stem just from a lack of understanding of the electoral mechanism, but this does not make it any less intense. Why else would we have the perennial complaints about "Tweedledum and Tweedledee," "*bonnet blanc et blanc bonnet*"? What is not clear is whether people object because they indeed value choosing or because they do not like the particular collective decisions that result from aggregating preferences

---

[1] One need not assume that people's preferences are independent of what parties propose, only that parties anticipate how people would end up voting for each platform after all is said and done.

that include some different from their own. Do people object that there is little choice or what the choices are?

Moreover, even if voters do face choices – parties do not in fact offer exactly the same platforms – none of us can individually cause a particular choice to be selected. The criterion of unanimity promised causal efficacy to each and every member of the collectivity and the only people who ever used this rule, Poles between 1652 and 1791, defended it vigorously until the death of their country in 1795 (Jędruch 1998). The nostalgia for effective participation continues to haunt modern democracies, but no rule of collective decision making other than unanimity can render causal efficacy to equal individual participation. Collective self-government is achieved not when each voter has causal influence on the final result, but when collective choice is a result of aggregating individual wills.

5.2 CHOICE IN ELECTIONS

Should democrats value choice? To study this question, we need a conceptual apparatus. Suppose each voter has an ideal policy in a particular realm: Think now that the ideal point represents the number of months up to which abortion is to be allowed. Then every voter will be able to vote for his peak preference only if there are as many competing parties as there are distinct ideal points in the electorate. But voters are aware that they have to make some compromises. As long as there is a platform sufficiently close to their preferences, they treat this platform as their own. For example, let the set of ideal points of seven voters be {1, 2, 3, 3, 4, 4, 5} and assume that voters see themselves as represented by a candidate who is not farther than one unit (month) away. Suppose that there are two parties, with platforms {2, 4}. The presence of 2 among the alternatives will satisfy the first four voters, while the presence of 4 the last five. The two platforms represent all seven voters, with five different ideal points.

As this example indicates, being able to vote for a platform one feels close to does not require everyone's peak preferences to be present among the proposed platforms. But even if voters are willing to tolerate some distance to treat the alternatives as theirs, the number of platforms must proliferate if voters are more heterogeneous. For example, if the ideal points are {1, 2, 3, 4, 5, 6, 7}, three platforms, {2, 5, 6}, are needed for all the voters to feel that their preferences are included among the alternatives presented to them.

Consider the French presidential election of 2002, in which sixteen candidates participated in the first round. The candidates who appeared to have no chance of winning whatever they would say actually said something, ranging across "stop globalization," "redistribute incomes," "give the vote to foreigners in local elections," "allow hunting," and "expel all immigrants," while the two major candidates limited themselves to statements such as "Youth is the smile of France." Standard political science considers voting for candidates who have no chance to win "expressive," as opposed to "instrumental," claiming that there is something irrational about it. Indeed, French polls showed that only some 20 percent of those who voted for the extreme candidates wanted them to actually become president. But these votes can be read differently. Whoever ends up governing must consider the full distribution of preferences, including the fact that some people have extreme views. Hence, even if voting for minor candidates does not influence who governs, it may affect how they govern. In this sense, it may be instrumental.

Yet even if these votes were noninstrumental, the mere fact that they were cast constitutes *prima facie* evidence that some voters value this opportunity. The French story highlights the importance of the process by which the choices are generated. Because the barriers to entry into the first round are very low in France, any alternative that enjoys some public support can enter the set of choices presented to voters. However, the same is not true of many democracies, notably the United States, where politics may be the most protected industry. When one's preferences are not recognized in the set of collective opportunities, one is excluded from the political community. Even if some people whose ideal point is included vote strategically, not for their first choice, they are the ones who decide how to vote. It is voters who should decide whether to maximize utility or to express their preferences in a noninstrumental way. When choices are restricted, they are denied this opportunity. This is why being free to form political parties is an empty freedom unless political parties are actually formed.

Nonetheless, because parties know that they have no chance to win if they propose a platform supported by few voters, there may well be ideal points that are not proposed by parties even in a multiparty systems. The reason parties propose platforms that offer meager choice to voters is intrinsic to electoral competition. One can think in several ways about the logic of elections. The simplest, most influential but least plausible view is that two parties that care only about winning compete in one issue dimension fully informed about the distribution of voters' ideal preferences. Under such conditions the parties converge to the same platform and the winner is chosen by a flip of a coin. The same is true if voters have ideosyncratic ideological preferences for one of the parties, only that then the decisive voter is the one with the mean, not the median, preference (Lindbeck and Weibull 1987). One can think that parties still compete in one dimension but they care about policies and are uncertain about voters; then they will offer somewhat distinct platforms (Roemer 2001). One can allow for the existence of more than two parties (Austen-Smith 2000).[2] One can also more realistically view elections as entailing several issue dimensions.[3] Nonetheless, however one thinks of electoral competition, the core intuition derived from the simplest perspective, due to Downs (1957), survives: Whether parties care only about winning or also about the welfare of their constituents, whether they know everything or only something, whether there are two or more of them, whether they compete in one dimension or in several, they can win only if they propose platforms somewhere in the political center. And if all parties that have a chance to win move to the center, the choice facing voters is circumscribed. There may be rare moments in which voters are offered a choice, not an echo, but they are indeed rare. Most of the time, parties propose and partisan governments implement policies that differ little from those of their opponents.

This logic can be observed by a glance at economic policies in Western Europe since World War I. This history consists of long periods during which most governments, regardless of their partisan stripes, pursued similar economic policies, interrupted by only sporadic policy innovations, followed again by periods when policies converged across partisan lines. Between the end of World War I and the 1930s, governments followed the golden principles of a balanced budget, deflationary anticrisis policies, the gold standard, and so on. Because everyone believed that capitalist economies obey natural laws, there was nothing anyone could do to counteract economic fluctuations. Socialists did want to nationalize industry but could not, because they held office only as minority governments or as members of coalitions. Because bourgeois parties viewed nationalization

---

[2] In Austen-Smith's model (2000: 1259), the decisive voter is the person with the mean income among those who would be employed after the tax rate has been set.
[3] To understand what will happen in such cases, we need to assume that parties cannot move freely across the policy space but this assumption, however it is motivated, is only realistic. In Roemer's (2001) party unity Nash equilibrium (PUNE), parties are restricted in the proposals they make by the requirement that different factions within them must unanimously agree about the best response to the platform of the other party. In the candidate–citizen model (Besley and Coate 1996; Osborne and Sliwinsky 1996), candidates cannot move across policy space at all.

as an anathema, there were no nationalizations. The major innovation of Social Democrats was the idea that capitalist economies can be controlled by an active state. With the rise of Keynesianism, governments, regardless of partisan orientations, learned that they could counteract fluctuations of the capitalist economy by managing demand. They also found that by providing public goods and infrastructural investments, correcting for externalities, and regulating natural monopolies, they could compensate for market inefficiencies. Finally, they came to believe that by subsidizing some investments and protecting some industries, governments can promote growth. The major innovation of neoliberals was the claim that well-designed market institutions spontaneously maximize the welfare of society, or at least "efficiency." Neoliberals believe that private ownership is more efficient than other forms of property, that the state is "too big," that macroeconomic balances drive investment, and, perhaps most consequentially, that anticyclical policies only increase inflation, without having an effect on employment. Hence, they privatize, reduce public expenditures, observe macroeconomic discipline, and let "the market" do the rest.

The history of economic policies thus may have the following dynamic. A government comes to office, makes a major successful policy innovation, and develops a story about the secret of its success. The opposition party campaigns in elections by criticizing the incumbent, but everyone knows that if elected the new government would follow the same policy. The difference between the two parties is so small that voters base their decisions on accidental issues – a scandal, personalities, a television debate – and at one time the incumbent loses. The victorious party follows the policies of its predecessor. Partisan control alternates without policies changing until, at some time, someone introduces a major policy innovation, this policy is successful, and the story repeats itself.

If this is true, different parties offer and implement similar policies not only because of the exigencies of electoral competition but also because they do not know what else to do. Skidelsky (1970: 6), writing about interwar Great Britain, observed that "The English political culture was relatively homogeneous. There were certain leading ideas, or patterns of thought, which all sensible men accepted. This applied particularly to economic thinking. Politicians in the 1920s deployed a stock of economic wisdom which was a kind of codification of what they assumed to be the successful practice of the 19th century." During a parliamentary debate in Sweden in 1925, when the Social Democratic Prime Minister Sandler was ironically needled by the Liberal leader, he responded that Liberals should be satisfied that Social Democracy assimilated liberal ideas, continuing to note that "when the gunpowder smoke surrounding the political struggles has dispersed it may easily happen, as in the case of sensible people sitting down at the table and arguing economics, that they are thinking alike in many important respects" (Tingsten 1973: 260). Exposed to the same experiences, believing that they are bound by the same constraints, reasonable people choose the same course of action. They dare to innovate only if the status-quo policies manifestly fail, if they truly believe that they have a better idea, and if they believe that voters will believe that they do have a better idea. But voters will not believe parties that have not shown themselves to have been responsible in the past by following the same policies as their opponents: this is the only way parties can acquire a reputation of being responsible. Parties emerging from the political wilderness can offer brilliant ideas but voters will dismiss them.

But even if parties offer little choice for good reasons, bells toll alarms about the functioning of democracy and about the legitimacy of electoral institutions. We are repeatedly told that when parties propose the same policies, there is nothing to choose; when they follow the same policies in office, electoral choices are inconsequential. Democracy is "anemic." Particularly now, when we repeatedly hear that globalization restricts choices and renders democratic politics meaningless, one is struck by how old is this complaint.

First, during a 1922 budgetary debate in the Swedish parliament, the Liberal leader, Eden, observed that the Social Democratic government was "bourgeois to an unexpectedly high degree," to which Prime Minister Hjalmar Branting replied, "I believe that amongst the Swedish labouring masses who have given their votes to our party there exists a high political training and an insight into the exigencies of the situation. I think that in relying upon this we have dared to put into practice a policy that is (to quote Herr Eden) as 'bourgeois' as it could possibly be, in accordance with his own description" (Tingsten, 1973: 251).

Second, leftist analyses of the MacDonald government as well as of the Front Populaire blamed them for not breaking with the standard economic wisdom of the time, accused them of "selling out," and questioned whether elections can make a difference in a capitalist economy (Miliband 1959).

Third, the so-called Keynesian welfare state evoked the same reaction, which exploded in 1968. The Cohn-Bendit brothers (1968) saw electoral competition as a choice between "gin and tonic and tonic and gin."

Fourth, and now again, the perception that all governments follow similar policies is widespread. Even *The Economist* (May 2, 1995) triumphantly observed that "the differences between New Labour and watered-down Thatcherism are far more of style than of substance." The diagnosis is shared by critics of globalization: "Two things tend to happen: your economy grows and your politics shrinks. . . . The Golden Straitjacket narrows the political and economic choices of those now in power to relatively tight parameters. . . . Once your country puts on the Golden Straitjacket, its political choices get reduced to Pepsi or Coke" (Friedman 2001).

What is not clear is whether the dissatisfaction with democracy arises from the meagerness of partisan differences or from policies enclosed within the partisan spectrum. Do citizens feel politically impotent because there is little room between the walls or because the walls are in a bad place? Do they object against not having a choice or against the policies they can choose?

To clarify what is entailed, it is useful to examine first the value of choice when each individual decides independently what is best for him or her. Suppose that you prefer x to $y, x \succ y$. There are two possible states of the world. In one, you get x. In the second, you choose between x and y. Does being able to choose have an inherent value for you?

To move to the collective level, suppose there are two types of people. Some prefer x to y, while others y to x. The collective decision determines whether x or y is chosen for everyone. There are more people who prefer x, so that x is the majority winner. Do you care whether two parties both propose x, so that your opportunity set is $\{x, x\}$, or they make distinct proposals, $\{x, y\}$? Whether you are of type x or y, do you care whether or not you were offered a choice?

To introduce the value of choosing, consider voting over tax rates. Your own peak preference is for the rate τ. The question is, would you rather have two parties propose $\{\tau, \tau\}$ or $\{\tau - c, \tau + c\}$? Note that if they propose $\{\tau, \tau\}$ you are certain that your ideal point will be selected. If they propose $\{\tau - c, \tau + c\}$, the outcome will be some distance, namely c, from your ideal point but you will have been given a choice. Do you value choosing enough to give up your most preferred alternative? You cannot be helped in answering this question in general because a transitive and complete ordering of such opportunity sets is not possible (Barbera, Bossert, and Pattanaik 2001). Sen (1988: 292) argues that fasting is preferable to starving because even if in either case I consume the same number of calories, fasting is a result of choice, while starving is not, and choosing is valuable in itself. Nonetheless, this example, heralded as it is, offers no help because it does not compare the opportunity sets in which you can choose only among alternatives you do not like and those in which you have no choice but you get what you want.

This example serves to elucidate the ambiguity inherent in the voices just heard here. Note that the set of alternatives $\{\tau - c, \tau + c\}$ has two properties; its central location is τ and its range is $2c$. Say your peak choice is $\tau = 0.45$. You may be unhappy because the choice is narrow, say $\tau = 0.45, c = 0.01$, with platforms $\{0.44, 0.46\}$, or because proposed tax rates are too low, with platforms $\{0.2, 0.4\}$. Przeworski and Meseguer (2006), for example, argue that the effect of globalization may be to make redistribution more expensive and thus to make both left- and right-wing parties propose lower tax rates while the difference between them becomes larger because of increased inequality.

The only bit of evidence I know of has been provided by Harding (2009). Having examined individual survey data from forty surveys in thirty-eight countries, Harding discovered the following: (1) Respondents who recognized at least one competing party as being close to their preferences were more likely to be satisfied with democracy. (2) Winners, people who voted for one of the parties that entered the government as the result of a legislative election, were more likely to be satisfied with democracy than losers. (3) Winners were more likely to be satisfied with democracy if they perceived more distinct parties among the competitors while losers cared only that at least one party was close to them but did not care how much choice was available. These are findings of deep significance. They say first that people do value having their views appear in the public sphere, the presence of some party to which they feel close. However, they also indicate that choice is a luxury good, valued only by those who got what they wanted. People who obtained their "essential element" are more satisfied with democracy if what they obtained resulted from a larger choice set, but people who did not get their most preferred choice do not care how many choices there were. In the end, the answer to the question "Do people value choice?" seems to be "Yes, if they get what they want anyway." Yet even if choice is a luxury, the fact that democracy provides it makes democracy valuable.

There are good but also bad reasons for excluding some options as choices offered to voters. If an option is not feasible, this is a good reason not to propose it even if it is included among voters' peak preferences. Nevertheless, we have seen in the previous chapter that choices offered to voters in elections can be distorted, perhaps literally bought, by money.

If powerful interest groups influence the platforms of all major parties, not only the options offered to voters are meager but the collectivity as a whole does not even get a chance to choose what it most wants. When left-wing parties echo the language of trade-offs – between taxes and investment, equality and efficiency, redistribution and growth – voters are unable to exercise their preferences for taxation, equality, or redistribution. Because this language serves the interests of the wealthy, one can only wonder whether left-wing politicians truly believe that such trade-offs are inevitable, whether they think that moving to the center is necessary to win elections, or whether they are responding to pressures by special interests. I am not claiming the latter: Perhaps political leaders themselves cannot isolate the effects of technical beliefs about policies, electoral considerations, and interested pressures to which they are constantly exposed. They know that to compete in politics they need resources, they know that resources follow some policy stances and not others, and perhaps they come to believe what is convenient to believe. All we can say is that choices offered to voters may be, and probably often are, distorted under the impact of money.

Dunn's (2000) analysis of British politics offers yet another cautionary tale about bad reasons. In his story, the stealth opening of capital account by Mrs. Thatcher changed the trade-offs between redistribution and growth and thus forced both major political parties to reduce the extent of redistribution they proposed. What is striking is that the opening of capital account was not an issue in the election of 1979 when Mrs. Thatcher came to office. Nonetheless, once the decision was made, the entire spectrum of feasible policies was moved. Even left-wing voters had to opt for less redistribution because redistribution became more costly. Hence, the decision about capital account was not a collective decision but it shaped subsequent collective decisions. Here is Dunn's (2000: 152) analysis:

In retrospect Mrs. Thatcher's most decisive political act was the complete dismantling, at the very beginning of her first term of office as Prime Minister, of all controls over capital movements into and out of the economy. What this did was to establish a space of political competition between capital and organized labour in which, in the end, the latter could only lose, and in which it was relatively simple to present its predestined loss as unequivocally in the interest of the population at large.

Now, if you think that Mrs. Thatcher was, as she never tired of repeating, elected to do whatever she wanted, then the fact that redistribution of income ceased to be an option is not a bad limitation on choices. Voters gave Mrs. Thatcher a mandate to do whatever she thought was best and, after she did it, some people did not like the choices they had: Too bad. But if you think that people faced with the option of dismantling capital controls would have rejected it, anticipating the opportunity set they would face as the result, then the meagerness of options is a bad limitation. If people bind themselves knowingly, they should not complain even if they do not like their bounds. If, however, they are bound involuntarily, then they have every right to be mad. The implication for self-government I draw from this example is that it is viable only when governments do not make decisions that are not a result of collective choice if – and to be realistic one has to say only if – such decisions restrict future alternatives.

5.3 DEMOCRACY AND PARTICIPATION

Should democrats value participation? This is a different question than the one just posed, in which we asked whether people should value having something to decide in elections. The question now is whether they should care whether the outcome is a causal effect of their actions or independent of what each person does. As long as I live under a social order that I *would* choose, does it matter that I *did* choose it, that is, that I did something that caused it to prevail?

Following Rousseau, Kelsen (1949: 284) claimed that "Politically free is he who is subject to a legal order in the creation of which he participates." If preferences over legal orders are in conflict, however, the criteria of participation and autonomy need not lead to the same conclusion about freedom. Consider three possible states of the world: (1) I participate and my preferences prevail; (2) I participate and find myself on the losing side; (3) the legal order is the one I prefer without my participation, dictated to me. The first possibility is clearly superior to the second by the criterion of autonomy. In turn, it is superior to the third by the criterion of participation. Nevertheless, the ranking of the second and the third possibility is ambivalent and, I suspect, historically contingent. Some people, under some historical conditions, may care only about the values embodied in the legal system under which they live: religion, communism, trains running on time, or whatever. Other people, under other circumstances, may care about participation independently of the outcomes it generates.

When individuals make private choices, they cause outcomes. One could argue, as does Sen (1988), that being an active agent, a chooser, has an autonomous value for us, that a result obtained by my actions is more valuable to me than the same result generated independently of them. Why would it matter, however, that I had voted rather than just observed that a coin landed on the side I prefer? It cannot be a causal difference; the probability that my vote matters is miniscule in any large electorate. From an individual point of view, the outcome of an election is a flip of a coin, independent of one's action. It bears emphasis that I am not arguing that voting is individually irrational. I may believe that the fate of humanity is at stake in an election and attach to this fate such importance that would I vote on purely instrumental grounds even if the probability that what I do matters is 10^{-8}. All I am pointing out is that no one can say "I voted for A, therefore A will win"; the most each of us can do is to cast our ballot, go home, and impatiently wait in front of a television set to see how others have voted. When collective decisions are made by using a simple-majority rule by many individuals endowed with an equal influence over the outcome, no individual has a causal effect on the collective decision.

The program of "participatory democracy," which springs up inter-mittently around the globe,[4] is thus not feasible at the national scale. If participation is to mean causal impact on the exercise of government by equal individuals, then "participatory democracy" is an oxymoron. Only a few can causally affect collective decisions. These few can be selected by elections or they can buy "influence."[5] They can be those who are excep-tionally vociferous or perhaps exceptionally brilliant. Everyone, however, cannot be equally efficacious. If everyone is equal, each one is condemned to causal impotence. In spite of valiant efforts (Barber 2004; Roussopou-los 2003), the circle just cannot be squared.[6]

Again, a clarification is required. Think of democratic politics as a process of competition among several groups for political influence (Becker 1983). These groups know how much they can lose and gain from government policies and expend resources to tilt these policies in their favor. In Becker's model the resources that groups spend depend only on what they expect to gain or lose and on what other groups spend. No group is budget constrained. In the real world of politics, however, the resources that different groups can muster are distributed unequally.

---

[4] Googling "participatory democracy" returns 177,000 items in English and 276,000 in Spanish.

[5] I put "influence" in quotation marks because during the eighteenth century it was a euphemism for what was later recognized as corruption.

[6] Moreover, as Mutz (2006) reveals, people are even less likely to vote when they are exposed to views different from theirs, so that deliberation and participation stand in conflict.

Hence, increased participation by those previously excluded may have an equalizing effect – except that if everyone were equal, no one would be effective. Equality and effectiveness are incompatible; inequality and effectiveness are not.

Pace Berlin (2002: 49), participation cannot be the reason to value self-government. No rule of collective decision making other than unanimity can render causal efficacy to individual participation. Collective self-government is achieved not when each voter has causal influence on the final result, but when collective choice is a result of aggregating individual wills. The value of the mechanism of voting rests in the ex post correspondence between the laws everyone must obey and the will of a majority: Selecting governments by elections does maximize the number of people who live under laws to their liking, even if no individual can treat these laws as a consequence of his or her choosing. Hence, even if individuals see their own vote as ineffective, they may value voting as a procedure for making collective choices, and there is dramatic evidence that they often do. To value the mechanism even in the face of individual impotence, it is sufficient that, to cite Bird (2000: 567), "Both governors and governed must recognize 'will-revealing' procedures and view them as communicating instructions, which governing agencies are then expected to execute as a matter of course."

But the appeal of this conception of self-government is much weaker than that of the original ideal. Under the original conception, a legal order could prevail only if everyone consented to it. The criterion of unanimous consent promised causal efficacy to each and every member of the collectivity. The nostalgia for effective participation continues to haunt modern democracies, in which – as Kelsen (1988: 35) was forced to concede – "political rights – which is to say liberty – are reduced in the essential to a simple right to vote."

5.4 THE ROLE OF THE PEOPLE BETWEEN ELECTIONS

The distinctive feature of democracy is that rulers are selected through elections. Perhaps this explains why descriptions of democratic politics often create an impression that elections are all there is to democracy. In elections the people is omnipotent; between elections it is impotent. This is how many theorists of democracy thought democracy should be. While O'Donnell (1994) diagnosed this reduction of politics to elections as a Latin American pathology, "delegative democracy," for Madison this was how representative government should function: The people should have no role in governing. Lippman (1956) insisted that the duty of citizens "is to fill the office and not to direct the office-holder." Schumpeter (1942) admonished voters that they "must understand that, once they elected an individual, political action is his business not theirs. This means that they must refrain from instructing him what he is to do."

As a description, this picture is obviously inaccurate. Conflicts over policies, competition for political influence, are the bread and butter of everyday politics. Political activities are not limited to elections, not even to efforts oriented to influence outcomes of future elections. But competition for political influence occurs in other political regimes as well. Is the role of the people between elections distinctive under democracy? Manin's (1997: 167) claim – "Since the end of the eighteenth century, representation has been accompanied by the freedom of the governed at all times to form and express political opinions outside the control of the government" – notwithstanding, we have seen that the U.S. founders were at best ambivalent about this role while the French ones were simply intolerant of it. Although the idea that opposition to government policies does not necessarily signify treason or obstruction was first recognized in Great Britain in a parliamentary speech of 1828, democracy grants no specific right to oppose. Most democracies do grant rights to speak and to associate, but even these rights have been extremely tenuous (Loveman 1993 on Latin America; Rosanvallon 2004 on France; Stone 2004 on the United States). Hofstadter's (1969: 7) observation merits repetition: "The normal view of governments about organized opposition is that it is intrinsically subversive and illegitimate."

Note that what is at stake is not "the right of resistance" as this right was formulated in the medieval and early modern constitutional theory (Carvajal 1992; Franklin 1969). The question posed there was whether either the people or some institutional bodies, such as assemblies or courts, have the right to depose a monarch who violates the conditions on which his authority was granted. A sixteenth-century French political thinker, Theodore Beza (1969 [1574]), influentially claimed that the right of revocation is implicit in the act of election. The exercise of this right, however, had to be qualified and institutionalized, otherwise "a thousand tyrants would arise on the pretext of suppressing one." Poland is to my best knowledge the only country where this right was constitutionalized: After 1505, several *pacta conventa* specified a procedure whereby a special committee of the Senate could authorize the nobles to rise in arms against the elected king (Bardach, Leśnodorski, and Pietrzak 2005; Jedruch 1982; Roháč 2008). The right to depose rulers who arbitrarily exceed their authority was broadly recognized throughout the history of representative institutions. While Hannah Arendt famously discovered that the etymology of the word "revolution" is a return to *status quo ante*, this was the standard usage in nineteeth-century Latin America (Sabato 2008; Sabato and Lettieri 2003). Thus, for the Argentine Radical Party in the 1890s, "revolution . . . meant the legitimate use of violence to free society from an unlawful government and return it to a previous political order: the restoration of old traditions and the constitution" (Alonso 2000: 111). *La revolución* was an act of defense of the constitution against usurpation of power by elected governments, and a government that came to power as a result of a successful revolution would portray itself as a *gobierno constitucional.* While the methods of deposing presidents have become less violent, mass movements and congressional oppositions have continued to force Latin American presidents out of office.[7]

The right to depose rulers was made almost automatic by the institution of periodic elections. The question here is whether people who have views different from those of the elected governments can and should be able to influence policies during periods between elections. I take it for granted that the opposition is free to compete in future elections. I also bracket political activities targeted at influencing the way people vote; such activities have already been covered here. But what should be the political role of the people between elections? Is it a duty of those who lost an election to suffer in silence until the next election arrives, or do they have the right to oppose by means other than changing governments through elections? Does a defeat in an election impose an obligation on the minority to accept the policies of the elected government? Should one not think, as did J. McGurk, the chairman of the Labour Party in 1919 (quoted in Miliband 1975: 69), that "We are either constitution-alists or we are not constitutionalists. If we are constitutionalists, if we believe in the efficacy of the political weapon (and we do, or why do we have a Labour Party?) then it is both unwise and undemocratic because we fail to get a majority at the polls to turn around and demand that we should substitute industrial action"? Can the people embark, in Dahl's (1966: xix) words, on "a deliberate course of action intended to modify

---

7 Hochstetler (2005) documents that 40 percent of post-1978 presidents in South America were challenged by civilian actors to leave office early and 23 percent did leave it, to be replaced by civilians. Moreover, she emphasizes that street demonstrations were a crucial factor. Alvarez and Marsteintredet (2007) show that the factors precipitating depositions of presidents by civilians were the same as those that in the past led to military interventions.

the conduct of the government"? What kind of opposition is loyal and what kind subversive? Must opposition to government policies be channelled through the framework of representative institutions, or can people act in any way they please? Ambedkar, one of the fathers of the Indian constitution, thought that while civil disobedience was appropriate under colonial rule, it is "nothing but the Grammar of Anarchy" under democracy (Guha 2008: 132). Does self-government require governments to respond to voices expressed publicly through mechanisms other than elections? The founders of representative institutions were highly ambivalent about these questions (Morgan 1988, Chapter 9; Wood 1969, Chapter IX) and, I believe, we are not any clearer about them today.

Why would an opposition between elections arise to begin with? Within the framework of institutions in which governments are selected through periodic elections, people choose at best among bundles of issues, electoral platforms. Hence, even if a government was elected by a majority, it need not mean that majorities support every policy of the government. Suppose there are two policies and four kinds of voters. The policies are taxing and spending, and each can be characterized as high or low. The distribution of voters' preferences is as follows:

	Tax High	Tax Low	Total
Spend high	0.36	0.34	0.70
Spend low	0.04	0.26	0.30
Total	0.40	0.60	1.00

In elections, candidates propose themselves by revealing their true preferences and voters vote for candidates who are closest to their preferences (the citizen–candidate model). The party that proposes to tax and spend high amounts is then the winner. Note, however, that while high expenditures are preferred by a majority, a majority also prefers low taxes.

Now, in the face of a majority opposed to taxation, the newly elected government may decide to abandon its electoral platform and to spend without taxing. Elections, though, are not a series of independent referendums bunched together in one choice. They authorize governments to govern, not only to listen to voices of public opinion. After all, we look with disdain at governments that guide their actions by public opinion polls. The voice of public opinion may or may not be countable, but even when it is, as in the public opinion polls, other manners of counting have neither the authority nor the reliability of elections. Moreover, intense minorities can garb the cloak of majorities. Neither elections nor other ways of aggregating preference allow preferences to differ in intensity. Intense minorities are just numerical minorities. We may not like this fact. Indeed, reasonable people may say "Because I do not really care one way or another while she cares intensely, her view should prevail." One could think of a reflective equilibrium based on this principle. Nevertheless, the impossibility of interpersonal comparisons of intensity is inexorable and the strategic issues are patent. Self-governments can be a system only of counting heads, perhaps enlightened heads, but heads nevertheless.

Suppose that the government perseveres with a policy that is unpopular. If this policy is subject to legislative approval, the government may fail in the parliament. Opposition parties may persuade government supporters to modify their views; they can exercise their institutional prerogatives to block some legislation (in Germany, presidencies of parliamentary committees are distributed proportionately to party strength; in the United Kingdom the Committee of Public Accounts is always controlled by the opposition); they can threaten with obstructive tactics (a government proposal to privatize an electric utility company was met with thousands of amendments in France; filibuster in the U.S. Senate); and they can threaten with noncooperation at lower levels of governments they control. Governments do not always get what they want in the legislatures: According to Saiegh (2009), democratic legislatures approved only 76 percent of bills proposed by the executive branch during 783 country-years for which these data are available.

But can people outside the parliament effectively influence government decisions? Manin (1997: 170), for one, makes this argument:

Freedom of public opinion is a democratic feature of representative systems, in that it provides a means whereby the voice of the people can reach those who govern.... Representatives are not required to act on the wishes of the people, but neither can they ignore them: freedom of public opinion ensures that such wishes can be expressed and be brought to the attention of those who govern. It is the representatives who make the final decision, but a framework is created in which the will of the people is one of the considerations in their decision process.

How does opposition to a policy become a consideration in the decision making by governments? One way public opinion can influence government policies is simply by providing information about their effects. Sen's (1981) famous observation that democracies do not experience famines because of the role of the local press is telling. Holmes (1995, 2007) has argued forcefully that active opposition reduces the likelihood that governments would make blunders. It is also easy to believe that, to the extent to which expressions of public opinion portend electoral reactions to the particular policies, anticipating retrospective judgments at the time of elections, incumbents may modify them so as to maximize their chances of reelection. In fact, governments do often respond to the voices expressed through nonelectoral mechanisms, not only to private voices of lobbyists but also to public voices shouted in demonstrations, political strikes, road blockages, and so on. To this extent, therefore, sporadic reactions of public opinion, whatever forms they assume, influence government policies. Nevertheless, other than referendums, our representative systems have no institutional mechanisms to guarantee that the opposition be heard, still less that it would prevail, however intense it might be.

In my view, the main reason governments pay heed to active opposition is the threat that if the opposition is ignored then conflicts may spill beyond the institutional framework. Governments can enforce laws and implement policies only if the system of representative institutions is able to structure and absorb whatever conflicts arise in society and is able to process them according to preestablished rules. In turn, representative institutions have the capacity to absorb conflicts only if everyone has the right to participate within these institutions, if conflicts are structured by organizations that have an institutionally constituted access to the representative system, mainly political parties, and if these organizations have the incentives to pursue their interests through the representative system. Finally, institutions are able to regulate conflicts only if the conflicting political forces can expect that they may be successful, at the present or at least in some not too distant future. Institutions "govern and shape the interactions of human beings" – their definitional feature according to Lin and Nugent (1995: 2,306) – only when all potential conflicts are processed according to rules, rather than spill into sporadic violence.

Prima facie observation indicates that particular institutional systems differ significantly in these capacities. Counting the average annual incidence of "unrest" – the sum of mass demonstrations, riots, and national strikes (Banks 1996) – under democratic regimes in Latin America between 1946 and 1996 shows the range to be from 0.47 in Costa Rica to 3.41 in Argentina. In Argentina almost every contentious issue finds thousands of people on the Plaza de Mayo, tractors blocking roads, and pickets occupying a bridge in Neuquen. In Costa Rica, in contrast, almost all conflicts are disciplined by political parties and processed through the congress, the presidency, or the courts. The contrast between European extremes is even sharper, with 5.84 annual instances of unrest in Italy and 0.10 in Norway.

Why does it matter? When conflicts spill outside the representative framework, a government has only two choices: Either persevere with its policies while reverting to repression or tolerating disorder, or abandon its policies in order to placate the opposition. Neither alternative is attractive. The spirals of repression and breakdowns of order undermine democracy, while repeated concessions render governments unable to implement any stable policies.

5.5 VOTING, ELECTING, AND CIVIL PEACE

Elections are the fundamental institution of self-government: Self-government consists of electing those who rule on behalf of the people. Moreover, among all mechanisms of political participation, voting is the most egalitarian one. The mere possibility that we can choose and replace our rulers appears sufficient to render plausibility to the myth that we are ruling ourselves.

Nevertheless, the relation between elections and the selection of rulers is not as straightforward as it may intuitively appear. Just think of elections in one-party systems, without opposition. Because people vote, we still call such events "elections." but no one is selected as their result. Such elections only ratify, under the shadow of force, choices made elsewhere. The siren of elections seduces only if voting entails collective choosing. Democracy, I am forced to repeat myself (1991), is when incumbents lose elections and winners assume office. Given that partisan alternation in office is now the bread and butter of democratic politics, we take it for granted that this is what democracy is all about. But it turns out that, throughout history, partisan alternations in office through elections have been a rare feat. In most places around the world, most of the time, incumbents repeatedly won elections and resisted leaving office if they surprisingly lost. There is nothing new about electoral authoritarianism.

5.5.1 Voting and Electing

What do people do when they vote? Voting is a physical act: shouting someone's name, raising a hand, placing a piece of paper in a box, pulling a lever, touching a screen. However, both the political consequences and the cultural interpretations of this act differed profoundly across countries and epochs. Voting is not the same as electing; indeed, it may have no relation to electing.

The clearest case in which voting does not have the sanction of electing are the events called "elections" in one-party systems, in which no one is selected as their result. The communist practices, though, were not an historical aberration. The idea of an official government list submitted to voters for a plebiscitary approval was already present in France under the Directorate (Crook 2002), used under the Restoration, and perfected under Napoleon III (Zeldin 1958). The Spanish monarchy gained in this way such a complete control over voters that between 1876 and 1917 it was able to orchestrate a system in which governments alternated in every election according to a prearranged agreement between parties. The same was true in Portugal between 1851 and 1869. Promoting government candidates was not a transgression but a duty of public officials: In 1822, French Prime Minister de Vilèlle issued a circular instructing "All those who are members of my ministry must, to keep their jobs, contribute within the limits of their right to the election of M.P.s sincerely attached to the government" (quoted in Zeldin 1958: 79). Partisan use of public administration was ubiquitous in Latin America as well as in Europe. Following Chile after 1831 (about which see Valenzuela 1995), several Latin American countries established stable systems of succession in which incumbent presidents completed their terms, faithfully obeying term limits, chose their successors, and used governmental power to ensure their victory at the polls. The stability of such systems of oligarchical pluralism – Chile between 1831 and 1891 and again until 1924, Nicaragua between 1856 and 1890, Brazil between 1894 and 1930, Argentina between 1890 and 1916, Uruguay between 1898 and 1932, and Mexico between 1934 and 2000 – was remarkable. Indeed, in the entire history of Latin America, only three incumbent presidents who presented themselves for reelection ever lost. As Halperin-Donghi (1973: 116) observed, "Among the many ways of overthrowing the government practiced in postrevolutionary Spanish America, defeat at the polls was conspicuously absent."

The mere occurrence of elections is thus not sufficient to make them competitive. Consider all the instruments at the disposal of incumbents. If they fear losing, they may simply abstain from taking the risk, not holding elections at all. Francisco Franco never did during the thirty-six years he ruled as *Generalissimo*. The *Barisan Nasional* (Alliance) Party in Malaysia carelessly held an election in 1969 but, when confronted with an unpleasant result, simply rewrote the rules to make sure that the experience would not be repeated, and thus far it has not. António Salazar was more prudent, making it sure that elections would generate the correct results by reverting to fraud, a practice dear to the Mexican

Partido Revolucionario Institucional. Sheer force, manipulation of rules, and fraud can keep incumbent rulers in power independently of the voice of the people.

Elections must inextricably follow some rules that regulate who can vote; whether voting is direct or indirect, secret or public, compulsory or voluntary; how votes are aggregated; and so on. And rules affect outcomes. Even minute details, such as the form or the color of ballots, the location of the polling places, or the day of the week when voting takes place can affect the result. Hence, elections are inextricably manipulated. Manipulation, however, can be more or less blatant. Perhaps the most flagrant example of manipulation is the law introduced by President Putin to prohibit "negative campaigning," by which he meant any criticism of the government. Somehow we feel that carving electoral districts in the form of a salamander is excessive, while making districts nicely square does not raise anyone's eyebrows. Hence, manipulation is a matter of degree.

Manipulation is not the same as fraud.[8] Manipulation consists of establishing rules while fraud entails breaking rules, whatever they may be. Furthermore, setting rules and breaking rules are subject to different sanctions even if they have identical consequences for electoral results. The same physical act – a campaign contribution – has a different meaning and is subject to different reactions when it is permitted by law and when it is illegal: "institutional facts have some autonomy with regard to brute facts" (Sánchez-Cuenca 2003: 81–2). Most importantly, even if their consequences may be difficult to assess, rules must be visible, while acts of fraud are clandestine. Even when the incumbents manipulate openly – in France the electoral rules have changed eleven times since 1875 – they do not want to be caught breaking their own rules. Breaking into the office of the opposition party to steal its secrets is fraud because it violates a general prohibition against burglary. Buying votes constitutes fraud when it is prohibited by specific rules. So is casting the votes of people whose spirits have passed to a better world. Fraud is best exemplified by a story told about Anastazio Somoza, who is alleged to have informed his defeated opponent, "Indeed, you won the voting, but I won the counting." The technology of fraud is highly varied (Lehoucq 2003; Simpser 2006), but, in almost all of its forms, fraudulent activity is secret.

While some voices claim that we are currently witnessing an emergence of a qualitatively new phenomenon, "electoral authoritarianism," such

---

[8] On the difficulties of defining fraud, see Annino (1995: 15–18). On corrupt electoral practices in Latin America, see Posada-Carbó (2000).

TABLE 5.1: *Events Surrounding Elections*

Incumbent	Winner				
	Assumed Directly	Assumed Indirectly	Did not Assume	Unclear	Total
Won	1,999	9	95		2,103
Lost	473	19	53		545
Total ran	2,472	28	148		2,648
Did not run	84	6	22		112
Unclear	15	3	8	7	33
Total	2,571	37	178	7	2,793

regimes have been the prevalent form of political organization through-out history. Nothing is new about Putinism.[9] The outcomes of elections are eloquent in showing that electoral defeats of incumbents have been historically rare and peaceful alternations in office even more so. Table 5.1 summarizes the outcomes of elections in which the office of the chief executive was at stake, as well as the subsequent events. The "incumbent" is not necessarily the same person; he or she may be a member of the same party or an otherwise designated successor. "Winner," as well, may be a person or a party. Note that if the incumbent won, he is the winner; if the incumbent lost, the winner is someone else. "Assumed indirectly" stands for sequences in which the winner assumed office but only after someone else – the loser or a third party – held it unconstitutionally in the immediate aftermath of an election. "Assumed," whether directly or not, indicates that the winner held office for at least one year, but not necessarily that she completed the constitutionally specified term.

The frequency with which incumbents won elections is striking: 2,103 out of 2,648 cases in which they ran, which means that the probability that incumbents would win an election is 0.79 and the odds of winning are 4:1.

Yet even with all the manipulation and fraud, incumbents sometimes lose elections. What are they to do then? They can accept the defeat and yield, but they can also attempt to prevent the winners from assuming office. Note that partisan alternations in office are peaceful only if

---

[9] Here is how the governor of Murmansk, Jurij Jewdokimow, described the practices of his own party, Only Russia, in the municipal election of March 15, 2009: "Employees of municipal enterprises are being forced to staff mailboxes with fliers calling for voting for the 'proper' candidate. Pre-school teachers have to distribute to parents agitational materials" (*Gazeta Wyborcza*, Warsaw, Poland, March 17, 2009).

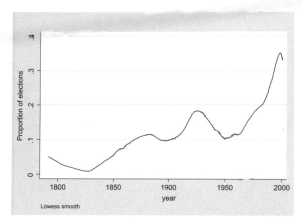

FIGURE 5.1 Partisan alternations in office.

the incumbent loses and the winner assumes office, which occurred in $473/2,648 = 0.18$ cases, or 1 in 5.6 elections. Moreover, even if the first partisan alternation in history occurred in the United States in 1801, peaceful alternations were rare until the last quarter of the past century (see Figure 5.1).

There is also strong evidence that the frequency of peaceful alternations rises steeply with per capita income (see Figure 5.2). The intuitive explanation is that, when incomes are higher, people care less about increasing them through violence, and if the cost of violence is constant, above some income level they obey even if they lose (Benhabib and Przeworski 2006; Przeworski 2005).

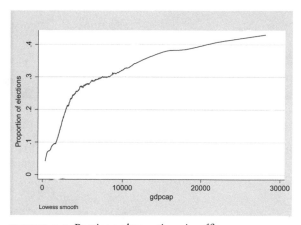

FIGURE 5.2 Partisan alternations in office.

The general picture that emerges from these facts appears quite bleak. Obviously, incumbents may have been repeatedly winning elections because they were authentically popular. But given all the manifestations of manipulation, fraud, and outright repression, it is more plausible that incumbents are frequently able to orchestrate or simply mute the voice of the people. The mere fact that people vote need not mean that they have the power to elect.

5.5.2 Elections and Civil Peace

The magic of elections is that they enable intertemporal horizons. A party that loses in any conflict may be prone to revert to force if it expects the defeat to be permanent or just indefinite, yet it may respect the result if it believes that at some fixed time it will have a chance to win. This is what elections enable: the prospects of alternation in power. This mechanism works, however, only if the electoral chances of different parties do not diverge too far from their ability to impose themselves by force.

Think as follows. Parties participate in elections to determine some policy – whether the rate of redistribution, regulation of abortion, or separation of church and state – over which they have conflicting interests. Having observed the result of an election, they decide whether to respect the outcome or to try to impose their will by force. The probability that the current incumbent would be reelected is given as is the probability that the incumbent would prevail in a violent conflict. Hence, political actors face two lotteries with different payoffs and different probabilities: elections and violent conflict. The generic conclusion of this way of thinking is that outcomes of elections are obeyed only if electoral chances reflect relative military power, which means that if one party dominates militarily it must also dominate electorally. Already Herodotus (quoted in Bryce 1921: 25–6) thought that in a democracy "physical force of the citizens coincides (broadly speaking) with their voting power," while Condorcet (1986: 11) observed that in ancient, brutal times, "for the good of peace and general utility, it was necessary to place authority where the force was." Nevertheless, the relation between military force and electoral chances becomes less important when people value less whatever they can acquire by fighting. Hence, if conflicts concern income, peace is easier to maintain in wealthier societies.

To pinpoint the role of elections in processing conflicts, think somewhat differently. Two groups in society are in conflict over a policy. They can obtain their ideal outcomes by fighting, with known probability that one would prevail. If they want to avoid violence, then given this probability they could agree to some rules according to which they would alternate in office and thus solve the conflict peacefully. But Fearon (2006) is correct to point out that the desire to solve conflicts peacefully is not sufficient to justify elections. If everyone knows everything, then they also know the expected value of the policy outcome associated with the relations of physical force. Why then hold elections, rather than simply agree to the policy that reflects their relative military power? Moreover, if people are risk averse, then agreeing to a fixed policy is superior in welfare terms to policies chosen by alternating parties (Alesina 1988). Hence, additional reasons must be adduced to understand why, to be peaceful, conflicts must be processed by elections. Elsewhere I argue (Przeworski 2005) that the policy could not be completely specified and rulers would use their residual power to deviate from any agreement. Fearon (2006) sees elections as a device to coordinate revolt in case the incumbent abuses his or her power. Londregan and Vindigni (2006) think that elections are a cheap way to learn the military strength of the parties, which was already the view of Simmel (1950: 241–2): "because the voting individuals are considered to be equals, the majority has the physical power to coerce the minority. . . . The voting serves the purpose of avoiding the immediate contest of forces and finding out its potential result by counting votes, so that the minority can convince itself that its actual resistance would be of no avail."

There are two ways to think about the relations of military force. One is that when governments abuse their authority, the people rise in unison against the transgression (Weingast 1997). In Fearon's (2006) view, elections play a specific role in enabling such resistance, because their results may reveal to isolated individuals that some large numbers of others are dissatisfied with the government and thus provide a signal that a coordinated revolt would be effective when the incumbent seeks to remain in power. The same may be true when the incumbent government claims to have won the election but there is a widespread perception that it committed fraud (Gandhi and Przeworski 2009) or when the government manipulates the rules to such an extent that the opposition has no chance to win. The problem with this way of thinking is that it assumes that the people who benefit from the transgression are willing to join those who are hurt by it in common defense of democratic institutions. This assumption, in turn, can be justified if everyone thinks in intertemporal terms and if the current beneficiaries expect that one day they may find themselves on the losing side. Nevertheless, if incumbents transgress by manipulating elections, committing fraud, or simply usurping power, they may remain in power for a long time, so that those who benefit from their illegitimate tenure have no incentives to resist.

An alternative perspective on military power is to think of parties as armies. Violence is then seen as just an extension of electoral competition. As Bravo (2003: 248) observed with regard to the mid-nineteenth-century Argentine province of Tucumán, "war constituted a functional recourse of politics, in that it defined or modified electoral results." In this perspective, results of elections are obeyed, regardless of how they were generated, if the party that claims victory is sufficiently strong militarily so that violent resistance has little chance of success. This perspective, which was an explicit understanding of politics in nineteenth-century Latin America (Sabato 2008; Sabato and Lettieri 2003), becomes less plausible once the exercise of violence becomes technologically advanced and once the control over the means of violence becomes a specialized domain of specific apparatuses: the military and the police. Once this occurs, the chance that the incumbent government will remain in power by force depends on the partisan attitudes of these apparatuses: they can unconditionally support one party regardless of what happens in elections or they can be "constitutionalist," that is, give equal support to whoever wins clean elections. In addition, there are good reasons to think that electoral defeats induce splits within the ruling block (Magaloni 2007). When a ruler holds an election and is unable to secure a victory or can obtain it only by a manifest use of manipulation and fraud, members of the coercive apparatus must envisage the possibility that the ruler may fall and they may be held individually responsible for acts of repression. Hence, they become hesitant to take this risk (Przeworski 1988): After General Pinochet lost the 1989 plebiscite to extend his term, the other members of the Chilean junta refused to override the result by force (Barros 2002). Hence, when incumbents are unable to win competitive elections, their military power may be undermined and they may be forced to obey the rules of democratic competition.

As Bobbio (1984: 156) put it, "What is democracy other than a set of rules . . . for the solution of conflicts without bloodshed?" This does not mean that elections are always competitive, not even that they are free and fair, that the people can always choose their rulers when they vote. Still, elections are a peaceful way of processing conflicts that otherwise may have or would have been violent. To the extent that electoral chances reflect the relations of physical force, elections occur under the shadow of violence. But under this shadow, there is peace.

6

Agency

6.1 INTRODUCTION

Our institutions are representative. Citizens do not govern; they are governed by others, perhaps different others in turn, but others nevertheless. To assess whether we collectively govern ourselves when we are governed by others, we need to consider two relations: among different parts of the government and between citizens and governments. The structure of government is logically prior to its connection with citizens and it was considered as such. This is because that which citizens can demand or expect of governments depends on what governments can and cannot do. In turn, what they are able to do depends at least to some extent on the way they are organized.

Systems in which different branches of government must consent and cooperate if an action is to be taken are de facto supermajoritarian. By multiplying the number of "veto players," they privilege the status quo (Tsebelis 2002). Hence, governments may be unable to respond to the will of the majority as expressed in elections, specifically to a mandate for change. The condition of neutrality is violated to varying degrees in almost all democracies by various institutional arrangements that are equivalent to supermajority rules. Indeed, Rae (1971) wanted to measure approximations to the ideal of democracy by the extent to which decision rules deviate from simple majority. Perhaps most noteworthy is the fact that bicameralism is under general conditions equivalent to supermajority rule, a fact already noted by Condorcet (1986 [1787]). McGann (2006) argues that only countries with proportional electoral systems, unicameral legislations, and without an executive veto and other contramajoritarian devices in fact use simple-majority rule. In his count, such countries are few.

Whether this is good or bad by some other criteria is not the issue here: We have seen repeated claims that the people as an entity has to be protected from itself, at least from its temporary passions or its wanton preferences.[1] However, if the status quo is privileged, one of the conditions for self-government as defined by May's axioms – neutrality[2] – breaks down. This may only mean that self-government should be understood differently; one might argue that when the people, as a constituent power, structure the government in this way, for some reasons they do not want the voice of the majority to be implemented unless all the powers of government agree that it should be. Nonetheless, it is striking that institutional features such as bicameralism or executive veto power extend the protection to the status quo on all issues, not only those explicitly subjected to special procedures or delegated to specialized agencies. Rights can be and most often are guarded separately. The supermajoritarian protection of the status quo extends to purely distributive issues that do not entail any fundamental rights. As several critics of the U.S. constitution have argued, the system of checks and balances may prevent a government from abusing its power but it may also paralyze it from doing what it should be doing.

In turn, the responsiveness axiom means roughly that government policies follow collective decisions of citizens. This axiom can hold only if there are some collective decisions that can be followed, if results of elections can be read as expressing some kind of a will. I believe they can be: By their inherent logic, elections structure individual wills into collective support for particular parties. Hence, although I agree with all those who observe that no government can represent the will of everyone, parties and partisan governments can represent the collective will of their supporters. It is a different matter whether they in fact do. Some agency costs are inevitable; if for any reason, bad or good, a government wants

---

[1] Indeed, Madison's claim reduces his concern about factions in *Federalist* #10 by saying that minorities do not matter because relief against them is "supplied by the republican principle." His target is majority rule. See Dahl (1956, Chapter 1).

[2] Note that what is entailed here is the axiom of neutrality, not of responsiveness. Say the rule is that status quo prevails unless two-thirds support an alternative. Then, if one of the majority opting for change already satisfies the criterion and an additional person joins this majority, the alternative still prevails. If this person is pivotal, then the status quo loses when this person shifts in favor of change. See May (1952, 1953) for cases in which neutrality is violated and responsiveness is not.

something different than what the people who elect it want, then the government must be offered incentives so as not to deviate too far from its popular mandate. Governments must be able to govern, even if some of the governing is dedicated to the pursuit of their own interests at the cost of their constituencies.

Once again, these arguments are developed in what follows.

6.2 THE STRUCTURE OF GOVERNMENT

6.2.1 The Problem to be Solved

The very act of creating government was necessary because without it people would do nasty things to one another. The government, unfortunately, can do some nasty things as well. On the one hand, we heard that "It is of great importance in a republic, not only to guard the society against the oppression of its rulers; but to guard one part of the society against the injustice of the other part" (*Federalist #51*). On the other hand, we were warned that "Individual liberty has much more to fear from the undertakings of the officials charged with exercising whatever part of the public power" (Sieyes, quoted by Pasquino 1998: 76). If the government has the power to govern, must it not also have the power to abuse? If the government has no power to abuse, can it govern? The balance was not obvious. Getting the institutional design right turned out to be a subtle undertaking.

There is something prescient in Bolívar's (1819) dictum that while tyranny is a weight, liberty is a balance. Authoritarian governments can impose order by oppression. Democracies face a much more delicate task. They must guard liberty, but they must also maintain order. As Lechner (1975) argued in a penetrating analysis of the advent of the 1973 dictatorship in Chile, democracy cannot survive if there is no order on the streets. Nonetheless, maintaining order entails force. Bobbio's parenthetical addition bares a crucial aspect of democracy: "by 'democratic system'," Bobbio (1984: 93) says, "I mean one in which supreme power (supreme in so far as it alone is authorized to use force as a last resort) is exerted in the name of and on behalf of the people by virtue of the procedure of elections." Democracy is a form of rule: "Not any more than any other political system, democracy cannot avoid that men would be not be commanded by those like them" (Kelsen 1988: 23). Ruling entails coercion: Governments, the rulers, can seize money from some and give it to others, put people in jail, and sometimes even take their lives. In

Locke's words (*Second Treatise*, ¶11), the government is but a "Magistrate, who by being Magistrate, hath the common right of punishing put in his hands."

The framers thought they knew how to prevent abuses of power: All they needed to do was to follow Montesquieu. The solution offered by Montesquieu was to separate the powers of government. Separation, his theory went, is necessary to balance powers; the balance of powers leads to moderation; and moderate governments protect liberty.

6.2.2 Functions and Powers

Having listed three dangers to liberty, Sieyes (quoted in Pasquino 1996: 19) offered what would become the standard solution: "The separation, and a good constitution of public powers are the only guarantee that Nations and Citizens might be preserved from this extreme evil."

The point of departure for everyone was Montesquieu (1995 [1748]: XI, 3):

When the legislative and executive powers are united in the same person or in the same body of magistrates, there can be no liberty; because apprehensions may arise, lest the same monarch or senate should enact tyrannical laws, and execute them in a tyrannical manner. Again, there is no liberty if the judiciary power be not separated from the legislative and the executive. Were it joined with the legislature, the life and liberty of the subject would be exposed to arbitrary control; for the judge would be then the legislator. Were it joined to the executive power, the judge might behave with violence and oppression. There would be an end of everything, were the same man or the same body, whether of the nobles or the people, to exercise those three powers, that of enacting laws, that of executing the public resolutions, and of trying the causes of individuals.

The authority of Montesquieu was so preponderant that everyone felt compelled to justify one's own ideas as consistent with those of the "celebrated oracle." As Manin (1994: 27) reports, "At times the constitutional debate of 1787 came close to an exegesis of Montesquieu's theories."

The essence of Montesquieu's hypothesis was that a government that is divided would be moderate or limited. Note first that read literally this is not what he said. His argument was couched in the negative: It asserts that a government that is not divided will be despotic, rather than that a government that is divided will be moderate. In neither reading, however, does this hypothesis appear to be true. There is no reason, I believe, to think that observing whether powers are formally divided or even whether they are actually balanced permits us to predict whether the government will be limited or oppressive. I have no systematic evidence to offer, only logical arguments spiced with historical anecdotes. But these are sufficient in my view for us to be skeptical about the validity of Montesquieu's hypothesis. First, however, this hypothesis has to be separated into two steps. One is that if powers are divided, they will be balanced. The second is that if powers are balanced, the government will be limited or moderate. They are discussed in turn.

Montesquieu's prescription assumes that the exercise of power consists of distinct and separable functions. Their standard list includes legislating, executing, and adjudicating. This list is not as obvious as it may appear given its historical patina: One can add and one can disaggregate functions. What about controlling the executive? Day-to-day administration, as distinct from the execution of laws? Educating the people to act as citizens? More importantly, these functions are not easy to demarcate. Madison (*Federalist #37*), for one, had doubts: "no skill in the science of government has yet been able to discriminate and define, with sufficient certainty, its three great provinces, the legislative, executive, and judiciary.... Questions daily occur in the course of practice, which proves the obscurity which reigns in these subjects, and which puzzles the greatest adepts in political science."

Even with this ambiguity, however, most people accepted Montesquieu's principle that functions should be allocated to distinct powers. The design of the government was thus an allocation of powers to functions. The powers, branches, departments, authorities, or "organs" included the (perhaps bicameral) legislature, some kind of an executive organ, the courts, but in some cases also a "moral power" (called *poder moral, poder censor, or poder conservador* in various Latin American constitutions), "necessary for a people which aspires to be virtuous," in the words of Bolívar's constitutional project of 1818 (Soriano 1969: 27), or a body that would control the expenditures by the executive, such as *Contaduria Mayor de Cuentas* in the 1812 Cádiz Constitution.

This mapping of powers on functions can be done in many ways. One is "strict separation." Here the mapping is one to one: Each organ is supposed to perform one function without interference from any other branch. The legislature legislates, the executive executes, the judicial organ adjudicates, perhaps the *poder moral* educates. Strict separation is also compatible with many (powers)-to-one (function) models that separated the legislature into two bodies with identical prerogatives. Under strict separation, each function is still performed by separate bodies, except that some functions are performed by more than one body. Strict separation, in turn, stood in contrast to the system that we now call "checks and balances," in which the mapping is many to many, including all to all. All powers of the government participate in different ways in the performance of all functions. Whether the latter model satisfied Montesquieu's requirement was intensely controversial in the United States (see Manin 1994), but this is not our problem.

The model of pure separation of powers was feared as granting excessive power to the legislature. Madison (*Federalist #51*), in particular, thought that legislative power would dominate all others: "In republican government, the legislative authority necessarily predominates." If the executive does something the legislature does not like, the legislature can modify laws to prohibit it. The same is true with the courts. True, the power of the legislature can be weakened by dividing it into chambers that would check one another. In the United States it was divided into the independently elected Senate and House. According to the 1914 Constitution of Norway, the legislature was to divide itself into the *Lagting* (one-fourth of the members) and *Odelsting* (three-fourths); bills were to be proposed by the *Odelsting* and if approved sent to *Lagting*. The danger of uncontrolled expansion by the legislature still remains. In Condorcet's (1986 [1787]: 243) words, "Any body that has an unlimited power to make laws is dangerous for liberty, whatever its form."

The strict separation of powers seems to have been adopted in countries dominated by fear of the executive. The French revolutionaries feared executive encroachments.[3] Moreover, they thought that because the executive function is exercised on a day-to-day basis while the legislative power is exercised only intermittently, the former would dominate. Thus, the National Assembly adopted in 1789 the principle of strict separation, dividing the legislative from the executive power. According to Sieyes, who was the architect of this system, the people delegate the legislative power to the unicameral assembly and the executive power to the King (Vile 1967: 204–5). Each of these powers has a representative character and each enjoys equal status. In turn, each power must be limited to its proper function and prevented from interfering with the other, which meant that there should be no checks or balances. This principle collapsed in practice almost as soon as it was adopted: By September of 1792, the

---

[3] Vile (1967: 193) first atributes the French devotion to the doctrine of strict separation to the influence of Rousseau: "This part of the explanation of the intensity and persistence of the theory must be sought in the way in which the thought of Jean-Jacques Rousseau was ovelaid upon that of Montesquieu." However, when he gets to the discussion of deliberations of the Constituent Assembly, he observes that the majority was "afraid of royal domination" (1967: 204).

National Convention monopolized all the powers. The principle of separating powers was all but abandoned in the Montagnard Constitution of 1793 and was restored in the form of strict separation with a bicameral legislature in 1795, but having set the stage for conflicts between the legislature and the executive, this constitution turned out to be equally short lived.

Reflecting on his experience as a minister, Mexican constitutionalist Lucas Alamán (2008 [1832]) argued that the strict separation of powers is untenable because the predominance of the legislature leaves the executive without sufficient power to govern. Aguilar (1998: 74) observes that in Mexico "It was thought that the major weight assigned to the legislature in the Constitution of 1857 was due to the memory of the dictatorship of Santa Anna [that] forewarned the constituents about the risks of strong executive power." He claims, disputed by Gargarella (2002), that this model was ubiquitous in Latin America. Citing a prominent Mexican constitutionalist, Emilio Rabasa, to the effect that "The complete separation of the two powers would not assure its equilibrium," Aguilar argues that the system of strict separation had to deteriorate into regimes of exception, in which the legislature temporarily but repeatedly delegated its powers to the executive. He points out that in 50 of the 120 months of the Restored Republic (1867–72), the government acted with extraordinary powers.

The model of checks and balances was adopted after an intense controversy in the United States, where the main fear was of the legislature. Even with these safeguards, the legislature was additionally weakened by being split into two chambers. As it finally developed, the U.S. model gave all of the organs of the government some role in performing all of its functions. This solution, however, did not establish a balance either: By 1792 the Federalists controlled all of the powers, and after their defeat in 1800, the Republicans did.

6.2.3 The Balance of Powers

Separation, whether in its strict form or as a system of mutual checks, was to ensure a balance of powers. But what is the "balance of powers"? A purely linguistic comment is first in order. The word used in several languages, English included, was "equilibrium." The framers, however, did not conceive of it, as at least some would today, in a game-theoretic sense of a situation in which no one wants to deviate from a particular course of action given how others act. They meant "balance" in a sense derived from physics, an equality between a weight and a counterweight, a state of repose achieved by a vector of conflicting forces.[4] If one power pushes too hard on one end of the scale, an other power(s) steps on the other end to restore the balance. Applied to government, though, balance meant something more specific.

To say that powers are balanced is to say that only those actions and all those actions that obtain cooperation of all the qualified branches of government are undertaken. To use a generic example, a citizen is jailed only if the legislature passed a law that qualified a particular action as so punishable, if the courts decided that the particular action violated this law, and if the executive placed the individual behind bars. Had the legislature passed a law making it punishable to engage in activities protected by the constitution, had the court sentenced someone for an action that was not previously qualified as punishable, or had the bureaucracy imprisoned someone without being so directed by the courts, we would say that the balance of powers broke down. One of the powers had acted unilaterally, that is, without the authoritative consent of other powers. Note, however, that we should say the same had any of the branches failed to act upon the authoritative instructions of other branches: had the courts failed to sentence someone who committed a legally qualified offense or had the executive failed to implement the orders of the legislature or the courts, had the government as a whole failed to act because of a unilateral inaction by one of its branches. In the case of unilateral actions, the breakdown of the balance of powers leads the government to take abusive, in this example oppressive, actions; in the case of unilateral inaction, it renders the government ineffectual, in this case unable to ensure order.

Once the functions of government are allocated to different powers, what would keep the system working as it was intended to? What are the mechanisms that would maintain the proper balance among these powers? These mechanisms can be external or internal to the government. In turn, the way that may operate depends on whether each branch of the government represents a particular social group or all branches represent the entire people.

In the theory of mixed government dating to Aristotle and Polybius and revived by Machiavelli, each power of the government represented a different social group. In Florence these were the *grandi* and *popolo*: the

---

[4] This intuition of "equilibrium" was still present in the functionalist sociology of Parsons (1951) and his followers in political science. For Easton (1953), for example, the equilibrium meant equality of "inputs" and "outputs."

wealthy and the people. The estate systems that gained preponderance during the eighteenth century were based on this kind of representation. Legislatures, in the theory of the time, should be based on two chambers, one representing the aristocracy and the second, if not quite the poor, some broader group. Thus, Mably (1783) believed in a two-chamber system by which "aristocracy and democracy are held in equilibrium" (Palmer 1959: 270). In the Whig theory of the British King in the Parliament model, the King was the embodiment of the nation, the unelected Lords represented the aristocracy, and the elected Commons the people.

This theory was rejected by democrats, both in the United States and in France. As Manin (1994: 30) observes, "The theorists of the mixed constitution held that to prevent abuses of power the various governmental bodies should be capable of actively resisting and counterbalancing each other. In addition, the traditional doctrine of balanced government prescribed that the different branches of the government should represent distinct social forces. The modern conception of checks and balances, however, did not retain the latter aspect." Democrats thought that the entire government, all its branches, should equally represent all the people. As Hamilton emphasized at the Philadelphia Convention, "A democratic assembly is to be checked by a democratic senate, and both these by a democratic chief magistrate" (quoted in Wills 1982: xvi). Branches of government were distinguished by their functions and their prerogatives, not by their constituencies. To cite Manin (1994: 29) again, "The Federalists indeed broke away from the classical Whig doctrine that the popular branch of the legislature (the lower house) was the privileged or even the exclusive representative of the people. They considered instead every branch of the government as equal agents of the people."

Now, one might think that if different chambers represent different social groups then the balance between them can be maintained only by the force of these groups. Indeed, in most versions of the theory of mixed government, the balance between the powers was a sort of a class compromise. Yet Pasquino (1999) claims that, in contrast to Aristotle and Machiavelli, Polybius, while recognizing that different powers represent different groups, had no role for active citizenry in his model. The balance was to be maintained by the mutual checks among the institutions.

These two dimensions – external versus internal checks and class versus democratic representation – are in principle independent. An estate-based government can maintain balance by institutional, internal checks, or by mobilizing the force of the respective constituencies. A government in which each branch represents all people can, in turn, again maintain balance by internal checks or because the people react against usurpations of power by any of the branches. Conversely, institutionally designed checks and balances may suffice to maintain the balance of power, whether each branch represents a different constituency or whether all branches represent all the people.

But how can a balance be maintained? Because democrats rejected the legal distinctions of social status that underlaid the estate-based bodies, the only issue they faced was whether the institutional checks would be sufficient to maintain the balance of powers or an external intervention of the people would be necessary. As Palmer (1959: 262) summarizes,

> The real problem (and it was a real problem) was to prevent the powers thus constituted from usurping more authority than they have been granted. According to one school, the several constituted powers of government, by watching and balancing and checking one another, were to prevent such usurpation. According to another school, which regarded the first school as undemocratic or mistrustful of the people, the people itself must maintain a constant vigilance and restraint upon the powers of government.

The issue was a subject of a polemic by Madison against Jefferson (see Manin 1994). The device that was considered, "as a provision in all cases for keeping the several departments of power within their constitutional limits" (*Federalist* #49), were periodical constitutional conventions. Madison rejected this solution because he thought that such a convention would collude with one of the powers, namely the legislature.[5] As Manin (1994: 55) points out, "By this crucial observation, Madison was denying that in the final analysis constitutional convention could be a true system of exogenous enforcement." The idea of an external force, a third party, that would have the role of keeping the legislature and the executive within their proper limits also surged in France, in Condorcet's 1793 proposal as a "national jury" and in Sieyes's later suggestion as *jurie constititionnaire*. Yet neither of these proposals was adopted.

Montesquieu (1995 [1748]: Book XIX, Chapter XIX) did briefly consider the threat to the balance of powers originating from political parties, having in mind Tories and Whigs. However, he did not see it as a mortal threat. As Madison would when the Federalists monopolized all the powers, Montesquieu found a role for the people in government – restoring balance between powers: "Because these parties are composed of men who are free, if one were to take too much of an advantage, the effect of

---

[5] Montesquieu (1995 [1748]: 593), however, thought that the more popular branch would be the executive, which "disposes of all the employment."

liberty would make that this advantage would be reduced, while citizens, like the hands that rescue the body, would come to raise the other." Even if the people were to misapprehend the danger, as they are likely to, they could rely on their enlightened representatives. Furthermore, if a power succeeded to violate fundamental laws, "everything would unite against it"; there would be a revolution, "which would not change the form of government or its constitution: for revolutions shaped by liberty are but a confirmation of liberty."

The assumption Montesquieu makes is that the people would not ally with the transgressing power against other powers. He supports this assumption by claiming that people would often change partisan loyalties. Why, however, would people turn against a party that acts in their interest, even when violating laws? The same problem plagues a solution offered two centuries later by Weingast (1997). Suppose that the government transgresses the limits set by the constitution, acting in the interest of the current majority against the rights of the current minority. Such transgressions can be stopped, Weingast argues, if the current majority acts against them, fearing that if it were to become a minority the government would turn against it. Yet the difficulty is that there is nothing to guarantee that majorities would change and in this case the government and the permanent majority would collude against the minority. One could argue, as does Holmes (1995: 165–6), that the people want to keep the government divided, applying in a reverse direction the principle of *divide et impera*. Hence, any time one branch of government tries to gain predominance, the people would act to restore the balance. Nevertheless, this argument assumes again that even the people who are advantaged by the violation would be willing to act against it. I am not claiming that they would not, only that one cannot base this argument on interests. As long as interests are at stake, there are no "external" enforcers.

Having rejected external mechanisms, Madison (*Federalist* #49) turned to internal ones. He wanted to solve the problem "by so contriving the interior structure of the government as that its several constituent parts may, by their mutual relations, be the means of keeping each other in their proper places." Such a solution requires two components. The first one is motivation: Why would the individuals who populate the particular branches want to keep others in their proper places? As is well known, Madison assumed that occupants of positions in the departments of government would be motivated only by their institutional positions: "The interest of the man must be connected with the constitutional rights of his place." As each occupant of an institutional position would seek to safeguard or even extend the power of his institution, "each department should have a will of its own."[6] Once they have the motivations, they need instruments, and this is what the procedures inherent in the system of checks and balances would provide. The result is an often cited passage from *Federalist #51*: "But the great security against a gradual concentration of several powers in the same department consists in giving to those who administer each department the necessary constitutional means and personal motives to resist encroachments of the others.... Ambition must be made to counteract ambition." It is remarkable how closely this statement echoes Montesquieu's (1995: 326) insistence that "For the abuse of power to be impossible, it is necessary that by the disposition of things, the power stop the power."

Whether or not it was persuasive to his contemporaries, Madison's motivational assumption appears rather flimsy. Why would ambitions be compartmentalized by branches of government? Why would not legislators seek favors from the executive or the executive from some legislators? Why would the ambition not be to make the government as a whole powerful against the people? Finally, to introduce the shadow that hangs over the entire conception of balanced powers, why would ambitions not be partisan rather than institutional?

6.2.4 Divided Implies Limited?

A formal separation of powers, whether in its strict version or as checks and balances, may, but need not, generate their balance. One of the powers can acquire political dominance in spite of all the separating and balancing mechanisms. Suppose, though, that the powers do maintain their balance. Are governments that maintain a balance among powers necessarily moderate? One obvious possibility is that they collude and abuse the power they hold in common. As Mill (1859: 6–7) comments, the idea of separation of power emerged to protect liberty from governments that were antagonistic to the people. However, once rulers are no longer independent, because they are elected and can be revoked, "some people began to think that too much importance had been attached to the limitation of the power itself." By delegating it through elections, it was thought, the people retain power and "the nation did not need to be protected against its own will." Nevertheless, Mill goes on, "such phrases

---

[6] One can find echoes of this assumption in Persson, Roland, and Tabelini (1996), where "the legislature" plays a game against "the executive."

as 'self-government,' and 'the power of the people over themselves,' do not express the true state of the case." He concludes that the rule of the majority may be as oppressive as the rule of a tyrannical government. Hence, precautions against "the tyranny of the majority" are "as much needed against this as against any other abuse of power."

This entire discussion, which I tried to keep within the perspective of the early framers, is so anachronistic that it would be pointless to continue. It just makes no sense, and perhaps it did not from the onset, to analyze the separation of powers and the actions of governments without acknowledging the role of political parties. Parties, under most circumstances, render the focus on the separation of powers largely immaterial. If the same party or a coalition thereof controls the legislature, the executive, and appoints the judges, there is only one power: the majority. The functions are still distinct and it is still true that different branches do different things; even in the pure parliamentary system, the parliament legislates, the government executes, and the courts adjudicate. Moreover, members of the same party may still take the interests of the power in which they serve to heart. Nonetheless, the parliament legislates and the government executes the will of a partisan majority.

The central problem with the separation of powers is that it is a blunt instrument. The choice to which it is addressed is whether the government – any government – should be enabled or disabled. This choice can be guided only by the expectation of whether future governments will be good or bad.[7] If we were sure that they would be good – meaning that they would not want to encroach on individual liberties even if they could – there would be no reason to separate and check powers. However, because violations of liberty are the greatest evil to be avoided, uncertainty about the character of future rulers is sufficient to justify precaution. Hence, just in case, it is better to make it difficult for governments to take concerted actions.

The consequence of the system of checks and balances, however, is that governments are incapacitated not only from doing bad but also good things. The problem inherent in the separation of powers is that it lacks the means for uniting the actions of government. Vile (1967) observes that when Montesquieu confronted this problem, he solved it with a wave of hand, saying that the government will act together by the "necessary movement of things." At least one eminent student of the U.S.

---

[7] For a model that applies this reasoning to the choice of constitutions, see Laffont and Tirole (1994, Chapter 11).

constitution thought that the framers' "fear of the government's doing harm ... incapacitated it for doing much good" (McIlwain 1939: 246). Finer (1934: 85), who was no admirer of Montesquieu, complained that the latter converted "all discussion of government into one of despotism.... It was a good solvent, but, as a creative agent, deficient." As a result, Finer (1934: 89) diagnoses, "the Constitution succeeded in making government next to impossible, by certain checks and balances." Vile (1967: 15) concluded that "The concern to prevent the government from encroaching upon individual liberty leads to measures which weaken it to the point where it is unable to act in order to provide those prerequisites of social and economic life which are essential if an individual is to be able to make proper use of his faculties."

A divided government may be limited in the sense of not being able to do some bad things but also unable to do what citizens want it to do. If the nominal separation of powers is really effective, if it is not dominated by partisan politics, the scope of government actions may be limited but so is its ability to respond to the majority will.

6.3 PROTECTING THE STATUS QUO

6.3.1 Neutrality and Supermajority

A collective decision-making rule is neutral if this does not privilege any choice on prior grounds. This property distinguishes simple-majority rule from the other decisive, anonymous, and responsive rules (May 1952). In turn, simple-majority rule has an attractive property, namely that it maximizes "autonomy" in the sense of Rousseau, Kant, and Kelsen, that is, the proportion of the collectivity that likes the collective decision (Kelsen 1988; Rae 1975).

In spite of this attractiveness, neutrality can be rejected on a number of grounds.

The first is deontological. One may maintain that some choices, singled out as rights, should be privileged by any collective decision-making procedure. To use the example of one of the two basic liberal rights, property should be protected from simple majorities. Hence, neutrality should not apply to issues that entail property.

The second is epistemic. Some decisions may be known to be "correct" independently of the distribution of individual preferences. "God's will" may be one source of such knowledge; the opinion of experts may be another.

The third is prudential. Committing some errors may be thought to be more undesirable than committing other errors. For example, we may want to maintain the presumption of innocence, meaning that the verdict of innocence should be privileged with regard to that of guilt. More generally, a known state of the world may be privileged with regard to innovations on the ground of risk aversion.

Regardless of the position one takes, however, these reasons identify potential exceptions; that is, they indicate when neutrality should not be applied.

A rule that is decisive, anonymous, and responsive but not neutral is a supermajority rule. In turn, supermajority rule protects the status quo. Now, the relation between supermajority rule and the status quo is not a logical one. One might imagine rules that would state that whenever a choice that qualifies as privileged confronts one that does not, the privileged choice should prevail as long as it has support of some qualified minority, regardless whether or not it is the status quo. For example, intellectual property rights should be extended or abortion should be curtailed with regard to the status quo unless a two-thirds majority objects. I do not know, however, any examples of such rules. In turn, in most democratic political systems altering the status quo requires supermajority support.

Note that risk aversion is not the same as stability. One common argument in favor of legal stability is that it allows people to plan their lives. Nonetheless, this argument does not require reverting to supermajority rule. If people value legal stability, then simple majorities should be hesitant to change laws even if they do somewhat prefer another legal order over the status quo. Hence, simple-majority rule is sufficient to prevent capricious legal changes.

6.3.2 Bicameralism and Supermajority Rule

The point I am about to make is so obvious that I am embarrassed to state it. Moreover, it is not even original: See Levmore (1992). Nevertheless, it bears repeating.

Bicameralism[8] is a supermajoritarian device: A motion that would pass under a simple-majority rule in a unicameral legislature need not pass under the same rule separately in two houses of legislature drawn from the same unicameral house. If the sorting into bicameral legislature is not

---

[8] For a brief sketch of the history of bicameralism and of the arguments in favor of it, see Muthu and Shepsle (2007).

random – so that the houses are "diversely arranged," in the language of Buchanan and Tullock (1962) – then more than a simple majority of a unicameral legislature is required for the motion to pass two houses.

To make the point starkly, I am keeping voters out of the story. All voters do is to elect a unicameral legislature of the size $H = L + U$. I refer to L as the lower and to U as the upper house, but they are in fact identical in their powers, differing at most in size. The house H consists of Y representatives who support the motion and N who oppose it, $Y + N = H$. Once the house H is elected, its members are sorted into L and U. A motion is passed by the unicameral legislature if $Y > H/2$. It is passed by a bicameral legislature if and only if $Y_L > L/2$ and $Y_U > U/2$, where the subscripts indicate the respective houses.

The key to the story is obviously the sorting process. Let p be the probability that a Y representative is drawn into the lower house. For a motion to be approved by a bicameral legislature, it must be true, therefore, that $pY > L/2$ and $(1 - p)Y > U/2$.

Note that when $Y = H/2 + \varepsilon$, where ε is an arbitrarily small number, then the only p for which the motion is passed in both houses is $p = p^* = L/H$.[9] In other words, if a bare majority in the joint house supports the motion, then the motion will pass a bicameral legislature if and only if the legislatures are sorted randomly, independently of their positions on issues.

It is more interesting to look at this relation conversely: If the probability of entering either house does not depend on the position of the legislator on the issue, a bare majority in the single house is sufficient to pass the motion in the divided house. Yet suppose that sorting is nonrandom: There is something about the electoral system, whatever it might be, that allocates representatives to the two houses differently. The preferences of the electorate are fixed. The division is due entirely to the electoral system. Now the question is this: If the sorting probability is not random, $p > p*$, what is the majority of the entire house required to pass the legislation in both houses?

Because $p > p^*$, a motion that gets a majority in the joint house is certain to pass in the lower house. To pass in the upper house it must be true that $(1 - p)Y > U/2$ or $(1 - p)(Y/H) > (1 - p^*)/2$ or

$$\frac{Y}{H} > \frac{1}{2}\frac{1 - p^*}{1 - p}.$$

---

[9] This is because $p^*Y = (L/H)(H/2 + \varepsilon) = L/2 + \varepsilon(L/H) > L/2$ and $(1 - p^*)Y = (U/H)(H/2 + \varepsilon) = H/2 + \varepsilon(U/H) > H/2$.

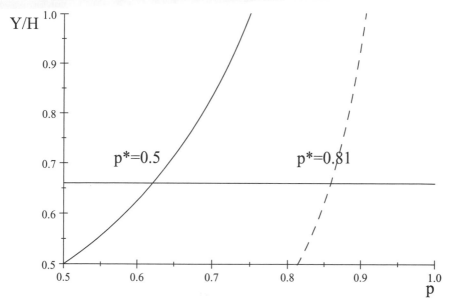

FIGURE 6.1 Supermajorities required in bicameral legislatures.

Figure 6.1 shows majorities necessary to pass legislation in two houses depending on their relative sizes (p^*) and the extent to which sorting is nonrandom. When the two houses are of equal size, $p^* = 0.5$; in the United States, $p^* = 0.81$. Think of $p - p^*$ as the bias that consists of sending supporters of Y disproportionately into the lower house. The horizontal line represents a supermajority of two-thirds; you can see that a relatively small bias is needed to make the required supermajority that large.

More sophisticated models of the legislative process generate the same conclusion. Cuttrone and McCarthy (2006: 184), for example, conclude that "If the median legislators in the two chambers differ in their preferences, then no status quo that lies between them can be defeated by two separate majority votes." Iaryczower, Katz, and Saiegh (2009) show that 25 percent of the bills that pass the House of Representatives are heavily amended in the Senate, while a "staggering" 45 percent never come up for the vote. They study a model in which the size of the majority in the House informs the members of the Senate about the quality of the bill. They learn that a four-fifths majority in the House is necessary for the Senate to pass a bill originating in the House. Given the sizes of the two bodies, these numbers translate into a supermajority of 74.4 percent.

TABLE 6.1: *Composition of Legislatures and Veto Powers (Annual Observations)*

Houses	Veto Power		Second House		Total
	Only One	Upper Cannot	Suspensive	Derogative	
I	7,031				7,031
2		75	1,291	4,653	6,019
3				28	28
Total	7,031	75	1,291	4,681	13,078

6.3.3 Some Facts

Bicameralism is thus a method for protecting the status quo. Another instrument is the veto power of some actor outside the legislature: Even if a bicameral legislature passes a law, the change of the status quo can still be prevented by a president, a monarch, or a judicial body.

The frequency of such devices is striking. Table 6.1 provides information about legislatures in the world for all the years for which we have this information after 1788. Unicameral legislatures prevailed only in slightly over one-half of the total annual observations. In turn, in almost all bicameral legislatures both houses could influence legislation; in about 20 percent of such years, one of the houses could only delay or ask for reconsideration ("suspensive" veto), but in the remaining cases both had to agree for legislation to become valid.

Table 6.2, in turn, shows the frequency with which legislation passed by different types of legislatures could be blocked by some actor outside them, not including the courts. Only in about 25 percent of the cases could legislation not be blocked; the remaining cases split almost evenly between those in which the veto was suspensive and those in which it was derogative.

TABLE 6.2: *Blocker Outside the Legislature (but not Courts)*

Houses	Veto Power	Outside Legislature		Total
	None	Suspensive	Derogative	
I	1,184	1,990	2,984	6,158
2	1,763	2,993	1,822	6,578
3	5	5	22	32
Total	2,952	4,988	4,828	12,768

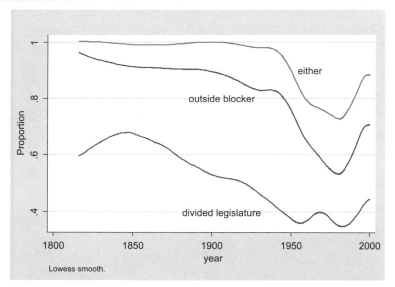

FIGURE 6.2 Supermajoritarian mechanisms, by year.

Finally, Figure 6.2 shows the frequency of these mechanisms over time. At least one of these two mechanisms was present in almost all representative institutions until the 1950s. So-called divided legislatures – parliaments composed of more than one chamber with power to influence legislation – became less frequent from the middle of the nineteenth century. Blockers external to legislatures (always not counting courts), in turn, became sharply less frequent after the emergence of new states in postcolonial Africa. Nevertheless, even at the end of the past century, at least one of these mechanisms was present in about 80 percent of representative institutions.

6.3.4 Democracy and Majority Rule

A simple majority of those elected to a single house is unable to win in two houses if they are "differently arranged." As Levmore (1962: 151) observed, "There will almost surely be less government intervention, less hasty legislation, and more preservation of the status quo if proposals must pass two hurdles rather than one."[10]

---

[10] The only nonconservative defense of bicameralism I found is by Buchanan and Tullock (1962): Because under plurality electoral systems one-fourth of voters can elect a

Few existing democracies are based on simple-majority rule. Constitutionally qualified majorities, judicial review, bicameralism, independent authorities, autonomous bureaucracies: Protections from simple majorities are numerous, complex, and obscure. Bicameralism may not be "the" preferred means of conservatism, as Levmore wants it, but he is right that it "is more subtle, while supramajority requirement appears terribly undemocratic" (1992: 155). What I find striking is that these supermajoritarian devices provide a blanket protection for the status quo in all realms, whether the status quo is good or bad by some criterion other than simple majority. Supermajority rule protects not just rights – rights are protected by special procedures and special bodies – but ordinary vested interests.

Obviously, who the beneficiaries of this protection are depends on the status quo, on the interests that are vested. Historically, they have been the propertied. As Cuttrone and McCarthy (2006: 180–1) observe, "One of the most common arguments for the emergence of bicameralism in Britain and in American colonies is ... ensuring that upper-class elements of society are protected." Moreover, Kiewet and McCubbins (1988) find that the U.S. presidents use veto power asymmetrically to reduce expenditures: "the president's veto threat works only when the president wants a budget smaller than the one preferred by the Congress." In turn, empirical evidence seems to indicate that unicameral systems without external veto power and even without a constitutional review are not more prone to violations of rights or to capricious policies (McGann 2006). Interestingly, Dixit, Grossman, and Gul (2000: 535–6) come to the conclusion that the supermajoritarian rule tends to generate more unequal outcomes: "those [supermajoritarian] devices intended to protect the welfare of minorities do not necessarily succeed in doing so; in fact, the division of the pie will be more uneven (and hence less efficient) in a regime of supermajority than in one of simple majority rule."

The point made by Dixit, Grossman, and Gul (2000) is more general. As long as voters' utility functions are concave, voters prefer policies that do not change drastically each time partisan control changes hands to policies that implement ideal points of the victorious parties

majority of the legislature, bicameralism is just a form of protection from minority rule. Bicameralism is thus an institutional patch designed to plug the hole created by the electoral system. I find this argument peculiar; the simplest way to protect from minority rule would be to institute a proportional electoral system. Moreover, the Buchanan–Tullock defense is feeble: It can be shown that when the two houses are differently elected, a supermajority of voters, not just representatves, is still required to pass legislation.

(Alesina 1988). Such policies are enforceable by the threat that voters would not support a party that adopts extreme policies even if such policies are close to their own preferences. Hence, the prospect of alternation in office forces the incumbent majorities to consider the preferences of minorities, even without any exogenous devices intended to protect minorities from simple-majority rule. Compromise, as it were, is induced by the prospect of alternation in office, even without any contramajoritarian devices. Furthermore, it is the prospect of alternation that induces moderation: "The ruling individuals must perceive an appreciable chance that their power will come to an end. . . . And they must foresee a possibility of regaining power once it is lost" (Dixit, Grossman, and Gul 2000: 533).

I am not claiming that a sufficiently large majority cannot get its way under democracy. Neither am I arguing in favor of a pure majority rule; majorities can be foolish, ephemeral, and vicious. But rather than erect hidden trenches around property, explicit rules should regulate which issues should be decided by which criteria.

6.4 CITIZENS AND GOVERNMENTS

"Representation," or its cognates, is frequently treated as quintessential, if not definitional, for democracy: Dahl (1971: 1) observes that "a key characteristic of a democracy is the continued responsiveness of the government to the preferences of its citizens"; Riker (1965: 31) asserts that "democracy is a form of government in which the rulers are fully responsible to the ruled"; while Schmitter and Karl (1991:76) maintain that "modern political democracy is a system of governance in which rulers are held accountable for their actions in the public realm by citizens." Note first that the relation between citizens and actions of government is variously described as responsiveness, responsibility, or accountability. While this is not the place to delve into these distinctions (for which see Przeworski, Stokes, and Manin 1999), what is crucial is that some agency costs are inevitable unless governments want exactly the same as their supporters.

Although governments cannot represent the will of all the people, supporters of particular parties may be sufficiently homogeneous to render meaning to a notion of partisan interest. True, even the will of supporters of particular parties is still likely to be multidimensional, so partisan interest need not be uniquely determined. But given the platform of other parties – by which I mean both the issues on which to take a position and the positions taken – the platforms to which supporters of a particular party would agree are circumscribed.[11] In elections, people sort themselves out by their distinct wills in response to proposals of parties, which, in turn, must anticipate how people would sort themselves out. In the end, "the electoral equilibrium," people vote for particular parties because they think that these parties will represent them better than others. Hence, partisan interests are distinct.

To understand this process, consider electoral competition between two parties (or coalitions) that choose policies from a single dimension, say the extent of redistribution. As long as parties propose or implement different platforms, almost all voters, except for those whose ideal preferences are equidistant from the proposals of the two parties, strictly prefer one party over another. However, even if the two parties offer the same platform (as in the median voter model), parties still represent different constituencies. The electoral constraint pushes the parties to the position of the median voter. Nevertheless, the parties are still distinguishable as "left" and "right," which can be seen as follows. If the electoral constraint were relaxed by a notch, so that both parties would have had the same chance to win the election (which in this story is 50/50) if they proposed to implement the ideal preference of the voter removed from the median by one to the left, then the left party would move to this voter while the right party would not. Hence, even when parties converge, they converge "from the left" and "from the right." And voters know it. Parties may change their objectives and voters may change their preferences from one election to another, so that different groups of voters may be represented by different parties at different times. At each time, however, interests and values align along partisan lines.

This is not to say that governments can admit that they act in partisan interests. The censoring power of the concensualist ideology recurrently conflicts with the partisan nature of elections. Elections must carve the electorate into partisan constituencies; the elected governments must each time stitch together the electoral wounds. After an exceptionally divisive campaign, Jefferson was the first to do so in 1801 by offering concessions to the Federalists. After an almost equally conflictive election in 2004, having appealed to extreme religious groups, George W. Bush rushed

---

[11] These intuitions, and they are only that, are based on Roemer (2001).

to preach "national unity" in his victory speech.[12] Salvador Allende's declaration, "*No soy Presidente de todos los Chilenos*" (I am not the President of all the Chileans), was an enormous blunder. The accusation that parties divide people is perennial in the history of democracy. Nevertheless, elections evolved to be partisan and governments learned that they would face elections, so they must act in partisan ways as well, even if they cannot admit it.

As long as government policies change in the same direction as the majority will expressed in elections, the axiom of responsiveness holds in the representative framework. All we need to assume is that if governments change, at least some policies tilt in the direction preferred by the people who elected them. Only if policies change in a perverse direction, self-government does not hold (even if voters change their mind ex post, as in Stokes 2001).

Responsiveness, however, does not require that governments be perfect agents. To understand what is entailed, consider the simplest possible model of accountability. Suppose that a government is elected for a term of T years and that during this term it can extract as rents some amount $S(T)$ taken away from the citizens. Anticipating this possibility, citizens (either homogeneous or pivotal) set an incentive scheme according to which if the government extracts in rents no more than R then it remains in office, but if it extracts more than R it is voted out. Assuming that politicians want to extract as much as possible, the incumbent government faces a choice between extracting $S > R$ and being voted out after one period or extracting R and remaining in office. The amount of rents that makes the government indifferent is then given by the solution to

$$U(S) = \frac{1}{1-\rho}U(R),$$

where $\rho < 1$ is the rate at which politicians discount the future.[13] The solution to this equation, R, represents the rents that citizens must give to governments as an incentive to work on the citizens' behalf. This agency cost, "efficiency wage" in the language of Shapiro and Stiglitz (1986), is

---

[12] How empty was this "unity" talk was immediately manifested by Bush's invitation to "all those who share our goals." As one Republican operative indiscreetly admitted, "Politics is not about uniting people. It's about dividing people. And getting your fifty-one percent" (*New Yorker*, June 2, 2008).

[13] If the government stays in the office one term, it gets $U(S)$. If it extracts R, it is reelected forever and gets $\sum_T \rho^T U(R) - [1/(1-\rho)]U(R)$. These utilities are standardized in such a way that politicians who are voted out get zero from then on.

inevitable, even though it may vary depending on the motivations of the incumbents as well as on the institutional arrangements, such as judicial scrutiny, transparency, and so on.

In this simple form, accountability models generate the countrary-to-fact conclusion that incumbents always respond to the incentive scheme and the voters always adhere to it, so that incumbents are always reelected. But it is sufficient to allow governments to be uncertain about citizens' preferences or citizens to change their minds and the argument becomes probabilistic. Note that citizens are in no way bound by their promises – in fact, they do not write contracts and even if they did there would be no one to enforce them. Citizens can base their votes on any considerations they want; failure in the World Cup or even shark attacks (Achen and Bartels 2002) may incline them to oust the rascals, even if the poor government officials have nothing to do with it. However, if citizens cannot be relied on to reelect governments that behave well, they must provide more generous incentives for governments to do so.

This model can be and has been complicated in innumerable ways, but the essence of the accountability mechanism remains the same:

1. The government is induced to respond to the will of the majority by the threat that, if it does not, it will be voted out of office.
2. The government is never a perfect agent; citizens must be willing to suffer agency costs to make the incentive scheme effective.

These agency costs arise if governments have some interests of their own but also if they have preferences that differ from those of the majority that supports them. Agency costs mean simply that citizens must tolerate some latitude in governing, that their mandates are not exactly imperative. They are not the same as corruption, which is an excess of material rents above the inevitable amount that citizens must and want to tolerate. Responsiveness, therefore, does not preclude agency costs. Agency costs are inevitable in any system of government, but not all governments are responsive.

7

Liberty

7.1 INTRODUCTION

Autonomy is a particular kind of liberty – the freedom to live under laws one wants to live under given that living under laws one must. The argument, from Rousseau to Kelsen, has been that because to live together we must live under laws, this is the only kind of freedom possible. Liberty cannot mean freedom in the state of nature. Legal order enables actions that are not feasible in the state of nature: In the latter each individual is exposed to aggression or exploitation by others, so that no one is free from interference. Freedom is possible only in society, not outside of it.

But necessity does not freedom make. Rousseau's promises notwithstanding – that we would be as free "as before" – counterfactual comparisons are irrelevant. Any legal order is a form of oppression. Even if we were to agree unanimously to a particular order, it docs not mean that each individual enjoys being subject to it. A legal order is but cooperation imposed by a threat of force. An order imposed by a majority is even more onerous, because it is just one way of imposing cooperation among several possible.

Moreover, some legal orders are more onerous than others. Even if we must live under a system of laws, not all aspects of our lives must be regulated. As Condorcet (1986 [1787]: 206) observed, "There arc two distinct parts in all legislation: deciding which objects can be legitimately legislated, deciding what the laws should be." The axiom of decisiveness does not imply that everything must be or should be subject to collective decisions, only that once preferences are revealed, we know what should be done. People often have different preferences as to what should be subject to public regulation; sexually explicit materials, drug use, and forms of cohabitation are recent examples. A collective decision-making rule is decisive if it unequivocally indicates whether or not drug use should be decriminalized, that is, left to individual discretion, not only whether drug use should be subject to twenty or thirty years in jail. The framers of the U.S. Constitution, for example, decided not to legislate on matters of religion (Holmes 1988), while in some democracies the state recognizes some religion as official.

One implication of the possibility of leaving some matters outside the scope of laws is that, contrary to Dahl (1989: 142 ff.), autonomy is not a welfarist criterion. Welfare is defined over objects from which individuals derive utility. Because laws distribute consumption and allocate resources between public and private goods, one could think that a preference for a legal order is just a preference over distributions of welfare. Legal systems, however, differ not only in what they generate but in what they allow individuals to achieve by their own actions; they differ in the extent to which they allow individual choice. A law may order individuals with particular incomes to pay a specific amount of taxes, or it may leave to individual discretion how much they contribute to the welfare of others (the latter was an idea of President Bush Sr.). A law may force all people to read *The Bible* or it may leave to their discretion whether they read *The Bible* or *Lady Chatterley's Lover*, neither, or both. Laws shape what Sen (1988) refers to "capability sets," defined as bundles of "functionings" that a person may achieve by one's own actions. Because capability sets include the ability to exercise choice, they are not exhausted by the consumption of commodities or leisure, Rawlsian primary goods, or utilities. Autonomy, thus, is not a welfarist criterion because laws determine what one can, not only what one does, achieve.

Liberty must mean more than Rousseau or Kelsen meant by autonomy: the freedom awarded by living under laws but also the freedom from interference by the government: freedom through law and freedom from law. These two freedoms are not easily compatible and their proper balance has never been obvious. Hence, one way to characterize real democracies is by posing the question of Berlin (2002: 35): "How much am I governed?" From Tocqueville (1986 [1835]) to Marcuse (1971), students of democracy raised the specter that it would regulate too much, that the tyranny of one would be replaced by the tyranny of many. The founders, for whom liberty was "everything," vacillated between a desire for security guaranteed by a legitimate application of laws and a resistance to interference in private lives. This issue gave rise to political divisions between "conservatives" and "liberals" that in many countries became organized along partisan lines. It continues to be a deep political fault line in many contemporary democracies.

7.2 DISABLING IS ENABLING

Why are laws necessary to enable people to be free? The argument is best seen by applying an anachronistic analytical instrument: game theory.

Laws can make us free in situations in which the pursuit of individual interests leads to an outcome that is collectively suboptimal. Such situations are typified by the prisoners' dilemma:

		j	
		Cooperate	Defect
	Cooperate	3, 3	1, 4
i			
	Defect	4, 1	2, 2

Examine this situation. There are two individuals, called i and j, each of whom can defect or cooperate. Each prefers a larger payoff to a smaller one. Whatever i does, j wants to defect; whatever j does, i wants to defect; hence, the outcome is that they both defect and each gets a payoff of 2. But given all the exogenous conditions, each could have gotten a payoff of 3. Each and all individuals are worse off than they could be. Examples abound: The classical one is that people grab each other's property and, fearing that their property would be taken away, no one invests. Because this topic is a matter of frequent confusion, let me just emphasize that nothing is assumed here about the content of these preferences: If all people are perfectly altruistic and only want others to enjoy property, all will end without any. What matters here is that each person behaves independently, not what the content of preferences is.

How can we remedy this situation? We can adopt laws. The law would say that everyone must cooperate and that violations would be subject to punishment. Suppose we were to vote whether to adopt this law or to leave things "as before," allowing each individual to make decisions independently. Because compliance with this law makes each and all of us better off than in the state of nature, the vote for the law would be unanimous. Our common interest is for everyone to get 3 and our general will is that everyone should cooperate. Moreover, individuals are free to cooperate *only* if the law compels everyone to act in this way. In the state of nature, I would know that if I invest then others will grab my property, so that I could not, would not be free to, invest.

However, getting a payoff of 3 is not the best for each individual. If you keep away from my property, I am still better off grabbing yours; if you cooperate, I still want to defect. We have to be compelled not to defect, against our individual will. The general will is not an aggregation of particular wills.[1]

The collectively beneficial outcome can be supported by rational moral- ity. Suppose I ask myself, "What is it that I would not want others to do to me?," the answer to which is "defect." The rule of conduct I would want everyone else to adopt is thus "do not defect." Each individual would want all others to adopt this rule. This, then, is the only rule that can be adopted universally and, if we are guided by universal reason, we would all adopt it.

Is this what Rousseau, or Kant, had in mind? Because this is not a history of thought, I ultimately do not care. There are certainly enough passages in Rousseau to indicate that he would not have objected to this interpretation, which was deliberately couched in his language.[2] Rousseau did think that the social contract must be Pareto superior to the state of nature; otherwise, it would not be voluntarily concluded. He also thought that "as the particular will cannot represent the general will, in turn, general will, cannot without changing its nature become partic- ular will" (1964: 129). What matters is that both the idea that in some situations individuals must be compelled to act in their own good and the idea that each individual would want to compel himself or herself by adopting laws are perfectly coherent. Whether they remain "as free as before" is another matter; what is clear is that once they live in society, people would not want to be free in the way they were before. To pursue the common good, individuals must act on the basis of the general will, as instituted in laws, even against their particular wills.

To put it in a broader perspective, the argument is that disabling some actions enables people to engage in actions that would not have been

---

[1] On this issue, see the polemic between Grofman and Feld (1989), Eastlund (1989), and Waldron (1989).

[2] As for Kant (1881 [1793]: 34–5), here is the relevant passage: "Right in general may be defined as the limitation of the Freedom of any individual to the extent of its agreement with the freedoms of all other individuals, in so far as this is possible by a universal Law.... Now as all limitations of freedom by external acts of the will of another, is a mode of *coercion* or *compulsion*, it follows that the Civil Constitution is a relation of *free* men who live under coercive Laws, without prejudicing their Liberty otherwise in the whole of their connection with others."

possible otherwise and that make them better off. Skipping centuries, this was the view of Rousseau, Burke (1790: 152), Shelling (1954), Elster (1985), Hardin (1989; 1999: 134), and Holmes (1995, 2003). Here are some applications of this hypothesis:

1. The obligation of kings to assume the debts of their predecessor – the context in which the idea of commitment seems to have first originated (Pusendorf, according to Holmes 1995) – enabled kings to borrow.
2. Delegating the power of the purse to the Parliament enabled the king to raise revenues to conduct wars (North and Weingast 1989).
3. Prohibition against interstate tariffs – Hardin's (1989; 1999: 96) favorite example – enabled the states to exploit gains from trade.
4. Prohibition against the suppression of free speech enables each person and all of us as a collectivity to make better informed and reasoned decisions. This is a main theme of J. S. Mill (1859).

I cite all these applications because the idea is powerful. Even if the laws that we are forced to observe are not of our own making, being ruled by laws allows us to do things we want to get done. As Holmes (1995: 153) summarized Madison's view, "If we take for granted certain procedures and institutions fixed in the past, we can achieve our present goals more effectively than we could if we were constantly being sidetracked by the recurrent need to establish a basic framework for political life." Moreover, Hardin (1999, but see Goodin 2001 for a critique) claims that once people are forced to cooperate in a particular way, one of several possible, then they have an incentive to adhere to this form of cooperation: The constitution becomes a "convention."

Laws, then, do make us free. They make us free to cooperate with the security that we would benefit from the fruits of cooperation.

7.3 "LIBERTY IS EVERYTHING"

Liberty was the ultimate value that motivated the men who sought to establish representative government. Liberty was "everything," as in "Everything would be lost" if the same body exercised the three powers of government (Montesquieu 1995: 328). "Liberty," Patrick Henry would orate in 1788, is "the greatest of all earthly blessings" (Ketchum 1986: 200). Loss of liberty, Sieyès would say, is "the extreme evil." But if liberty was everything, what was "liberty"?

This is a dangerous question to pose, for it is vulnerable to anachronisms. In the aftermath of Isaiah Berlin's 1958 lecture and the vigorous debate it engendered, it is not easy to think about the concept of liberty without all the distinctions and arguments this discussion illuminated. And this is not the only danger. We must also beware of excessively relying on views of philosophers, whose logical coherence was not always imitated in the passions of those who risked their lives to make everyone free. One thinks differently in Königsberg or Geneva than on the battlefields of Concord or Ayacucho or even in the halls of Philadelphia or Tucumán. Syllogisms enlighten but do not inspire, and the cry for liberty was a shout, not a logical argument.

A view systematized by philosophers was that liberty consists of security or tranquility guaranteed by the legitimate exercise of power by the government. When government acts only according to laws that in turn express the popular will, people are free. Such laws, properly adopted and executed, maintain the social order under which the people want to live, protect them and their property from one another and from arbitrary actions by the government.

Note that the danger to security can originate from two sources. To use Dunn's (1999) enlightening turn of phrase, having government transforms a "horizontal" into a "vertical" danger: If the government has the power to maintain order, it must also have the power to oppress. The dual nature of the danger was apparent. "We are cautioned," Patrick Henry observed, "against faction and turbulence: I acknowledge that licentiousness is dangerous and that it ought to be provided against. I acknowledge also the new Government may effectually prevent it. Yet, there is another thing it will as effectually do: it will oppress and ruin the people" (in Ketchum 1986: 201). Hobbes emphasized the first, "horizontal," danger; Montesquieu and his numerous followers, the latter.

While Montesquieu observed that liberty is not the same as independence (1995 [1748]: 325), he focused only on the former. What he says about liberty I find confusing. Because I am not a philosopher, I suspect that more competent scholars can tease out a coherent interpretation of his thought. However, I am not less of a philosopher than the people who populated the halls of the Philadelphia Convention or the Paris Assemblée, so I find no reason to think that they could have derived a clearer lesson. Perhaps anticipating Constant (1997 [1819]) and Berlin (2002 [1958]), Montesquieu drew a distinction between what he called "philosophical freedom," which is "the exercise of one's will, or at least . . . the opinion that one exercises one's own will," and "political freedom," which "consists of security, or at least the opinion one has of one's security" (1995 [1748]: 376). He left philosophical freedom aside and spelled out what he meant by political freedom: "Political liberty in the citizen," he defined, "is this tranquility of spirit which comes from the opinion which each has of his security; and for this liberty to exist, it is necessary that the government would be such that one citizen could not fear another citizen" (1995 [1748]: 327). Governments must protect citizens from one another; this is why we have governments.[3] Montesquieu seems to take for granted that a government would neutralize the horizontal danger. He does not say that a unified, strong government is better equipped to maintain order, to ensure the security of citizens from one another. His entire preoccupation is with preventing tyranny, with protecting citizens from their rulers. This is why he says that there can be no liberty unless the powers of the government are divided.

Liberty cannot and did not mean acting against laws. As Montesquieu (XI, IV) insisted, "if a citizen could do what they [laws] forbid, he would no longer be possessed of liberty, because all his fellow-citizens would have the same power." Even if individuals would want to act against laws, if people acted against the laws which they unanimously support, society would disintegrate. This much we know again from Rousseau and Kant.

Liberty is thus neither the natural freedom nor the right to act against laws. It is the security of living under laws. Something like this must have been in the minds of the founders. However, it sat uneasily in their minds, for it could not have been all.

Montesquieu (1995 [1748]: 325), echoed again by Rousseau and Kant, also tells us that liberty cannot mean doing what one wants: It consists of doing all that one ought to want to do and not being forced to do what one ought not want to do. Being free in the sense of living under laws of our choosing is a liberty of citizens guided by universal reason, virtue, morality, or whatever that turns them into "copies of the species." It is not freedom of individuals distinguished by their wants, desires, interests, or fantasies. There are two possibilities: Either liberty is the security guaranteed to citizens by laws, as in the mature Locke's view

---

[3] I have no idea what to make of Chief Justice Rehnquist's opinion in the 1988 case of DeShaney v. Winnebago County Department of Social Services (57 US LW 4218, 4219), where he argues that the purpose of the Constitution "was to protect the people from the State, not to ensure that the State protected them from each other." If the State is merely a danger, why have the State?

that "Where there is no law, there is no freedom" (*Second Treatise*, ¶57), or it is whatever is left untouched by regulation, a view Laslett (1988: 20) attributes to the young Locke. This distinction – liberty of the ancients versus liberty of the moderns, positive versus negative freedom, freedom as liberty versus freedom as independence – has been made so many times and in so many different guises that it now appears intuitive. Constant (1997 [1819]: 603) thought that "The goal of the ancients was sharing of social power among all the citizens of the same country. It was this that they called liberty. The goal of the moderns is the security in the private happiness (*jouissances*); and they call liberty the guarantees granted by the institutions to such happiness." Berlin (2002 [1958]: 178 and 169) juxtaposed the positive sense of liberty, "derived from the wish on the part of the individual to be his own master," to the negative sense, which is "the degree to which no man or body of men interferes with my activity."

At least from Constant on, liberal thought recognized the divergence between these two freedoms: "We are moderns," Constant (1997 [1819]: 611) exclaimed, "who want to enjoy, each one, our rights; to develop, each one, our faculties as it seems good to us.... We are not willing to be subjected so that the nation would be sovereign, not willing for the individual to be a slave so that the people would be free." Liberty cannot mean only being secure under laws that promote the good of each and all. In a powerful passage, Constant (1997 [1819]: 616–17) anticipated the "pluralist liberalism" of Berlin:

Authorities... will tell us: 'What is at the bottom the goal of your efforts, the motive of your work, the object of your hopes? Is it not happiness? Well, this happiness, let us act, and we will give it to you.' No, Gentlemen, we will not let you do it. However touching may be an interest so tender, we ask authority to remain within its bounds. That authority limits itself to being just; we will occupy ourselves about being happy.

The problem the founders faced was to maximize both freedoms, to interfere in private lives as little as possible and to guarantee security as much as possible. The difficulty was, and is, that both cannot be maximized at the same time and the proper balance is neither obvious nor the same under different conditions. Take Voltaire's principle that "The freedom of one ends where the freedom of another begins." As the Prussian General Code of 1791 declared, "The laws and ordinances of the state should no further restrict the natural liberty and rights of citizens than the public welfare demands" (in Palmer 1959: 406). Somewhere there is a line dividing the actions that do not impinge on others and those that do affect them. If my actions do not have effects on the welfare of others, no externalities, then I should be free from the constraint of law to pursue them. Even in society we are not interdependent in all of our actions, and one is free in the sense of noninterference when laws do not impinge on actions that have no externalities.

Yet the line between your freedom and mine is imperceptible. We can err in one direction or another. And err we do. One can always find externalities. If I do not brush my teeth correctly, I will get cavities, and impose on society the cost of my dental care. If other children are allowed to read *Huckleberry Finn*, my child will be corrupted by them. Suppose that all our actions, even my manner of brushing my teeth, not to speak of my private reading of *Lady Chatterley's Lover,* are subject to laws. We are still free in the sense of Rousseau: Our liberty is enabled by laws. Yet the freedom from command no longer exists. Berlin (2002: 198), perhaps excessively generous toward Kant, was puzzled by the implications of this argument: "What can have led to so strange a reversal – the transformation of Kant's severe individualism into something close to a pure totalitarian doctrine on the part of thinkers some of whom claimed to be his disciples?" Remarkably, Constant (1997 [1819]: 604) observed the same with regard to Rousseau in 1819. "In transporting into our modern times the extent of social power, of collective sovereignty that belonged to other centuries, this sublime genius nevertheless furnished disastrous pretexts to more than one kind of tyranny." For this argument implies that, although people are free to cooperate, cooperate they must. As Berlin (2002 [1958]: 194) observed, in this conception "Liberty, so far from being incompatible with authority, becomes virtually identical with it." "Tyranny of the majority," or "totalitarian democracy," to use the language in which some German refugees from fascism (Fromm 1994 [1941]; Marcuse 1971) described the United States, is not an oxymoron. As Berlin (2002 [1958]: 209) put it, "An equal right to oppress – or interfere – is not equivalent to liberty." The title of Fromm's book was *Escape from Freedom.* Marcuse (1962), albeit in a framework of Freudian psychology, used a concept of "surplus repression": repression beyond that which is necessary to make people live together and cooperate. To put it in a different language, maximizing welfare is incompatible with tolerating heterogeneous preferences. This is Sen's (1970) impossibility of a Pareto liberal.

Constant, speaking in 1819, claimed originality when making his distinction between the two kinds of liberty. It was indeed first made by him in the unpublished 1806 *Principes de politique,* where he says that "the first difference between the social state of the ancients and the moderns" is that "the happiness of the majority is no longer placed in the enjoyment of power but in individual liberty" (Gauchet in Constant 1997: 834, ft. 2). If this distinction was as novel as Constant claimed, however, then what did "liberty" mean to those who were designing the government to protect it and enlarge it? Unfortunately, the only answer I can give is that I do not know. Indeed, the answer may have been "everything": the right to self-determination, the security afforded by living under duly implemented laws, the protection from undue interference, the freedom to choose one's own happiness. Searching for these distinctions in the minds of the founders seems a futile endeavor. Their views may have been much simpler than these distinctions allow. Order is necessary to reduce the horizontal danger; to maintain order, some amount of oppression of individual wants, desires, and even values is necessary. Nevertheless, order can extend beyond the realm of necessity and it may be arbitrarily administered. The ambivalence of the founders, as I see it, was between security and noninterference. This ambivalence is not easy to resolve and it can be never resolved once and for all.

7.4 LIBERTY AS ENUMERATED RIGHTS

In many constitutions the line beyond which individual lives should be protected from public interference is drawn at "rights." Rights, as we know, may include prohibitions against governments taking some actions with regard to citizens or injunctions about procedures governments must observe if they seek to take some actions, traditionally to imprison someone or to take away property, but also guarantees of equal and unobstructed influence over the process of making collective decisions.

Rights define domains to be excluded from ordinary politics, specifically from applying the simple-majority rule. As Holmes (1988: 196) observed, "The basic function of the constitution is to *remove* certain decisions from the democratic process." He cites Justice Robert Jackson's opinion in a 1943 case:

The very purpose of a Bill of Rights was to withdraw certain subjects from the vicissitudes of political controversy, to place them beyond the reach of majorities and officials and to establish them as legal principles to be applied by the courts. One's right to life, liberty, and property, to free speech, a free press, freedom of worship and assembly, and other fundamental rights may not be submitted to vote: they depend on the outcome of no election.

Yet even once rights are defined, two issues always remain open. Questions of what falls under their protection remain politically, not only legally, controversial. The right to hold and acquire property – a right ubiquitously enshrined in early constitutions – does not protect against all policies that reduce the value of property, say abolishing tariffs or issuing more taxi medallions. Income taxes, for example, have been generally considered to be compatible with the right to property, although uncompensated takings of property have not been (Halbac 2008). Perhaps more fundamentally, though, rights are almost always in conflict. Moreover, as Waldron (2006: 1352) observed, "the fact that people disagree about rights does not mean that there must be one party to the disagreement which does not take rights seriously."

The ambiguity inherent in delimiting the realm of majority rule as distinct from the realm protected by rights is often posed as an opposition between democracy and the rule of law, as a conflict between abstract principles of popular sovereignty and those of justice. According to Raz (1994: 260), "Legislatures because of their preoccupation with current problems, and their felt need to secure re-election by a public all too susceptible to the influences of the short term, are only too liable to violent swings and panic measures," and "The rule of law functions in modern democracies to ensure a fine balance between the power of a democratic legislature and the force of tradition-based doctrine" (1994: 361). Dworkin (1986: 376) goes even further: "Any competent interpretation of the Constitution as a whole must therefore recognize...that some constitutional rights are designed exactly to prevent majorities from following their own conviction about what justice requires." In such views, as Guarnieri (2003) observes, "Submitting the performance of public functions to the scrutiny of independent judges becomes an effective and essential check on the exercise of political power, ensures the supremacy of the law and guarantees citizens' rights."

What are the grounds, though, to counterpose intemperate legislators to oracles of "the law," "tradition," or even "justice"? Are we asked to believe that judges have no interests other than to implement "the law," that their decision power is nondiscretionary, that independence guarantees impartiality? The rule of judges need not be "the rule of law" (see several essays in Maravall and Przeworski 2003). Unembodied entities cannot rule: "rule" is a verb that can take only people as its subject (Sánchez-Cuenca 2003: 62). Neither "law" nor "justice" can rule; only people can. Conversely, as Waldron (2006: 1349) forcefully argued, legislatures are not necessarily less deliberate nor less respectful of rights than courts. There is no evidence that institutional systems that give more power to majorities are more abusive or capricious than those that impede governments from acting by checks and balances. Courts and legislatures are "populated institutions." Their conflict is "political in the sense that it is rooted in desires to maintain or increase authority and is not necessarily connected to norms of legality themselves" (Ferejohn and Pasquino 2003). Yet the voices that want to constrain or even counteract majority rule continue to be vociferous: Rosanvallon (*Le Monde*, April 29, 2009), for example, thinks that "Now power is not considered fully democratic unless it is submitted to the tests of control and validation at the same time concurrent and complementary to the majoritarian expression." The fear of the people seems to be congenital among the ideologists of self-government of the people: It was one of the contradictions at the onset and it is alive and well today.

Courts – I am following Waldron (2006: 1370) again – may have an important role to play in focusing political attention on those aspects of ordinary legislation or of executive actions that concern rights. Courts can inform, even instruct, legislatures and executive agencies. Nevertheless, the ultimate decision power must rest in the hands of elected representatives. The ideal of autonomy can be advanced in heterogeneous societies – societies in which views about rights conflict – only if laws are nothing else than the will of the majority structured within an institutional framework.

8

Democracy as an Implementation of Self-Government in Our Times

Is "democracy," as we understand the term today, an implementation of "self-government," as this ideal was formulated when representative institutions were first established? The evidence is mixed. Reading backwards, our contemporary understanding of democracy into the intentions of the founders of representative institutions is anachronistic. Their ideals – self-government, equality, and liberty – were seminal. During more than 200 years they animated the evolution of representative institutions into what we now see as democracy. This is why we venerate the founders. Unfortunately, some of their ideas were logically incoherent and practically unfeasible, and some manifestly rationalized interests.

Let me reiterate that the issue of intentions cannot be resolved. Wood (1969: 383), for example, makes this claim:

The Americans were not simply making the people a nebulous and unsubstantial source of all political authority. The new conception of a constitution, the development of extralegal conventions, the reliance on instructions, the participation of the people in politics out-of-doors, the clarification of the nature of representation, the never-ending appeals to the people by competing public officials – all gave coherence and reality, even a legal reality, to the hackneyed phrase, the sovereignty of the people.

Yet this is a conclusion of a section that describes the ambiguities and the polemics concerning the relation between the people and their representatives, the role of the people between elections, the locus of sovereignty. Moreover, of this list only "the never-ending appeals to the people by competing public officials" survived the Constitution. Hence, it is easy to side with Morgan (1988: 82): "The problem of reconciling the wishes and needs and rights of actual people with the overriding will of a fictional sovereign people was not temporary. It was, indeed, inherent in the new fiction."

As Morgan (1988: 152) has it, "The problem was to develop institutions and habits of thought that would recognize popular power but at the same time direct expression of it to the support of existing authority." Systems of representative government were born under a fear of participation by the broad masses of the population, a large part of whom were poor and illiterate. One would not err much in thinking that the strategic problem of founders, pretty much everywhere, was how to construct representative government for the rich while protecting it from the poor. We have seen that in spite of lofty pronouncements, the original institutions were not egalitarian even in the political realm. Self-government meant, for the founders, government of those endowed with reason and virtue, but reason and virtue were to be reserved for those distinguished by wealth, gender, and race. While governments were to be selected by elections – elections were the only source of authorization to govern – their role was merely to ratify the superiority of those qualified to govern by their social and economic position. Created under a shadow of religious and economic conflicts, representative institutions were designed to bar or at least minimize the voice of the people between elections, treating all "intermediate organizations" – clubs, associations, trade unions, as well as political parties – as a danger to civil peace. Intended as a bulwark against despotism, they were designed to disable governments from doing much of anything, bad or good, by checking and balancing powers, by protecting the status quo from the will of the majority. Inspired by the value of vaguely understood liberty, many ended up quite authoritarian, infusing moral and even explicitly religious values into the institutional design.

The benevolent guise of paternalism, whether extended to the poor, women, or people who were not "civilized," was a veneer covering interests. And the veneer was thin: It wore off as soon as it touched on property. The relation between power and property was intimate and often unabashed. Naked force stood as the ultimate bulwark against threats to property. Institutional systems often provided sufficiently effective trenches. The poor were instructed that their interests are represented by the wealthy, women that their interests are guarded by men, the "uncivilized" that they need to be guided by their colonizers. When the fear for property would take hold, self-government, equality, and liberty were dressed up in elaborate intellectual constructions to make them compatible with rule by a few. This is why some voices are so revealing; they only bared the true beliefs, real intensions. The people cannot be trusted because it can "err": James Madison said it, Simon Bolívar said it, and so did Henry Kissinger. Furthermore, the gravest error they can commit is to use political rights in the quest for social and economic equality, to associate in pursuit of higher wages, decent working conditions, material security, to encroach on "property." Even when the poorer classes could no longer be excluded, a plethora of inventive devices neutralized the effects of their political rights. When most people acquired the right to vote, the relation between voting and electing was protected by various institutional rules as well as by the political muscle of the incumbents. As one speaker observed in the Spanish parliamentary debate about universal suffrage in 1889, "We are going to establish universal suffrage, and then what is going to happen in our national political history? Nothing ... the Congress of Deputies will continue working as it is doing now; the legislative power will be wielded by the Crown with the Cortes; the Crown will have ... all the guarantees and privileges given by the Constitution of 1876" (cited in Garrido 1998: 213).

Clearly, property was not the only divisive issue. Representative institutions emerged in the shadow of religious wars: As Christin (1997) shows, political institutions became autonomous in sixteenth-century Europe as a framework for regulating conflicts over religion. The conflicts between conservatives and liberals in Latin America had more to do with religion than with economic interests. Moreover, power is valued by politicians for its own sake as well as an instrument to promote interests. And the quest for power was relentless. Rulers used every instrument at their disposal – monopolizing political rights, manipulating procedures, outright fraud, blatant partisan use of government prerogatives – to hold on to power. In retrospect it is just amazing how successful they were, how rarely their political opponents could displace the incumbents according to institutional rules.

Several of these institutional features linger today, but both ideological and actual transformations have been profound.

Consensualism – the assumption that people endowed with reason and virtue would arrive at the same conclusion about the common good of all – fell apart in the face of conflicts based on material and cultural divisions. The rise in the second part of the nineteenth century of the socialist movement, with its emphasis on the inevitability of class conflict, threatened the very foundation of societies based on private property. The specter of socialism forced to the forefront of the political agenda the question of how societies could survive in peace in the presence of profound conflicts. It was easy to say "United we stand" but much harder to see how we could still stand divided. Hence, while the nostalgia for consensus still persists among some political philosophers, we came to see democracy as a method for processing conflicts, in a peaceful way and according to rules. It took almost 200 years for partisan alternation in office to become something we take as a natural. Today, however, we know that even if we are ruled by others, we can be ruled by different others in turn if we so wish.

While conflicts became attenuated as societies became wealthier, so that they are generally processed in peace, economic inequality continues to be sufficiently pervasive to belie the fears of some and the hopes of others that economic differences would succumb to popular will. Even in the most equal democratic societies, a fair dose of inequality persists and there are reasons to expect that it will continue to persist. Nevertheless, we no longer see inequality as a fatalistic consequence of economic laws. Indeed, as many public opinion surveys testify, people around the world expect democracy to promote economic and social equality. And, perhaps most radically, we are no longer willing to accept that economic, indeed any kind of social inequality would be institutionalized or transformed in other ways into political inequality.

We now demand that governments do something more than just protect people from one another. While we continue to be wary that governments may abuse their powers, today we see the state as an institution that can promote prosperity, regulate markets, and ensure the economic welfare of all citizens. I am not claiming that we have reached a consensus about the role of the state, but on the historical scale the ideological as well as the real transformations have been enormous. Today, towns of 100,000 around the world employ as many people as the United States government did in 1789. We expect governments to be acting to improve our lives; we judge them by their actions and their effect on our welfare. At the same time, being treated equally by the state has become an enforceable right: Democracy has become, à la Weber, synonymous with equal treatment by bureaucracy.

Liberty assumed an institutional form of entrenched rights, protected by special institutions and procedures. These rights include not only protection of the private realm from intrusions by governments but also the right to oppose elected governments between elections, the freedom of public opinion, the freedom to assemble and to petition. Moreover, we have learned, perhaps I should put it in the present, we are learning, that rights are not enough, that the exercise of rights requires resources, and that state institutions must actively provide these resources if rights are to be effective (Holmes and Sunstein 1999).

It is thus certain that contemporary democracies would not have been recognized by the ideologues of self-government as anything they intended to institute. Why, then, insist that contemporary democracies bear any relation to "self-government of the people"? Why not just say that this particular ideal was abandoned in favor of ideas that recognize the inevitability of partisan divisions, that no longer tolerate political inequality, that place emphasis on governments being able to do something to make our lives better, that entrench political liberty?

It is useful to distinguish two roles of "the people" in the notion of self-government: as the political subject and as the source of the authorization to govern. As the former, the people are divided, atomized. They can be glued together only by being organized by the "intermediate bodies" that were banned by the French Revolution and feared elsewhere. The theoretical reconstitution of the people as the political subject is difficult in the face of the fact that individual people differ in their interests, values, and passions. I have argued that many still do not understand how the people's rule is exercised in systems in which they are ruled by others, who are selected through elections. Many are dismayed at not being offered clear choices; many feel impotent that their political acts have little if any efficacy. They value the democratic mechanism but not their own role in making it function.

Yet even if "the people" is divided along partisan lines as a political subject, it is the only referent in terms of which contemporary democracies are legitimized. The founders everywhere said "No representation without elections" and no democrat today could say anything else. Certainly, invocations of the will of God cannot serve as the source of democratic authorization. Neither can order or rationality, promised by authoritarians of different stripes. There are still some who seek legitimacy in unembodied "justice," but justice and democracy cohere at best uneasily (Shapiro 1999). We are ruled by others, and the only authority that justifies this fact is that the rulers act on bequest of "the people" expressed in elections.

The most banal definition of democracy is one according to which decisions implemented by governments reflect or correspond to what citizens want. This, however, is not a demanding criterion. Under this definition, democracy can be and is claimed by almost all rulers. Almost invariably, rulers assert that they govern at the bequest of and on behalf of "the people." Nevertheless, while this claim today is almost universal, actual forms of political regimes differ significantly across the world. As an exponent of the Russian conception of "sovereign democracy," Mikhail Leontiev, put it (in an interview with a Polish newspaper, *Dziennik*, from January 19, 2008), "The Russian political system – in its essence although not in form – does not differ in anything from real, serious Western democracies." But if the form differs, does the essence not differ as well? Hence the question: What evidence is required to support this claim?

To evaluate such claims, we need to step back to the methodological framework described in the Introduction. All political claims constitute "myths," in the sense of Morgan (1988), or "ideologies," in the sense of Gramsci (1971). They are myths, rather than scientific propositions, because they can be validated by everyday experience rather than by some formalized procedure. Myths, however, must find corroboration in some facts if they are to orient the life of a society, if they are to glue together individual people as "the people" in singular, if they are to enjoy what Gramsci calls "active consent."

What are the facts that can make credible the claim that "the people" rules? Note that some rulers assert their legitimacy without invoking democracy, claiming only that they provide what the people most want, mainly order and prosperity. The successes of Singapore or China are in many eyes sufficient to validate such claims, even when order is maintained by blatant repression. Huntington's (1968: 1) classical statement continues to find widespread echoes today: "The most important political distinction among countries concerns not their form of government but their degree of government. The differences between democracy and dictatorship are less than between those countries whose politics embodies consensus, continuity, legitimacy, organization, effectiveness, stability, and those countries whose politics is deficient in these qualities."

Now, in spite of Lincoln's cherished formula, democracy cannot constitute rule "by" the people. As J. S. Mill (1859) already observed, the "people" cannot rule. It can only be ruled by others. Hence, the only parts of this formula that can be subject to evaluation are "of" and "for." What, then, makes it credible that rulers act at the bequest of and on behalf of the people?

The only answer can be that the people could have thrown the rascals out and did not. Even if counterfactual potentialities are not easy to assess, the "could have" is decisive. Competitive elections – elections in which incumbents face a chance of being voted out of office if the people so decides according to reasonably fair rules and procedures – are the only credible test of the validity of the myth of government of the people. To reiterate Bobbio's (1987) distinction, there is difference between systems in which elites *propose* themselves and those in which they *impose* themselves.

Competitive elections matter because rulers who face the possibility of being removed by means of elections must anticipate this threat when they govern. Authoritarian rulers can also be removed. But revolutions, even when they are garbed in velvet, are painful and chaotic events. Elections are by far the least costly way to remove governments; hence, they constitute more of a check on rulers. True, one should not idealize the role of elections in enforcing accountability. Elections are a blunt instrument. Incumbents can manipulate electoral rules, manage public opinion by influencing the media, throw state resources behind candidates friendly to the government, and so on. Indeed, between 1788 and 2000, incumbents won about 80 percent of the elections in the world. Perhaps they won many of them because they enjoyed genuine popular support, but they must have also won quite a few because they could use the instruments at their disposal to influence their result. Nonetheless, if incumbents are prepared to hold elections that they may lose, then they have to worry about being voted out.

Consider governments that do maintain order and promote prosperity. Their claim to democracy is that they satisfy what people want and their evidence is that people eat and do not revolt. Elections may appear in this perspective as just a frivolous celebration of popular support. Nevertheless, most such regimes do hold "elections," except that they carefully see to it that no one is selected as their result. It bears emphasis that such elections are as old as the system of representative institutions: Only historical ignorance of U.S. political scientists could lead them to the discovery of "electoral authoritarianism" as something novel. But if the people are satisfied, if they get what they want, why would such rulers not brave exposing themselves to real competition, to the possibility of losing? As Ivan Krastev put it (in a review of "Sovereign Democracy" in *Dziennik*, August 28, 2006), "Creating a counterfeit democracy, the falsifier admits that the original is something desirable." If they are afraid to have the real thing, is it because rulers themselves do not believe in their claim?

Competitive elections are the only credible mechanism of making the people believe that their rulers govern at their bequest and on their behalf. They are a device of the skeptic. Elections authenticate the claim that governments govern with active consent because they repeatedly test this claim by counting heads. If governments that do not enjoy such consent can be voted out, the fact that they were not, that they have won a free and fair election, is informative. And it is the only source of credible information.

But when are elections competitive? Answers to this question are not obvious. Even international election observers do not completely agree about the criteria by which they certify elections: Americans like to classify them as "free and fair," while Europeans use the language of "competitive and accurate." The main difficulty is that the test of elections is conclusive only when incumbents lose an election and leave office peacefully. If they win, the evidence is silent; they may have won because the people so desired or because the people had no chance to defeat them. Leontiev (in the interview already cited) plays on this ambiguity: "I do not understand what is undemocratic in that some force enjoying overwhelming social support wins elections." Nevertheless, the use of government power to prevent electoral defeats is often flagrant. While elections must follow rules and rules can be manipulated, manipulation is at times so blatant that the opposition has no chance. Furthermore, fraud is sometimes used by incumbents when manipulation fails. At the very least, it must be true that everyone has an equal chance of expressing their partisan preference, regardless of what this preference is, and that the final outcome of the election would not have been different under different rules. This is what "free and fair" means.

The force of elections in perpetuating the myth of self-government, in rendering vitality to democracy, is nothing short of astonishing. Just a small possibility that the government may change as a result of an election is sufficient to kindle hopes. Elections are the siren of democracy: Whatever the past, regardless of how disgusted or jaded people are with politics, elections invariably renew hope. And perhaps for a good reason: Who would have ever thought that a country that elected and reelected Bush and Cheney could elect Obama? In the end, the mere possibility that a government may change one day as a result of the people's vote seems sufficient to render plausible all the myths about equality, accountability, representation, and the like.

This is why, in spite of all the ideological and real transformations, I see contemporary democracies as an implementation of the ideal of self-government of the people.

What I think has happened over the past 200 years is that we have made this ideal more coherent and more honest. We understood that some conflicts cannot be avoided and we learned that they are best organized by political parties. We called the founders' bluff about political equality. We learned that we are better off when governments are equipped to act to promote our welfare. We learned that liberty is best protected when it is formulated in terms of specific rights and that the exercise of these rights requires specific conditions.

In large parts of the globe we now have universal suffrage, parties that appeal to the poor and to women, reasonably competitive elections, reasonably effective institutions, attention to basic rights, and a fair degree of political freedom. The progress is evident. We are closer to the realization of these ideals than we have been in the past. Have we finally arrived, then, at self-government, equality, and liberty? The answer, I fear, is still not simple.

I have argued throughout this book that democracy has limits, that no political institutions of any form or fashion can reach, at least simultaneously, all the values we may cherish. In market economies there are purely technical, perhaps inexorable, limits to economic equality. Moreover, if the priority is to reduce poverty, economic growth may be a more effective instrument than redistribution of consumption. Nevertheless, many existing democracies are far from what is possible and in quite a few the extent of economic inequality is appalling. The fact that other forms of political arrangements fail in reducing inequality does not exonerate democracies. The fact that those endowed with disproportionate economic, ideological, and organizational resources use them successfully to defend their privileges does not render futile the struggle for economic and social equality. At the very least, we can actively combat the influence of money over politics, to equalize access to politics. The only limits to economic and social equality that are acceptable today are those that result from the fact that democracies function, and will continue to function, in market economies, not those that reflect political inequality.

I am skeptical about the attempts to enlarge the scope of political participation. Even if electoral participation is not quite equal, in the end elections are the most egalitarian political mechanism we have and can have. Too often the calls for increased participation privilege those who have more resources to participate. Participation just cannot be equal and effective. The Tocquevillian vision of associated, active citizens is obviously attractive, but the claim that participation is more effective in smaller communities hurls itself against the puzzle that turnout in local elections is everywhere lower than in national ones. What we can do is to enhance our efforts to keep elections free and fair.

I have no doubt that governments have a major role to play in enhancing general welfare by promoting development, equalizing opportunities to earn incomes, and protecting those whose incomes are insufficient. The architects of representative institutions were too skeptical about motives of the rulers and too eager to protect vested interests. Obviously, governments can act in their own interest or those of their cronies. They can also simply blunder. But with a proper institutional design, governments can be made simultaneously more effective and more accountable: We can increase their authority and the transparency of their actions simultaneously (Ferejohn 1999).

I have sympathy for the position according to which fundamental rights should be monitored by specialized bodies, but in the end the laws and public policies must be decided by majoritarian procedures. This issue has been warped by an ideological formulation that juxtaposes rule of the majority to "the rule of law," as if the law could be something independent of the will of the majority structured within the institutional framework. Yet there is no evidence that institutional systems that give more power to majorities are more abusive or capricious than those that impede governments from acting by checks and balances.

In the end, although some limits may be generic, each democracy suffers from its own deficiencies. Many countries suffer simply from poverty. Some – Brazil comes immediately to mind – exhibit intolerable economic inequality. In many, politics is dominated by money: Barring the access of money to political influence would be perhaps the most consequential reform in several countries. In other democracies – I am now thinking about Argentina as well as France – the party system and the institutional framework repeatedly fail to absorb social conflicts and to process them according to institutional rules. In some democracies – Sweden is often mentioned as a case – the administrative state penetrates too deeply into private lives. Indeed, some facts are still as shocking as they are puzzling. How is it possible that a country that has had representative institutions for more than 200 years would have the highest degree of economic inequality among the developed nations and the highest proportion in the world of people languishing in jails, higher than most repressive autocracies? How is it possible that almost one-half of the electorate in this country does not vote even once in four years? How is it possible that the people in this country tolerate the flagrant influence of money over politics?

One could go on, but I do not pretend to have accurately diagnosed the deficiencies particular to each democracy. All I want to emphasize is that recognizing that there are limits is not a call for complacency. We should be aware of the limits because otherwise we become prey to demagogical appeals, which more often than not mask a quest for political power by promises that cannot be fulfilled by anyone anywhere. We should recognize that the fact that things can be improved does not always mean that they would be. But some reforms are urgent and many reforms are feasible.

References

Aberdam, Serge et al. 2006. *Voter, élire pendant la Révolution française 1789–1799.* Paris: Éditions du CTHS.

Achen, Christopher, and Larry Bartels. 2002. "Blind retrospection: Electoral responses to drought, flu, and shark attacks." Paper presented at the Annual Meeting of the American Political Science Association, Boston, August 29–September 1.

Aguilar Rivera, José Antonio. 1998. "Oposición y separación de poderes. La estructura institucional del conflicto 1867–1872." *Metapolitica* 2: 69–92.

Aguilar Rivera, José Antonio. 1999. *Cartas Mexicanas de Alexis de Tocqueville.* Mexico City: Ediciones Cal y Arena.

Aguilar Rivera, José Antonio. 2000. *En pos de la quimera. Reflexiones sobre el experimento constitucional atlántico.* Mexico City: CIDE.

Aguilar Rivera, José Antonio. 2009. "Manuel Lorenzo de Vidaurre: la imaginación política y la república incierta." Mexico City: CIDE.

Alamán, Lucas. 2008 [1832]. *Examen imparcial de la administración de Bustamante.* Edited by José Antonio Aguilar Rivera. Mexico City: Conaculta.

Alaminos, Antonio. 1991. "Chile: transición politica y sociedad." Madrid: Centro de Investigaciones Sociologicas.

Alesina, Alberto. 1988. "Credibility and convergence in a two-party system with rational voters." *American Economic Review* 78: 796–805.

Alonso, Paula. 2000. *Between Revolution and the Ballot Box: The Origins of the Argentine Radical Party.* Cambridge: Cambridge University Press.

Alvarez, Michael E., and Leiv Marsteintredet. 2007. "Presidential interruptions and democratic breakdown in Latin America: Similar causes, different outcomes." Paper presented at GIGA, Hamburg, December 13–14.

Anderson, Perry. 1977. "The Antinomies of Antonio Gramsci." *New Left Review* 100: 5–78.

Anduiza Perea, Eva. 1999. *Individuos o sistemas? La razones de la abstención en Europa Occidental.* Madrid: CIS.

Annino, Antonio. 1995. "Introducción." In Antonio Annino (ed.), *Historia de las elecciones en Iberoamérica, siglo XIX.* Mexico City: Fondo de Cultura Económica.

Annino, Antonio. 1998. "Vote et décalage de la citoyenneté dans les pays andins et meso-americains." In Raffaele Romanelli (ed.), *How Did They Become Voters? The History of Franchise in Modern European Representation* (pp. 155–82). The Hague: Kluwer.

Arrow, Kenneth A. 1951. *Social Choice and Individual Values.* New Haven: Yale University Press.

Austen-Smith, David. 2000. "Redistributing income under proportional representation." *Journal of Political Economy 108:* 1235–69.

Austen-Smith, David, and Jeffrey Banks. 1988. "Elections, coalitions, and legislative outcomes." *American Political Science Review 82:* 405–22.

Austen-Smith, David, and Jeffrey Banks. 2000. *Positive Political Theory I: Collective Preference.* Ann Arbor: University of Michigan Press.

Bagehot, Walter. 1963 [1867]. *The English Constitution.* Ithaca, NY: Cornell University Press.

Bahamonde, Ángel, and Jesús A. Martinez. 1998. *Historia de España Siglo XIX.* Madrid: Catedra.

Ball, Terence. 1989. "Party." In Terence Ball, James Farr, and Russel L. Hanson (eds.), *Political Innovation and Conceptual Change* (pp. 155–76). Cambridge: Cambridge University Press.

Banerjee, Abhijit, and Esther Dufflo. 2003. "Inequality and growth: What can the data say?" *Journal of Economic Growth 8:* 267–99.

Banks, Arthur S. 1996. Cross-National Time-Series Data Archive. See http://www.databanks.sitehosting.net

Barber, Benjamin R. 2004. *Strong Democracy: Participatory Politics for a New Age.* Berkeley: University of California Press.

Barbera, Salomon, Walter Bossert, and Prasanta K. Pattanaik. 2001. *Ranking Sets of Objects.* Montreal: Cahier University of Montreal, Centre de recherche et développement en économique.

Bardach, Juliusz, Bogusław Leśnodorski, and Michal Pietrzak. 2005. *Historia Ustroju i Prawa Polskiego.* Warszawa: LexisNexis.

Barros, Robert. 2002. *Constitutionalism and Dictatorship.* New York: Cambridge University Press.

Bartels, Larry M. 2008. *Unequal Democracy: The Political Economy of the New Gilded Age.* New York: Russell Sage Foundation.

Becker, Gary S. 1983. "A theory of competition among interest groups for political influence." *Quarterly Journal of Economics 98:* 371–400.

Beitz, Charles R. 1989. *Political Equality.* Princeton: Princeton University Press.

Benabou, Roland. 1996. "Inequality and growth." In Ben S. Bernanke and Julio J. Rotemberg (eds.), *NBER Macro-Economics Annual 1996* (Vol. 11, pp. 11–92). Cambridge, MA: MIT Press.

Bénabou, Roland. 2000. "Unequal societies: Income distribution and the social contract." *American Economic Review 90:* 96–129.

Benabou, Roland, and Efe A. Ok. 2001. "Social mobility and the demand for redistribution: The PUOM hypothesis." *Quarterly Journal of Economics 116:* 447–87.

Benhabib, Jess, and Adam Przeworski. 2006. "The political economy of redistribution under democracy." *Economic Theory* 29: 271–90.

Benhabib, Jess, and Alberto Bisin. 2007. "The distribution of wealth: Intergenerational transmission and redistribute policies." Working paper, Department of Economics, New York University.

Beramendi, Pablo, and Christopher J. Anderson (eds.). 2008. *Democracy, Inequality, and Representation*. New York: Russell Sage Foundation.

Berlin, Isaiah. 2002 [1958]. *Liberty*. Edited by Henry Hardy. Oxford: Oxford University Press.

Bernstein, Eduard. 1961. *Evolutionary Socialism*. New York: Schocken Books.

Beza, Theodore. 1969 [1574]. *Concerning the Rights of Rulers over Their Subjects and the Duty of Subjects Toward Their Rulers*. New York: Pegasus Books.

Bird, Colin. 2000. "The possibility of self-government." *American Political Science Review* 94: 563–77.

Black, Duncan. 1958. *The Theory of Committees and Elections*. Cambridge: Cambridge University Press.

Bobbio, Norberto. 1987. *Democracy and Dictatorship*. Minneapolis: University of Minnesota Press.

Bobbio, Norberto. 1989. *The Future of Democracy*. Minneapolis: University of Minnesota Press.

Bolingbroke, Henry Saint-John Viscount. 2002 [1738]. "The patriot king and parties." In Susan E. Scarrow (ed.), *Perspectives in Political Parties* (pp. 29–32). New York: Palgrave Macmillan.

Bolívar, Simon. 1969. *Escritos politicos*. Edited by Graciela Soriano. Madrid: Alianza Editorial.

Booth, John A., and Mitchell A. Seligson. 2008. "Inequality and democracy in Latin America: Individual and contextual effects of wealth on political participation." In Anirudh Krishna (ed.), *Poverty, Participation, and Democracy: A Global Perspective* (pp. 94–124). Cambridge: Cambridge University Press.

Brandolini, Andrea, and Timothy M. Smeeding. 2008. "Inequality patterns in western democracies: Cross-country differences and changes over time." In Pablo Beramendi and Christopher J. Anderson. (eds.), *Democracy, Inequality, and Representation* (pp. 25–61). New York: Russell Sage Foundation.

Bratton, Michael. 2008. "Poor people and democratic citizenship in Africa." In Anirudh Krishna (ed.), *Poverty, Participation, and Democracy: A Global Perspective* (pp. 28–64). Cambridge: Cambridge University Press.

Bravo, María Cecilia. 2003. "La política 'armada' en el norte argentino: El proceso de renovación de la elite política tucumana (1852–1862)." In Hilda Sabato and Alberto Littieri (eds.), *La vida política en la Argentina del siglo XIX: Armas, votos y voces* (pp. 243–58). Buenos Aires: Fondo de Cultura Económica.

Bryan, Shari, and Denise Baer (eds.). 2005. *Money in Politics: A Study of Party Financing Practices in 22 Countries*. Washington, DC: National Democratic Institute for International Affairs.

Bruszt, László, and János Simon. 1991. "Political culture, political and economical orientations in Central and Eastern Europe during the transition to democracy." Manuscript. Budapest: Erasmus Foundation for Democracy.

Bryce, James. 1921. *Modern Democracies*. London: Macmillan.

Buchanan, James M., and Gordon Tullock. 1962. *The Calculus of Consent: Logical Foundations of Constitutional Democracy.* Ann Arbor: University of Michigan Press.

Burda, Andrzej. 1990. "Charakterystyka postanowień konstytucji PRL z 1952r." In *Konstytucje Polski: Studja monograficzne z dziejów polskiego konstytucjonalizmu* (Vol. 2, pp. 344–76). Warszawa: Państwowe Wydawnictwo Naukowe.

Burke, Edmund. 2002 [1770]. "Thoughts on the cause of the present discontents." In Susan E. Scarrow (ed.), *Perspectives in Political Parties* (pp. 37–44). New York: Palgrave Macmillan.

Burke, Edmund. 1774. Speech to the Electors of Bristol. See http://oll.libertyfund.org

Burke, Edmund. 1790. Reflections on the Revolution in France. See http://oll.libertyfund.org

Canedo, Leticia Bicalho. 1998. "Les listes électorales el le processus de nationalisation de la cityoennetè au Brésil (1822–1945)." In Raffaele Romanelli (ed.), *How Did They Become Voters? The History of Franchise in Modern European Representation* (pp. 183–206). The Hague: Kluwer.

Caramani, Daniele. 2003. "The end of silent elections: The birth of electoral competition, 1832–1915." *Party Politics* 9: 411–44.

Carvajal, Patricio A. 1992. "Derecho de resistencia, derecho a la revolución, desobedencia civil." *Revista de Estudios Politicos (Nueva Epoca)* 76: 63–101.

Cheibub, José Antonio. 2007. *Presidentialism, Parliamentarism, and Democracy.* New York: Cambridge University Press.

Cheibub, José Antonio, and Adam Przeworski. 1999. "Democracy, elections, and accountability for economic outcomes." In Adam Przeworski, Susan C. Stokes, and Bernard Manin (eds.), *Democracy, Accountability, and Representation* (pp. 222–50). New York: Cambridge University Press.

Christin, Olivier. 1997. *La paix de religion.* Paris: Éditions du Seuil.

Clogg, Richard. 1992. *A Concise History of Greece.* Cambridge: Cambridge University Press.

Cohen, Joshua. 1989. "The economic basis of deliberative democracy." *Social Philosophy & Policy* 6: 25–50.

Cohn-Bendit, Daniel, and Gabriel Cohn-Bendit. 1968. *Obsolete Communism: The Left-Wing Alternative.* New York: McGraw-Hill.

Collier, Simon, and William F. Sater. 1996. *A History of Chile, 1808–1994.* Cambridge: Cambridge University Press.

Collini, Stefan, Donald Winch, and John Burrow. 1983. *That Noble Science of Politics.* Cambridge: Cambridge University Press.

Condorcet. 1986 [1785]. "Essai sur l'application de l'analyse a la probabilité des décisions rendues a la pluralité des voix." In *Sur les élections et autres textes. Textes choisis et revus par Olivier de Bernon* (pp. 9–176). Paris: Fayard.

Condorcet, Marguis de. 1986 [1787]. "Lettres d'un bourgeois de New Heaven a un citoyen de Virginie, sur l'inutilité de partager le pouvoir législatif en plusieurs corps." In *Sur les élections et autres textes. Textes choisis et revus par Olivier de Bernon* (pp. 203–72). Paris: Fayard.

Constant, Benjamin. 1997 [1815]. "Principes de politique." In *Écrits politiques. Textes choisis, présentés et annotés par Marcel Gauchet* (pp. 305–588). Paris: Gallimard.

Constant, Benjamin. 1997 [1819]. "De la liberté des anciens comparée à celle des modernes." In *Écrits politiques. Textes choisis, présentés et annotés par Marcel Gauchet* (pp. 589–622). Paris: Gallimard.

Cox, Gary W. 1999. "Electoral rules and the calculus of mobilization." *Legislative Studies Quarterly* 24: 387–419.

Crook, Malcolm. 2002. *Elections in the French Revolution.* Cambridge: Cambridge University Press.

Cuttrone, Michael, and Nolan McCarthy. 2006. "Does bicameralism matter?" In Barry R. Weingast and Donald A. Wittman (eds.), *Oxford Handbook of Political Economy* (pp. 180–95). Oxford: Oxford University Press.

Dahl, Robert A. 1956. *A Preface to Democratic Theory.* New Haven: Yale University Press.

Dahl, Robert A. (ed.) 1966. "Introduction." In *Regimes and Oppositions.* New Haven: Yale University Press.

Dahl, Robert A. 1971. *Polyarchy: Participation and Opposition.* New Haven: Yale University Press.

Dahl, Robert A. 1989. *Democracy and Its Critics.* New Haven: Yale University Press.

Dahl, Robert A. 2002. *How Democratic is the American Constitution?* New Haven: Yale University Press.

Dardé, Carlos, and Manuel Estrada. 1998. "Social and territorial representation in Spanish electoral systems." In Raffaele Romanelli (ed.), *How Did They Become Voters? The History of Franchise in Modern European Representation* (pp. 133–54). The Hague: Kluwer.

Deininger, Klaus, and Lyn Squire. 1996. "A new data set measuring income inequality." *World Bank Economic Review* 10: 565–91.

De Luca, Miguel. 1998. "Los ejecutivos." In Hipólito Orlandi (ed.), *Las Institutciones Políticas de Gobierno* (Vol. I, pp. 89–132). Buenos Aires: Editorial Universitaria.

Derathé, Robert. 1964. "Introduction." In Jean-Jacques Rousseau, *Du contrat social.* Paris: Gallimard.

Descombes, Vincent. 2004. *Le Complément De Sujet: Enquête sur le fait d'agir de soi-même.* Paris: Gallimard.

Diniz, Hinemburgo Pereira. 1984. *A Monarquia Presidential.* Rio de Janeiro: Editora Nova Frontera.

Dixit, Avinash, Gene M. Grossman, and Faruk Gul. 2000. "The dynamics of political compromise." *Journal of Political Economy* 108: 531–68.

Downs, Anthony. 1957. *An Economic Theory of Democracy.* New York: Harper & Row.

Dunn, John (ed.). 1993. *Democracy: The Unfinished Journey, 508 BC to AD 1993.* Oxford: Oxford University Press.

Dunn, John. 1999. "Situating democratic political accountability." In Adam Przeworski, Susan C. Stokes, and Bernard Manin (eds.), *Democracy, Accountability, and Representation* (pp. 329–44). New York: Cambridge University Press.

Dunn, John. 2000. *The Cunning of Unreason.* Cambridge: Cambridge University Press.

Dunn, John. 2003. "Democracy before the age of the democratic revolution." Paper delivered at Columbia University.

Dunn, John. 2005. *Democracy: A History.* New York: Atlantic Monthly Press.

Dunn, Susan. 2004. *Jefferson's Second Revolution: The Election Crisis of 1800 and the Triumph of Republicanism.* Boston: Houghton Mifflin.

Dworkin, Ronald. 1986. *Law's Empire.* Cambridge, MA: Belknap Press.

Easton, David. 1953. *The Political System: An Inquiry into the State of Political Science.* New York: Knopf.

Elster, Jon. 1985. *Ulysses and the Sirens: Studies in Rationality and Irrationality.* New York: Cambridge University Press.

Ensor, R. C. K. 1908. *Modern Socialism as Set Forth by the Socialists in Their Speeches, Writings, and Programmes.* New York: Scribner's.

Estlund, David, Jeremy Waldron, Bernard Grofman, and Scott Feld. 1989. "Democratic theory and the public interest: Condorcet and Rousseau revisited." *American Political Science Review 83:* 1317–40.

Fearon, James. 2006. "Self-enforcing democracy." Working Paper No. 14, Institute of Governmental Studies, University of California, Berkeley.

Ferejohn, John. 1986. "Incumbent performance and electoral control." *Public Choice 50:* 75–93.

Ferejohn, John. 1995. "Must preferences be respected in a democracy?" In David Coop, Jean Hampton, and John E. Roemer (eds.), *The Idea of Democracy* (pp. 231–44). Cambridge: Cambridge University Press.

Ferejohn, John. 1999. "Accountability and authority: Toward a theory of political accountability." In Adam Przeworski, Susan C. Stokes, and Bernard Manin (eds.), *Democracy, Accountability, and Representation* (pp. 131–53). New York: Cambridge University Press.

Ferejohn, John, and Pasquale Pasquino. 2003. "Rule of democracy and rule of law." In José María Maravall and Adam Przeworski (eds.), *Democracy and the Rule of Law* (pp. 242–60). New York: Cambridge University Press.

Fernández Garcia, Antonio. 2002. "Introducción." In *La Constitución de Cádiz* (pp. 9–68). Madrid: Clasicos Castalia.

Finer, Herman. 1934. *The Theory and Practice of Modern Government.* New York: Dial Press.

Fontana, Biancamaria. 1993. "Democracy and the French Revolution." In John Dunn (ed.), *Democracy: The Unfinished Journey, 508 BC to AD 1993* (pp. 107–24). Oxford: Oxford University Press.

Frank, Thomas. 2004. *What's the Matter with Kansas? How Conservatives Won the Heart of America.* New York: Henry Holt.

Franklin, Julian H. (ed.). 1969. *Constitutionalism and Resistance in the Sixteenth Century. Three Treatises by Hotman, Beza, & Mornay.* New York: Pegasus Books.

Friedmann, T. 2001. *The Lexus and the Olive Tree: Understanding Globalization.* New York: Anchor Books.

Fromm, Erich. 1994 [1941]. *Escape from Freedom.* New York: Henry Holt.

Fuller, Lon. 1964. *The Morality of Law.* New Haven: Yale University Press.

Gallego, Jorge. 2009. "Self-enforcing clientilism." Manuscript. Department of Politics, New York University.

Gandhi, Jennifer. 2008. *Dictatorial Institutions*. New York: Cambridge University Press.

Gandhi, Jennifer, and Adam Przeworski. 2006. "Cooperation, cooptation, and rebellion under dictatorships." *Economics and Politics 18*: 1–26.

Gargarella, Roberto. 2005. *Los fundamentos legales de la desigualdad: El constitucionalismo en América (1776–1860)*. Madrid: Siglo XXI.

Garrido, Aurora. 1998. "Electors and electoral districts in Spain, 1874–1936." In Raffaele Romanelli (ed.), *How Did They Become Voters? The History of Franchise in Modern European Representation* (pp. 207–26). The Hague: Kluwer.

Goodrich, Melanie, and Jonathan Nagler. 2006. "A good model of turnout and a cross-national empirical analysis." Manuscript. Department of Politics, New York University.

Graham, Richard. 2003. "Ciudadanía y jerarquía en el Brasil esclavista." In Hilda Sabato (ed.), *Ciudadanía política y formación de las naciones: Perspectivas históricas de América Latina* (pp. 345–70). Mexico City: El Colegio de Mexico.

Gramsci, Antonio. 1971. *Prison Notebooks*. Edited by Quintin Hoare and Geoffrey Nowell Smith. New York: International Publishers.

Graubard, Stephen R. 2003. "Democracy." In *The Dictionary of the History of Ideas*. University of Virginia Library: The Electronic Text Center. See http://etext.lib.virginia.edu/cgi-local/DHI/dhi.cgi?id=dv1-78

Grofman, Bernard, and Scott Feld. 1989. "Rousseau's general will: A Condorcetian perspective." *American Political Science Review 82*: 567–76.

Grossman, Gene M., and Elhanan Helpman. 2001. *Special Interest Politics*. Cambridge, MA: MIT Press.

Goodin, Robert E. 2001. "Review of liberalism, constitutionalism, and democracy by Russell Hardin." *Journal of Philosophy 98*: 374–8.

Guarnieri, Carlo. 2003. "Courts as an instrument of horizontal accountability." In José María Maravall and Adam Przeworski (eds.), *Democracy and the Rule of Law* (pp. 223–41). New York: Cambridge University Press.

Guerra, François-Xavier. 2003. "El soberano y su reino: Reflexiones sobre la génesis del ciudadano en América Latina." In Hilda Sabato (ed.), *Ciudadanía política y formación de las naciones: Perspectivas históricas de América Latina* (pp. 33–61). Mexico City: El Colegio de Mexico.

Guha, Ramachandra. 2008. *India after Ghandi: The History of the World's Largest Democracy*. New York: HarperCollins.

Gutiérrez Sanin, Francisco. 2003. "La literatura plebeya y el debate alrededor de la propriedad (Nueva Granada, 1849–1854)." In Hilda Sabato (ed.), *Ciudadanía política y formación de las naciones: Perspectivas históricas de América Latina* (pp. 181–201). Mexico City: El Colegio de Mexico.

Halbac, Claudia. 2008. *Democracy and the Protection of Private Property*. PhD Dissertation, Department of Politics, New York University.

Halperin-Donghi, Tulio. 1973. *The Aftermath of Revolution in Latin America*. New York: Harper & Row.

Hanham, Harold J. 1990. "Government, parties and the electorate in England; a commentary to 1900." In Serge Noiret (ed.), *Political Strategies and Electoral Reforms: Origins of Voting Systems in Europe in the 19th and 20th Centuries* (pp. 118–26). Baden-Baden: Nomos Verlagsgesellschaft.

Hansen, Mogens Herman. 1991. *The Athenian Democracy in the Age of Demosthenes.* Oxford: Blackwell.

Hansen, Mogens Herman. 2005. *The Tradition of Ancient Democracy and Its Importance for Modern Democracy.* Copenhagen: Royal Danish Academy of Arts and Letters.

Hanson, Russell L. 1985. *The Democratic Imagination in America.* Princeton: Princeton University Press.

Hanson, Russell L. 1989. "Democracy." In Terence Ball, James Farr, and Russell L. Hanson (eds.), *Political Innovation and Conceptual Change* (pp. 68–89). Cambridge: Cambridge University Press.

Hardin, Russell. 1989. "Why a constitution?" In Bernard Grofman and Donald Wittman (eds.), *The Federalist Papers and the New Institutionalism* (pp. 100–20). New York: Agathon Press.

Hardin, Russell. 1999. *Liberalism, Constitutionalism, and Democracy.* Oxford: Oxford University Press.

Harding, Robin. 2009. "Freedom to choose and democracy: Addressing the empirical question." Manuscript. Department of Politics, New York University.

Haring, C. H. 1947. *The Spanish Empire in America.* New York: Harcourt, Brace & World.

Harrington, James. 1977. *The Political Works of James Harrington.* Edited by J. G. A. Pocock. Cambridge: Cambridge University Press.

Heinberg, John Gilbert. 1926. "History of the majority principle." *American Political Science Review* 20: 52–68.

Heinberg, John Gilbert. 1932. "Theories of majority rule." *American Political Science Review* 26: 452–69.

Hochstetler, Kathryn. 2006. "Rethinking presidentialism: Challenges and presidential falls in South America." *Comparative Politics* 38: 401–18.

Hofstadter, Richard. 1969. *The Idea of a Party System: The Rise of Legitimate Opposition in the United States, 1780–1840.* Berkeley: University of California Press.

Holmes, Stephen. 1988. "Precommitment and the paradox of democracy." In Jon Elster and Rune Slagstad (eds.), *Constitutionalism and Democracy* (pp. 195–240). Cambridge: Cambridge University Press.

Holmes, Stephen. 1995. *Passions and Constraints: On the Liberal Theory of Democracy.* Chicago: University of Chicago Press.

Holmes, Stephen, 2003. "Lineages of the rule of law." In José María Maravall and Adam Przeworski (eds.), *Democracy and the Rule of Law* (pp. 19–61). New York: Cambridge University Press.

Holmes, Stephen. 2007. *The Matador's Cape: America's Reckless Response to Terror.* Cambridge: Cambridge University Press.

Holmes, Stephen, and Cass R. Sunstein. 1999. *The Cost of Rights.* New York: Norton.

Hume, David. 2002 [1742]. "Of parties in general." In Susan E. Scarrow (ed.), *Perspectives on Political Parties* (pp. 33–6). New York: Palgrave Macmillan.

Huntington, Samuel P. 1968. *Political Order in Changing Societies*. New Haven: Yale University Press.

Iaryczower, Matias, Gabriel Katz, and Sebastian Saiegh. 2009. "The not-so-popular branch: Bicameralism as a counter-majoritarian device." Working paper, California Institutute of Technology and UCSD.

Jaures, Jean. 1971. *L'Esprit de socialisme*. Paris: Denoel.

Jędruch, Jacek. 1982. *Constitutions, Elections and Legislatures of Poland, 1493–1993*. New York: EU Books.

Jespersen, Knud J. V. 2004. *A History of Denmark*. New York: Palgrave Macmillan.

Johnson, Helen Kendrick. 1913. *Woman and the Republic*. See http://womans history.about.com

Kant, Immanuel. 1891 [1793]. "The principles of political right." In W. Hardie (ed. and trans.), *Kant's Principles of Politics*. Edinburgh: T & T Clark.

Kelsen, Hans. 1988 [1929]. *La Démocratie. Sa Nature-Sa Valeur*. Paris: Economica.

Kelsen, Hans. 1949. *General Theory of Law and State*. Cambridge, MA: Harvard University Press.

Ketcham, Ralph (ed.). 1986. *The Anti-Federalist Papers and the Constitutional Convention Debates*. New York: Mentor Books.

Kiewet, D. R., and Matthew McCubbins. 1988. "Presidential influence on congressional appropriation decisions." *American Journal of Political Science* 32: 713–36.

Klinghoffer, Judith Apter, and Lois Elkis. 1992. "'The petticoat electors': Women's suffrage in New Jersey, 1776–1807." *Journal of the Early Republic* 12: 159–93.

Konopczynski, Władysław. 1918. *Liberum veto: studyum porównawczo-historyczne*. Kraków: A. S. Krzyżanowski.

Konopnicki, Guy. 1979. *Vive le centenaire du P.C.F.* Paris: CERF.

Kowecki, Jerzy. 1991. *Konstytucja 3 Maja 1791*. Warszawa: Państwowc Wydawnictwo Naukowe.

Krishna, Anirudh. 2006. "Do poor people care less for democracy? Testing individual-level assumptions with individual-level data from India." In Anirudh Krishna (ed.), *Poverty, Participation, and Democracy: A Global Perspective* (pp. 65–93). Cambridge: Cambridge University Press.

Krukowski, Stanisław. 1990. "Mala Konstytucja z 1919 r." In *Konstytucje Polski: Studja monograficzne z dziejów polskiego konstytucjonalizmu* (Vol. 2, pp. 7–18). Warszawa: Państwowe Wydawnictwo Naukowe.

Laffont, Jean-Jacques, and Jean Tirole. 1994. *A Theory of Incentives in Procurement and Regulation*. Cambridge, MA: MIT Press.

Lakoff, Sanford. 1996. *Democracy: History, Theory, Practice*. Boulder, CO: Westview Press.

Laslett, Peter. 1988. "Introduction." In *Locke: Two Treaties of Government*. Cambridge: Cambridge University Press.

Latinobarómetro. 2002. *Informe de Prensa*. See www.latinobarómetro.org.

Lavaux, Philippe. 1998. *Les grands démocraties contemporaines* (2nd ed.). Paris: PUF.

Lechner, Norbert. 1977. *La crisis del Estado en América Latina*. Caracas: El Cid.

Lechner, Norbert. 1986. *La conflictive y nunca acabada construcción del orden deseado*. Madrid: CIS.

Lehoucq, Fabrice. 2003. "Electoral fraud: Causes, types, and consequences." *Annual Review of Political Science 6*: 233–56.

Lenin, V. I. 1959 [1919]. "Letter to the workers of Europe and America." In *Against Revisionism* (pp. 479–86). Moscow: Foreign Languages Publishing House.

Levmore, Saul. 1992. "Bicameralism: When are two decisions better than one?" *International Review of Law and Economics 12*: 145–62.

Li, Hongyi, Lyn Squire, and Heng-fu Zou. 1997. "Explaining international and inter-temporal variations in income inequality." *The Economic Journal 108*: 1–18.

Lin, Jeffrey, and Justin Nugent. 1995. "Institutions and economic development." In *Handbook of Development Economics* (Vol. 3A). New York: Elsevier.

Lindbeck, Assar, and Jurgen Weibull. 1987. "Balanced-budget redistribution as the outcome of political competition." *Public Choice 52*: 273–97.

Lindblom, Charles. 1977. *Politics and Markets*. New York: Basic Books.

Linz, Juan J. 2004. "L'effondrement de la démocratie. Autoritarisme et totalitarianisme dans l'Europe de l'entre-deux-guerres." *Revue Internationale de Politique Comparée 11*: 531–86.

Lippmann, Walter. 1956. *The Public Philosophy*. New York: Mentor Books.

Locke, John. 1988 [1689–90]. *Two Treaties of Government*. Cambridge: Cambridge University Press.

Londregan, John, and Andrea Vindigni. 2006. "Voting as a credible threat." Working paper, Department of Politics, Princeton University.

López-Alves, Fernando. 2000. *State Formation and Democracy in Latin America, 1810–1900*. Durham, NC: Duke University Press.

Loveman, Brian. 1993. *The Constitution of Tyranny: Regimes of Exception in Spanish America*. Pittsburgh, PA: University of Pittsburgh Press.

McGann, Anthony. 2006. *The Logic of Democracy: Reconciling Equality, Deliberation, and Minority Protection*. Ann Arbor: University of Michigan Press.

McIlwain, Charles H. 1939. *Constitutionalism: Ancient and Modern*. Cornell: Cornell University Press.

McKelvey, Richard D. 1976. "Intransitivities in multidimensional voting models and some implications for agenda control." *Journal of Economic Theory 12*: 472–82.

Macaulay, Thomas B. 1900. *Complete Writings* (Vol. 17). Boston: Houghton Mifflin.

Maddox, Graham. 1989. "Constitution." In Terence Ball, James Farr, and Russell L. Hanson (eds.), *Political Innovation and Conceptual Change* (pp. 50–67). Cambridge: Cambridge University Press.

Madison, James. 1982 [1788]. *The Federalist Papers by Alexander Hamilton, James Madison and John Jay*. Edited by Gary Wills. New York: Bantam Books.

Magaloni, Beatriz. 2007. "Elections under autocracy and the strategic game of fraud." Paper presented at the Annual Meeting of the American Political Science Association, Chicago, August 30–September 2.

Maier, Charles. 1975. *Recasting Bourgeois Europe*. Princeton: Princeton University Press.

Manela, Erez. 2007. *The Wilsonian Moment: Self-Determination and the International Origins of Anticolonial Nationalism*. Oxford: Oxford University Press.

Manin, Bernard. 1994. "Checks, balances, and boundaries: The separation of powers in the constitutional debate of 1787." In Biancamaria Fontana (ed.), *The Invention of the Modern Republic* (pp. 27–62). Cambridge: Cambridge University Press.

Manin, Bernard. 1997. *The Principles of Representative Government*. Cambridge: Cambridge University Press.

Maravall, José María, and Adam Przeworski (eds.). 2003. *Democracy and the Rule of Law*. New York: Cambridge University Press.

Marcuse, Herbert. 1962. *Eros and Civilization*. New York: Vintage Books.

Marcuse, Herbert. 1971. *Soviet Marxism: A Critical Analysis*. London: Penguin Books.

Markoff, John. 1999. "Where and when was democracy invented?" *Comparative Studies in Society and History* 41: 660–90.

Marx, Karl. 1844. *On the Jewish Question*. See http://csf.colorado.edu/psn/marx/Archive/1844-JQ

Marx, Karl. 1952 [1851]. *Class Struggles in France, 1848 to 1850*. Moscow: Progess Publishers.

Marx, Karl. 1934 [1852]. *The Eighteenth Brumaire of Louis Bonaparte*. Moscow: Progress Publishers.

Marx, Karl. 1971. *Writings on the Paris Commune*. Edited by H. Draper. New York: International Publishers.

May, Kenneth O. 1952. "A set of independent necessary and sufficient conditions for simple majority decision." *Econometrica* 20: 680–4.

May, Kenneth O. 1953. "A note on the complete independence of the conditions for simple majority decision." *Econometrica* 21: 172–3.

Maza Valenzuela, Erika. 1995. "Catolicismo, anticlericalismo y la extensión del sufragio a la mujer en Chile." *Estudios Politicos* 58: 137–97.

Meltzer, Allan G. and Scott F. Richards. 1981. "A rational theory of the size of government." *Journal of Political Economy* 89: 914–27.

Metcalf, Michael F. 1977. "The first 'modern' party system?" *Scandinavian Journal of History* 2: 265–87.

Michels, Roberto. 1962. *Political Parties: A Sociological Study of the Oligarchical Tendencies of Modern Democracies*. New York: Collier Books.

Miliband, Ralph. 1970. *The State in a Capitalist Society*. New York: Basic Books.

Mill, John Stuart. 1991 [1857]. *Considerations on Representative Government*. Cambridge: Cambridge University Press.

Mill, John Stuart. 1989 [1859]. *On Liberty and Other Writings*. Edited by Stefan Colini. Cambridge: Cambridge University Press.

Miller, Nicholas. 1983. "Social choice and pluralism." *American Political Science Review* 77: 734–47.

Montesquieu, Baron de. 1995 [1748]. *De l'esprit des lois*. Paris: Gallimard.

Mookherjee, Dilip, and Debraj Ray. 2003. "Persistent inequality." *Review of Economic Studies* 70: 369–93.

Moreno Alonso, Manuel. 2000. *Las Cortes de Cádiz*. Cádiz: Editorial Sarriá.

Morgan, Edmund S. 1988. *Inventing the People: The Rise of Popular Sovereignty in England and America*. New York: Norton.

Muthu, Abhinay, and Kenneth A. Shepsle. 2007. "The constitutional choice of bicameralism." Working paper, Department of Government, Harvard University.

Mutz, Diana C. 2006. *Hearing the Other Side: Deliberative versus Participatory Democracy*. New York: Cambridge University Press.

Neves, Lúcia Maria Bastos P. 1995. "Las elecciones en al construcción del imperio brasileño: Los límites de una nueva práctica de la cultura politica lusobrasileña 1820–1823." In Antonio Annino (ed.), *Historia de las elecciones en Iberoamérica, siglo XIX* (pp. 381–408). Mexico City: Fondo de Cultura Económica.

Norris, Pippa. 2002. *Democratic Phoenix: Reinventing Political Activism*. Cambridge: Cambridge University Press.

Norris, Pippa. 2004. *Electoral Engineering: Voting Rules and Political Behavior*. Cambridge: Cambridge University Press.

O'Donnell, Guillermo. 1985. "Argentina de nuevo?" Working paper, Helen Kellogg Institute for International Studies, University of Notre Dame.

O'Donnell, Guillermo. 1993. "On the state, democratization, and some conceptual problems: A Latin American view with glances at some postcommunist countries." *World Development* 21: 1355–69.

O'Donnell, Guillermo. 1994. "Delegative democracy." *Journal of Democracy* 5: 56–69.

O'Donnell, Guillermo. 1999. "Horizontal accountability and new polyarchies." In Andreas Schedler, Larry Diamond, and Mark Plattner (eds.), *The Self-Restraining State: Power and Accountability in New Democracies*. Boulder, CO: Lynne Rienner.

O'Donnell, Guillermo, Philippe C. Schmitter, and Laurence Whitehead. 1986. *Transitions from Authoritarian Rule: Tentative Conclusions about Uncertain Democracies*. Baltimore: The Johns Hopkins University Press.

Osborne, M. J., and Slivinski, A. 1996. "A model of political competition with citizen-candidates." *Quarterly Journal of Economics* 111: 65–96.

Paine, Thomas. 1989 [1776–94]. *Political Writings*. Edited by Bruce Kuklick. Cambridge: Cambridge University Press.

Palacios, Guillermo, and Fabio Moraga. 2003. *La independencia y el comienzo de los regímenes representativos*. Madrid: Editorial Sintesis.

Palmer, R. R. 1959. *The Age of the Democratic Revolution: Vol. I. The Challenge*. Princeton: Princeton University Press.

Palmer, R. R. 1964. *The Age of the Democratic Revolution: Vol. II. The Struggle*. Princeton: Princeton University Press.

Paolucci, Caterina. 1998. "Between *Körperschaften* and census: Political representation in the German Vormärz." In Raffaele Romanelli (ed.), *How Did They Become Voters? The History of Franchise in Modern European Representation* (pp. 251–94). The Hague: Kluwer.

Parsons, Talcott. 1951. *The Social System.* New York: The Free Press.

Pasquino, Pasquale. No date. "Penser la démocratie: Kelsen à Weimar." Paris: CREA.

Pasquino, Pasquale. 1996. "Political theory, order, and threat." In Ian Shapiro and Russell Hardin (eds.), *Political Order. Nomos XXXVIII* (pp. 19–41). New York: New York University Press.

Pasquino, Pasquale. 1997. "Emmanuel Sieyes, Benjamin Constant et le 'Gouvernement des Modernes'." *Revue Française de Science Politique 27:* 214–29.

Pasquino, Pasquale. 1998. *Sieyes et L'Invention de la Constitution en France.* Paris: Editions Odile Jacob.

Pasquino, Pasquale. 1999. "Republicanism and the separation of powers." Paris: CNRS.

Paz, Octavio. 1965. "A democracia en América Latina." *Caderno de Cultura de O Estado de São Paulo,* ano II, numero 128.

Payne, J. Mark, Daniel G. Zovatto, Fernando Carrillo Flórez, and Andrés Allamand Zavala. 2002. *Democracies in Development: Politics and Reforms in Latin America.* Washington, DC: Johns Hopkins University Press.

Persson, Torsten, Gerard Roland, and Guido Tabelini. 1996. "Separation of powers and accountability: Towards a formal approach to comparative politics." Discussion Paper No. 1475. London: Centre for Economic Policy Research.

Peter, Henry, Lord Brougham. 2002 [1839]. "Remarks on party." In Susan E. Scarrow (ed.), *Perspectives in Political Parties* (pp. 51–6). New York: Palgrave Macmillan.

Pierre, Jan, Lars Svåsand, and Anders Widfeldt. 2000. "State subsidies to political parties: Confronting rhetoric with reality." *West European Politics 23:* 1–24.

Piketty, Thomas. 1995. "Social mobility and redistributive politics." *Quarterly Journal of Economics 110:* 551–84.

Piketty, Thomas. 2003. "Income inequality in France, 1901–1998." *Journal of Political Economy 111:* 1004–42.

Piketty, Thomas, and Emmanuel Saez. 2003. "Income inequality in the United States, 1913–1998." *Quarterly Journal of Economics 118:* 1–39.

Pitkin, Hanna F. 1967. *The Concept of Representation.* Berkeley: University of California Press.

Pitkin, Hanna F. 1989. "Representation." In Terence Ball, James Farr, and Russel L. Hanson (eds.), *Political Innovation and Conceptual Change* (pp. 132–54). Cambridge: Cambridge University Press.

Posada-Carbó, Eduardo. 2000. "Electoral juggling: A comparative history of the corruption of suffrage in Latin America, 1830–1930." *Journal of Latin American Studies 32:* 611–44.

Prat, Andrea. 1999. "An economic analysis of campaign financing." Working paper, Tilburg University.

Przeworski, Adam. 1988. "Democracy as a contingent outcome of conflicts." In Ion Elster and Rune Slagstad (eds.), *Constitutionalism and Democracy* (pp. 59–80). Cambridge: Cambridge University Press.

Przeworski, Adam. 1991. *Democracy and the Market.* New York: Cambridge University Press.

Przeworski, Adam. 2003. "Freedom to choose and democracy." *Economics and Philosophy 19*: 265–79.

Przeworski, Adam. 2005. "Democracy as an equilibrium." *Public Choice 123*: 253–73.

Przeworski, Adam, and Michael Wallerstein. 1988. "Structural dependence of the state on capital." *American Political Science Review 82*: 11–30.

Przeworski, Adam, and Fernando Limongi. 1993. "Political regimes and economic growth." *Journal of Economic Perspectives 7*: 51–69.

Przeworski, Adam, Susan C. Stokes, and Bernard Manin (eds.), 1999. *Democracy, Accountability, and Representation*. New York: Cambridge University Press.

Przeworski, Adam, and Covadonga Meseguer. 2006. "Globalization and democracy." In Pranab Bardhan, Samuel Bowles, and Michael Wallerstein (eds.), *Globalization and Egalitarian Distribution* (pp. 169–91). Princeton: Princeton University Press.

Rae, Douglas W. 1969. "Decision rules and individual values in constitutional choice." *American Political Science Review 63*: 40–56.

Rae, Douglas W. 1971. "Political democracy as a property of political institutions." *American Political Science Review 65*: 111–19.

Rae, Douglas W. 1975. "The limits of consensual decision." *American Political Science Review 69*: 1270–94.

Rakove, Jack N. 2002. *James Madison and the Creation of the American Republic* (2nd ed.). New York: Longman.

Rakove, Jack N. 2004. "Thinking like a constitution." *Journal of the Early Republic 24*: 1–26.

Rakove, Jack N. Andrew R. Rutten, and Barry R. Weingast. 2000. "Ideas, interests, and credible commitments in the American revolution." Manuscript. Department of Political Science, Stanford University.

Raz, Joseph. 1994. *Ethics in the Public Domain*. Oxford: Clarendon Press.

Riker, William. 1965. *Democracy in America* (2nd ed.). New York: Macmillan.

Riker, William. 1982. *Liberalism against Populism: A Confrontation Between the Theory of Democracy and the Theory of Social Choice*. San Francisco: Freeman.

Rippy, Fred J. 1965. "Monarchy or republic?" In Hugh M. Hamill, Jr. (ed.), *Dictatorship in Spanish America* (pp. 86–94). New York: Knopf.

Ritter, Gerard A. 1990. "The electoral systems of imperial Germany and their consequences for politics." In Serge Noiret (ed.), *Political Strategies and Electoral Reforms: Origins of Voting Systems in Europe in the 19th and 20th Centuries* (pp. 53–75). Baden-Baden: Nomos Verlagsgesellschaft.

Roberts, Michael. 2002. *The Age of Liberty: Sweden 1719–1772*. New York: Cambridge University Press.

Roemer, John. 2001. *Political Competition*. Cambridge: Harvard University Press.

Rohác, Dalibar. 2008. " 'It is by unrule that Poland stands.' Institutions and political thought in the Polish-Lithuanian republic." *The Independent Journal 13*: 209–24.

Romanelli, Raffaele. 1998. "Electoral systems and social structures. A comparative perspective." In In Raffaele Romanelli (ed.), *How Did They Become Voters? The History of Franchise in Modern European Representation* (pp. 1–36). The Hague: Kluwer.

Rosanvallon, Pierre. 1992. *Le sacre du citoyen: Histoire du suffrage universel en France.* Paris: Gallimard.

Rosanvallon, Pierre. 1995. "The history of the word 'democracy' in France." *Journal of Democracy* 5(4): 140–54.

Rosanvallon, Pierre. 2004. *Le Modèle Politique Français: La société civile contre le jacobinisme de 1789 á nos jours.* Paris: Seuil.

Rosenblum, Nancy L. 2008. *On the Side of the Angels: An Appreciation of Parties and Partisanship.* Princeton: Princeton University Press.

Rousseau, Jean-Jacques. 1964 [1762]. *Du contrat social.* Edited by Robert Derathé. Paris: Gallimard.

Roussopoulos, Dimitrios, and C. George Benello (eds.). 2003. *The Participatory Democracy: Prospects for Democratizing Democracy.* Montreal: Black Rose Books.

Sabato, Hilda. 2003. "Introducción." In Hilda Sabato (ed.), *Ciudadanía política y formación de las naciones: Perspectivas históricas de América Latina* (pp. 11–29). Mexico City: El Colegio de Mexico.

Sabato, Hilda. 2008. *Buenos Aires en Armas: La Revolución de 1880.* Buenos Aires: Siglo XXI.

Sabato, Hilda, and Alberto Littieri (eds.). 2003. *La vida política en la Argentina del siglo XIX: Armas, votos y voces.* Buenos Aires: Fondo de Cultura Económica.

Saiegh, Sebastian. 2009. "Ruling by statue: Evaluating chief executives' legislative success rates." *Journal of Politics* 71: 1342–56.

Saint-John, Henry, Viscount Bolingbroke. 2002 [1738]. "The patriot king and parties." In Susan E. Scarrow (ed.), *Perspectives in Political Parties* (pp. 29–32). New York: Palgrave Macmillan.

Sánchez-Cuenca, Ignacio. 1998. "Institutional commitments and democracy." *European Journal of Sociology* 39: 78–109.

Sánchez-Cuenca, Ignacio. 2003. "Power, rules, and compliance." In José María Maravall and Adam Przeworski (eds.), *Democracy and the Rule of Law* (pp. 62–93). New York: Cambridge University Press.

Scarrow, Susan E. (ed.). 2002. *Perspectives in Political Parties.* New York: Palgrave Macmillan.

Schmitt, Carl. 1988 [1923]. *The Crisis of Parliamentary Democracy.* Cambridge, MA: MIT Press.

Schmitt, Carl. 1993. *Théorie de la Constitition.* Traduit de l'Allemand par Lilyane Deroche. Paris: Presses Universitaires de France.

Schmitter, Philippe, and Terry Lynn Karl. 1991. "What democracy is... and what it is not." *Journal of Democracy* 2: 75–88.

Schorske, Carl E. 1955. *German Social Democracy 1905–1917: The Development of the Great Schism.* New York: Harper & Row.

Schumpeter, Joseph A. 1942. *Capitalism, Socialism, and Democracy.* New York: Harper & Brothers.

Schwartzberg, Melissa. 2009. *Democracy and Legal Change*. New York: Cambridge University Press.

Sen, Amartya. 1970. "The impossibility of a Pareto liberal." *Journal of Political Economy 78:* 152–78.

Sen, Amartya. 1981. *Poverty and Famines: An Essay on Entitlement and Deprivation*. Oxford: Oxford University Press.

Sen, Amartya. 1988. "Freedom of choice: Concept and content." *European Economic Review 32:* 269–94.

Sen, Amartya. 2003 (October 6). "Democracy and its global roots: Why democratization is not the same as Westernization." *The New Republic.*

Seymour, Charles. 1915. *Electoral Reform in England and Wales: The Development and Operation of the Parliamentary Franchise, 1832–1885*. New Haven: Yale University Press.

Shapiro, Ian. 1999. *Democratic Justice*. New Haven: Yale University Press.

Shapiro, Carl, and Joseph E. Stiglitz. 1986. "Equilibrium unemployment as a worker disciplining device." *American Economic Review 74:* 433–4.

Sharp, Andrew. 1998. *The English Levellers*. Cambridge: Cambridge University Press.

Shelling, Thomas. 1954. *Strategy and Conflict*. Cambridge, MA: Harvard University Press.

Shklar, Judith N. 1979. "Let us not be hypocritical." *Deadalus 108:* 1–25.

Sieyes, Emmanuel. 1970. *Qu'est-ce que le tiers état?* Edited by Roberto Zapperi. Genève: Droz.

Simmel, Georg. 1950 [1908]. *The Sociology of Georg Simmel*. Translated, edited, and with an introduction by Kurt H. Wolff. New York: The Free Press.

Simpser, Alberto. 2006. "Making votes not count: Strategic incentives for electoral corruption." PhD Dissertation, Stanford University.

Skidelsky, Robert. 1970. "1929–1931 revisited. "*Bulletin of the Society for the Study of Labour History* 21: 6–8.

Skinner, Quentin. 1973. "The empirical theorists of democracy and their critics: a plague on both houses." *Political Theory 1:* 287–306.

Sobrevilla, Natalia. 2002. "The influence of the European 1848 revolutions in Peru." In Guy Thomson (ed.), *The European Revolutions of 1848 and the Americas* (pp. 191–216). London: Insitute of Latin American Studies.

Soriano, Graciela. 1969. "Introducción." In Simon Bolívar, *Escritos politicos* (pp. 11–41). Madrid: Alianza Editorial.

Stokes, Susan C. 2001. *Mandates and Democracy: Neoliberalism by Surprise in Latin America*. Cambridge: Cambridge University Press.

Stone, Geoffrey R. *Perilous Times: Free Speech in Wartime, From the Sedition Act of 1798 to the War on Terrorism*. New York: Norton.

Stratman, Thomas. 2005. "Some talk: Money in politics. A (partial) review of the literature." *Public Choice 124:* 135–56.

Sunstein, Cass. 1995. "Democracy and shifting preferences." In David Coop, Jean Hampton, and John E. Roemer (eds.), *The Idea of Democracy* (pp. 196–230). Cambridge: Cambridge University Press.

Teik, Goh Cheng. 1972. Why Indonesia's attempt at democracy in the mid-1950s failed. *Modern Asian Studies 6:* 225–44.

Ternavaso, Marcela. 1995. "Nuevo régimen representativo y expansión de la frontera política. Las elecciones en el estado de Buenos Aires: 1820–1840." In Antonio Annino (ed.), *Historia de la elecciones en Iberoamérica, siglo XIX* (pp. 65–106). Mexico City: Fondo de Cultura Económica.

Thach, Charles C., Jr. 1969 [1923]. *The Creation of the Presidency 1775–1789: A Study in Constitutional History.* Baltimore: The Johns Hopkins University Press.

Tingsten, Herbert. 1973. *The Swedish Social Democrats.* Totowa: Bedminster Press.

Tocqueville, Alexis de. 1961 [1835]. *De la démocratie en Amérique.* Paris: Gallimard.

Trębicki, Antoni. 1992 [1792]. "Odpowiedź autorowi prawdziwemu Uwagi Dyzmy Bończy Tomaszewskiemu nad Konstytucją i rewolucją dnia 3 maja." In Anna Grześkowiak-Krwawicz (ed.), *Za czy przeciw ustawie rządowej* (pp. 193–260). Warszawa: Institut Badań Literackich.

Törnudd, Klaus. 1968. *The Electoral System of Finland.* London: Hugh Evelyn.

Tsebelis, George. 2002. *Veto Players: How Political Institutions Work.* Princeton: Princeton University Press.

Ungari, Paolo. 1990. "Les réformes électorales en Italie aux XIXe et XXe siècles." In Serge Noiret (ed.), *Political Strategies and Electoral Reforms: Origins of Voting Systems in Europe in the 19th and 20th Centuries* (pp. 127–38). Baden-Baden: Nomos Verlagsgesellschaft.

Urfalino, Philippe. 2007. "La décision par consensus apparent: Nature et propriétes." *Revue Européenne des Sciences Sociales 95:* 47–70.

Valenzuela, J. Samuel. 1995. "The origins and transformations of the Chilean party system." Working Paper No. 215, Helen Kellogg Institute for International Studies, University of Notre Dame.

Verba, Sidney, Kay Schlozman, and Henry E. Brady. 1995. *Voice and Equality: Civic Voluntarism in American Politics.* Cambridge, MA: Harvard University Press.

Verney, Douglas V. 1957. *Parliamentary Reform in Sweden, 1866–1921.* Oxford: Clarendon Press.

Vile, M. J. C. 1998. *Constitutionalism and the Separation of Powers* (2nd ed.). Indianapolis: Liberty Press.

Waldron, Jeremy. 2006. "The core of the case against judicial review." *Yale Law Journal 115:* 1346–1406.

Washington, George. 2002 [1796]. "Farewell Address to Congress." In Susan E. Scarrow (ed.), *Perspectives in Political Parties* (pp. 45–50). New York: Palgrave Macmillan.

Weingast, Barry R. 1997. "Political foundations of democracy and the rule of law." *American Political Science Review 91:* 245–63.

Weisberger, Bernard A. *America Afire: Jefferson, Adams, and the First Contested Election.* New York: HarperCollins.

Wills, Garry. 1981. *Explaining America· The Federalist.* New York: Penguin Books.

Wills, Garry. 1982. "Introduction." In *The Federalist Papers by Alexander Hamilton, James Madison, and John Jay.* New York: Bantam Books.

Wills, Garry. 2002. *James Madison*. New York: Henry Holt.

Wood, Gordon S. 1969. *The Creation of the American Republic, 1776–1787*. New York: Norton.

Wootton, David. 1993. "The levellers." In John Dunn (ed.), *Democracy: The Unfinished Journey, 508 BC to AD 1993* (pp. 71–90). Oxford: Oxford University Press.

Yadav, Yogendra. 2000. "Understanding the second democratic upsurge: Trends of Bahujan participation in electoral politics in the 1990s." In Francine Frankel, Zoya Hasan, Rajeev Bhargava, and Balveer Arora (eds.), *Transforming India: Social and Political Dynamics of Democracy* (pp. 120–45). Oxford: Oxford University Press.

Young, Crawford. 1994. *The African Colonial State in Comparative Perspective*. New Haven: Yale University Press.

Zeldin, Theodore. 1958. *The Political System of Napoleon III*. New York: Norton.

Zolberg, Aristide. 1972. "Moments of madness." *Politics and Society* 2: 183–207.

Name Index

Subject Index

Country Index